THE MODERN THEATRE
Volume One

Eric Bentley is the author
of *What is Theatre?* and
other volumes.

THE

MODERN THEATRE

Volume One
Edited by

ERIC BENTLEY

Five Plays

WOYZECK

CAVALLERIA RUSTICANA

WOMAN OF PARIS

THE THREEPENNY OPERA

ELECTRA

Doubleday Anchor Books

DOUBLEDAY & COMPANY, INC., GARDEN CITY, N.Y.

ACKNOWLEDGMENTS

Acknowledgment of permission to reprint is to be found on the title page of each play.

Beyond these thanks to my authors, I owe thanks to my more secret collaborators. The MS of *The Threepenny Opera* was read by Mrs. Therese Dessau Pol and Mr. Theodore Hoffman, both of whom suggested changes which have found their way into the text; while Mr. Christopher Isherwood permitted me to pillage his versions of the songs (as found in *A Penny for the Poor*).

I also owe thanks to those of my authors who let *me* suggest—and even execute—changes in *their* scripts.

Many suggestions for titles in my modern anthologies come to me unsolicited—heaven-sent, as it were—from strangers. I would urge readers of the present volume to perpetuate this splendid, though not highly paid, practice. Here and now I must confine myself to thanking those whom I regularly "pump" for their opinions and even persuade to read plays which they might otherwise have lived happily without: Mr. Jacques Barzun, Mr. William Becker, and Mr. Theodore Hoffman.

My own editorial labors have been shared cheerfully—I should say gaily—by my wife, Joanne Davis Bentley. We, in turn, were assisted by Miss Violet Serwin, who can type from copy which your modern printer would probably take for pre-historic cave drawings.

That this series should exist at all was the idea of Mr. Jason Epstein of Doubleday & Company. The form it has finally taken was devised by him and myself in constant consultation—when not at length, then at long distance. If the result is something to be grateful for, it is clear that the gratitude should go, in a very large measure, to him.

E.B.

CONTENTS

ELECTRA
A Play in Two Acts by
JEAN GIRAUDOUX
English Version by Winifred Smith

195

NOTES
293

ADAPTATION VS. TRANSLATION
299

THE MODERN THEATRE
Volume One

WOYZECK

Twenty-six Scenes
by

GEORG BÜCHNER

English version by
Theodore Hoffman

Characters

WOYZECK*
THE CAPTAIN
ANDRES
MARIE
MARGRET
DRUM-MAJOR
MARIE'S CHILD
BARKER
AN OLD MAN
A YOUNG BOY
SERGEANT
THE DOCTOR
FIRST APPRENTICE
SECOND APPRENTICE
THE JEW
FOOL
AN OLD WOMAN
THREE LITTLE GIRLS
KÄTHE *pronounced pretty much like Katey*
INNKEEPER
TWO MEN
POLICEMAN

HORSE, MONKEY, COURT CLERK, DOCTOR, JUDGE, SOLDIERS, CHILDREN, APPRENTICES, STUDENTS, ORDINARY PEOPLE.

The action apparently takes place in Leipzig, 1824.

* Pronounced: Voyt-seck. (The form Wozzeck—pronounced Votseck—is still widely current. It has its origin in a misreading of the MS by its first editor.)

1 AT THE CAPTAIN'S

The CAPTAIN *in a chair;* WOYZECK *shaving him.*

CAPTAIN. Easy, Woyzeck, take it easy. One thing after the other! You're making me dizzy. You'll finish up early and what'll I do with ten minutes on my hands? Use your head, Woyzeck. You've got thirty years to live. Thirty! That's three hundred sixty months. And days! Hours! Minutes! What are you going to do with that horrible stretch of time? Figure it out for yourself, Woyzeck!

WOYZECK. Yes sir, Captain.

CAPTAIN. When I think about eternity, Woyzeck, this world gets me worried. Our task, Woyzeck! Our task is eternal. It's eternal, eternal! You know that? And then again, it's not so eternal. It's just a passing moment. Yes, a passing moment. Woyzeck, I get upset when I think it takes a whole day for the world to turn around just once. What a waste of time! And where does it get us? Woyzeck, I can get melancholy just looking at a mill-wheel.

WOYZECK. Yes sir, Captain.

CAPTAIN. Woyzeck, you always look so moody. A good man doesn't look moody; a good man is someone with a good conscience. Well, say something, Woyzeck! How's the weather today?

WOYZECK. Nasty, Captain, nasty. Wind.

CAPTAIN. Yes, I felt it before. It's really whizzing around. A wind like that has the same effect on me a mouse does. *Slyly.*
I think the wind's from the north-south.

WOYZECK. Yes sir, Captain.

3

CAPTAIN. Ha! Ha! Ha! north-south! Ha! Ha! Ha! Are you dumb! Disgustingly dumb!

Touched, but condescending.

Woyzeck, you're a good man, but

With dignity

you have no morals. Morals! That's what a man's got who behaves morally! Understand? It's a good word. You went and got yourself a child without the blessing of the Church, as our right reverend chaplain put it. "Without the blessing of the Church." Now, I didn't invent the phrase.

WOYZECK. Captain, the Good Lord's not going to be hard on the little worm, just because no one said Amen before they made him. The Lord said, "Suffer little children to come unto me."

CAPTAIN. What did you say? What kind of crazy answer is that? It's got me all confused, and by "it" I mean "you"! See?

WOYZECK. You see, Captain—with us poor people—it's money, money! If you don't have money . . . Well, you just can't have morals when you're bringing someone like yourself into the world. We're only flesh and blood. People like us can't be holy in this world—or the next. If we ever did get into heaven, they'd put us to work on the thunder.

CAPTAIN. Woyzeck, you have no virtue. You are not a virtuous man. Flesh and blood? Why, when I lie by my window after the rain and I see those white stockings flashing over the sidewalk—damn it, Woyzeck, then I know what love is too! I'm flesh and blood, too, Woyzeck. But virtue! Virtue! The things I could waste my time on! But I say to myself "You're a virtuous man!"

Moved.

A good man, a good man.

WOYZECK. Yes, Captain. Virtue. I don't have much of that. But you see, what happens to us ordinary people—that's just nature. Now, if I was a gentleman and wore a hat and a watch and a cane, and could talk smooth—well, I'd like to be virtuous too. It must be fine to be virtuous, Captain, but I'm just ordinary.

CAPTAIN. You're good, Woyzeck. You're a good man. But you think too much. It wears you out. You're always so moody. Well, this conversation has exhausted me too. You can go. But don't run. Take it easy, nice and easy, out into the street.

2 AN OPEN FIELD, THE TOWN IN THE DISTANCE

WOYZECK *and* ANDRES *cut kindling wood in the bushes.* ANDRES *is whistling.*

WOYZECK. You know, Andres, there's a curse on this place. You see that light spot on the grass down there, where the toadstools are sprouting? At night a head rolls around there. Someone picked it up once. Thought it was a hedgehog. Three days, three nights, and he was lying in a wooden box.
Low.
Andres, that was the Freemasons. I get it! The Freemasons!

ANDRES, *singing:*
    And there did sit two hares, Sir,
    A-tearing up the green, the greenest grass.

WOYZECK. Quiet. Listen, Andres, listen! Something's moving.

ANDRES.
    A-tearing up the green, the greenest grass,
    Until the ground was bare, Sir.

WOYZECK. It's moving behind me. Under me.
He stamps on the ground.
Hollow. Listen! It's all hollow under here. The Freemasons!

ANDRES. I'm scared.

WOYZECK. It's so queer, and quiet. Makes you want to hold your breath . . . Andres!

ANDRES. What?

WOYZECK. Say something!
  Stares around him.
  Andres, look how bright it is. It's all shiny over the city.
  There's a fire running around the sky, and a sound coming
  down like trumpets. It's closing in on us!—Come on. Don't
  look back!
  Pulls him into the shrubbery.

ANDRES, *after a pause.* Woyzeck! You still hear it?

WOYZECK. Quiet. Everything's quiet. Like the world was dead.

ANDRES. Listen! There's the drum. We've got to get back.

3 THE TOWN

  MARIE *with her child at the window,* MARGRET. *The Re-
  treat passes, the Drum-Major in front.*

MARIE, *dandling her child.* Hey, boy! Ta-ra-ra-ra! Hear them?
  Here they come!

MARGRET. What a man! Built like a tree.

MARIE. He handles himself like a lion.
  The Drum Major salutes her.

MARGRET. Ooh, he's giving you the glad eye, neighbor. I
  hardly expected it of *you.*

MARIE, *singing.*
  Oh, soldiers are such handsome guys.

MARGRET. Your eyes are still shining.

MARIE. Who cares? If you took yours to the pawnbroker's and
  had them polished up, maybe they'd shine enough to be
  sold for a couple of buttons.

MARGRET. What's that? Why, you! Listen, Mrs. Virginity, I'm

at least respectable. But you, everyone knows you could stare your way through seven pairs of leather pants.

MARIE. You bitch!

Slams the window.

Come on, little fellow. What do people want, anyhow? Maybe you are just a poor whore's kid, but your illegitimate little face still brings joy to your mother. Da, da, dum.

Singing:

Girlie, what's wrong in this house?
You've got a kid but no spouse.
Night-time I sing me a song.
Why let a man do me wrong?
Hush-a-bye, baby; baby, hurrah!
Let the men stay where they are.

Hansel, harness your six horses up.
They'd like to drink and to sup.
Oats they won't eat for you,
Water won't drink for you.
But lovely cool wine would do fine. Hurrah!
But lovely cool wine would do fine.

A knock at the window.

Who's there? That you, Franz? Come on in.

WOYZECK. Can't. Got roll call.

MARIE. Get the wood cut for the Captain?

WOYZECK. Yes. Marie.

MARIE. What's the matter, Franz? You look upset.

WOYZECK. Marie, it happened again. Plenty. Doesn't the good book say, "And behold, there was a smoke coming up from the land like the smoke of an oven?"

MARIE, Oh, you . . .
with pity.

WOYZECK. It followed me all the way into town. Something we can't understand, that drives you out of your senses. What's going to happen?

MARIE. Franz!

WOYZECK. I've got to go. See you tonight at the fair grounds.
I saved something up.

He goes.

MARIE. That man! He's seeing things. Didn't even notice his
own child. He'll crack up with these ideas of his. Why so
quiet, little fellow? Are you scared? It's getting so dark it's
like going blind. Only that street light shining in. It gives
me the creeps.

4 FAIR BOOTHS, LIGHTS, PEOPLE

OLD MAN *singing and* CHILD *dancing to a barrel-organ.*
Everything on earth fades fast,
Death will take us all at last,
That's a truth we know won't pass.

WOYZECK. Yahoo! A poor old man and a poor little boy. Fun
and trouble!

MARIE. Good God, if fools make sense, then we're all fools.
What a crazy world! What a beautiful world!

Both move on to a barker.

BARKER, *in front of a booth, with his wife in trousers and a
monkey in costume.* Ladies and gentlemen, if you looked
at this creature as God made him, you'd see nothing, absolutely nothing! Ah, but Art, look what Art has done for
him! He walks upright, wears a fancy jacket and tight
trousers, and carries a sword. This here monkey is a soldier!
He is no longer in the lowest ranks of the masculine gender.
Here, take a bow. There you are, the perfect gentleman.
Give us a kiss.

The monkey trumpets.

The kid is really musical. Ladies and gentlemen, inside
you will also see the little love birds and the astronomical
horse. Favorite of the crowned heads of Europe. Can tell
any one of you your age, number of children, and physical
ailments. The show is about to begin. We're going to begin

at the beginning. This is just the introduction to the introduction.

WOYZECK. Want to?

MARIE. It's all right with me. It should be good. Did you see the tassels on the man, and the wife wearing pants?
Both go in.

DRUM-MAJOR. Hey, hold it! Did you see her? What a piece!

SERGEANT. And how! Made for breeding whole regiments of cavalry.

DRUM-MAJOR. And reproducing Drum-Majors!

SERGEANT. Look at the way she holds her head up. You'd think all that black hair would weigh her down. And those eyes!

DRUM-MAJOR. Like looking into a well, or staring up a chimney. Let's go! After her!

5 INSIDE THE BRIGHTLY LIGHTED BOOTH

MARIE. What lights!

WOYZECK. Yeah, Marie. Black cats with burning eyes. Oh, what a night!

BARKER, *leading a horse.* Show your talent! Show your brute reason! Put human society to shame! Ladies and gentlemen, the animal you see here, four hoofs on the ground and a long tail on his body, is a member of all the learned societies, a professor here at our university, where he teaches the students to ride and to fence. There's simple intelligence for you. But he also thinks with double reason. Show what you do when you use double reasoning. For instance, among this learned company do you see one single donkey?
The nag shakes his head.
Now do you see the double reasoning? That's physiognomy for you. Yes, this is no mere specimen of a dumb animal. This is a human being! No, a human beast! But still a beast.

The horse mounts up indecently.

All right, put society to shame! This beast, as you can see
for yourselves, is still in a state of nature—not ideal nature
of course . . . Take a lesson from him. But first consult your
doctor. It may prove highly dangerous. Now, we have been
told, be natural! You are created from dust, sand, and dung.
Do you want to be more than dust, sand, and dung. See?
What a mind! He can do arithmetic, even if he can't count
on his fingers. Why? He just can't express himself, he just
can't explain. He's a metamorphosed human being. Tell
the audience what time it is. Have any of you ladies and
gentlemen got a watch? A watch?

SERGEANT. A watch?

*Pulling a watch out of his pocket with great deliberation and
dignity.*

There you are, sir.

MARIE. I'm not going to miss this.

She climbs on the front bench. The Sergeant helps her.

DRUM-MAJOR. What a piece!

6 MARIE'S ROOM

MARIE. *sitting, the child in her lap, a piece of mirror in her
hand. She looks at herself.* Don't the stones shine! What kind
did he say they were? Sleep, baby. Close your eyes, tight.

The child covers his eyes with his hands.

Tighter yet. That's it. Stay like that—or he'll get you.

Sings.

Quick, girl, lock the shutter tight.
A gypsy's on the road tonight.
He'll take you by the hand
Straight into gypsyland.

Looking at herself again.

They must be gold. Wonder how I'd look dancing in them?
Maybe people like us may only have a little corner of the
world and a little piece of mirror, but my lips are as red as

the finest ladies', with their top to bottom mirrors, and handsome gentlemen kissing their hands. And I'm just a common woman.

The child raises himself.

Quiet, boy. Close your eyes. There's the sandman running across the wall.

She flashes the mirror.

Close your eyes, or he'll look into them and strike you blind!

Woyzeck walks in, behind her. She jumps up, her hands over her ears.

WOYZECK. What have you got?

MARIE. Nothing.

WOYZECK. It's shining through your fingers.

MARIE. An earring. I found it.

WOYZECK. I never found anything that way, two at a time.

MARIE. I'm only human.

WOYZECK. Forget it, Marie. Look at the way that kid sleeps. Lift him up under the arms. The chair's hurting him. Those shiny drops on his forehead. Everything under the sun is work. Sweat, even in our sleep. Us poor people! Here's some more money, Marie. My pay and something from the Captain.

MARIE. You're too good, Franz.

WOYZECK. I have to go. See you tonight, Marie. Good bye.

MARIE, *alone, after a pause.* I'm such a rotten creature. I could stab myself. What the hell! Everything is going to the devil anyhow.

7 AT THE DOCTOR'S

WOYZECK, *the* DOCTOR.

DOCTOR. And what do I see, Woyzeck? You! A man of your word!

WOYZECK. What's that, doctor?

DOCTOR. I saw you, Woyzeck. You were pissing in the street.
You were pissing against the wall, like a dog! Three groschen
a day and board for that! Woyzeck, that was bad. The
world's going bad, very bad.

WOYZECK. But, Doctor, when Nature calls.

DOCTOR. When Nature calls! When Nature calls! Nature! Didn't
I prove that the *musculus constrictor vesicae* can be con-
trolled by the will? Woyzeck, Man is free! Through Man
alone shines the individual's will to freedom! Can't hold his
water!

*Shakes his head, puts his hands behind his back, paces up
and down.*

Have you been eating your peas, Woyzeck? Nothing but
peas. *Cruciferae.* Remember that! This will cause a revolu-
tion in scientific thought, I'll blow it to bits! Urea, o.10.,
Ammonium hydrochlorate, hyperoxidic. Woyzeck, can't you
piss again? Go in there again and try.

WOYZECK. Can't do it, doctor.

DOCTOR, *upset.* Pissing against a wall! Tsk, Tsk, tsk! I have it in
writing, the agreement's right here. And what do I see? With
my own eyes I saw it. I stick my nose out the window, letting
the sun's rays hit it to observe the process of sneezing, and
what do I see? Did you bring me any frogs? Tadpoles? Fresh
water polyps? *Cristatellum?* Keep away from the micro-
scope. I've got the thick back tooth from an infusorium under it. I'll blow them to bits, all of them! Pissing against a
wall indeed! And I saw it!

Bearing down on him.

No, Woyzeck. I'm not getting angry. Anger is unheathy,
it's unscientific. I'm calm, perfectly calm. My pulse is beating
its regular 60, and I'm addressing you in an absolutely cold-
blooded manner. Why get angry with a man, God forbid? A
man! Now if a Proteus should fail on you . . . But, Woyzeck,
you shouldn't have been pissing against that wall.

WOYZECK. Don't you see, Doctor? Some people are built like you

say—they have character, you might say. But it's something
else with Nature. You see, with Nature,

He snaps his fingers.

it's like that. How can I explain? For instance . . .

DOCTOR. Woyzeck, you're philosophizing again.

WOYZECK. Nature. Yes, doctor, when Nature gives way . . .

DOCTOR. Nature. What's that? When Nature gives way?

WOYZECK. When Nature gives way. That is, when Nature gives
way. The world gets dark and you have to feel around with
your hands, and everything keeps slipping, like in a spider's
web. That's the way it is when something's there but really
isn't, when it's all dark with only a red glow in the west, like
from a furnace.

He paces the room.

DOCTOR. You feel around with your feet as if you were a spider!

WOYZECK. Doctor, did you ever see anything with a double
nature? When the sun stops at noon, and it's like the whole
world's caught on fire? That's when a terrible voice spoke
to me.

DOCTOR. Woyzeck, you have an *aberratio.*

WOYZECK, *putting his finger to his nose.* In the toadstools, doctor, that's where it is. Did you ever notice the signs toadstools make growing in the grass? If only you could figure
out what they mean!

DOCTOR. Woyzeck, you have the most beautiful *aberratio men-
talis partialis,* secondary order, nicely developed. Woyzeck,
you're getting a raise. *Idée fixe,* of the second highest rank,
but with a tractable disposition. Doing everything as usual?
Shaving the Captain?

WOYZECK. Yes sir.

DOCTOR. Eating your peas?

WOYZECK. Everything's regular, doctor. The money goes to
Marie for the house.

DOCTOR. Going on duty?

WOYZECK. Yes, sir.

DOCTOR. You're an interesting case. Woyzeck, you're getting a
raise. Behave yourself. Let's feel your pulse. Yes.

8 MARIE'S ROOM

MARIE, *the* DRUM-MAJOR

DRUM-MAJOR. Marie!

MARIE. *Looking at him intently.* Stand up there!—A chest like
a bull and a beard like a lion. In a class by himself—no
woman is prouder than I am.

DRUM-MAJOR. But Sunday, when I'm wearing my white gloves
and the hat with the plume in it, hot damn! The Prince always says, "By God, there's a real man!"

MARIE, *mockingly.* Does he?
Steps up before him.
A real man!

DRUM-MAJOR. And you're a real piece of woman, too. Hell's
bells, let's raise a race of Drum-majors. Eh?
He embraces her.

MARIE, *moody.* Let me go!

DRUM-MAJOR. You wildcat!

MARIE, *violently.* Just touch me!

DRUM-MAJOR. You've got the devil in your eyes.

MARIE. What's the difference?

9 THE STREET

The CAPTAIN, *the* DOCTOR.

The CAPTAIN *comes panting along the streets, stops, pants, looks around.*

CAPTAIN. Don't run so fast, Doctor. Stop paddling your cane in the air like that. You're chasing your own death. A good man, with a clear conscience, doesn't run so fast. A good man . . .

He seizes the Doctor by the coat.

Doctor, permit me to save a human life.

DOCTOR. I'm in a hurry, Captain, a hurry.

CAPTAIN. Doctor, I'm feeling low. I get so sentimental. When I look at my coat hanging on the wall, I start crying.

DOCTOR. Puffy, fat, thick neck, apoplectic constitution. You're headed straight for *Apoplexia Cerebria*. You'll probably just get it on one side. Paralyzed down one side. Or, if you're lucky, just lose your mental faculties and go on vegetating. Those are your prospects for the next four weeks. I can assure you, you'll be a most interesting case. And if God wills that your tongue only gets half paralyzed, our experiments are immortal.

CAPTAIN. Don't frighten me, Doctor. People have died of fright, just plain fright!—I can see them already, with flowers in their hands. But they'll say: He was a good man, a good man —you coffin-nail devil!

DOCTOR, *showing him his hat.* Do you know who that is, Captain? That's Mr. Emptyhead, my dear Drill-killer.

CAPTAIN, *showing a button hole.* Do you know who this is, Doctor? That's Mr. Hole-in-theHead, my dear Coffin-nail. Hahahaha! No harm meant. I'm a good man, but I can play that game too.

Woyzeck tries to hurry past.

Hey, Woyzeck! Where are you rushing? Hang on, Woyzeck.

Why, he runs through the world like an open razor, you could cut yourself on him. He runs as if he had a regiment of eunuchs to shave and would be hung while the last hair was being cut. But what about long beards, Woyzeck? How shall I put it? Woyzeck, long beards . . .

DOCTOR. A long chin beard. Now Pliny mentions that, how soldiers should be broken of the habit.

CAPTAIN, *continuing*. Ah, yes, long beards. Woyzeck, how come you haven't found the hair from a beard in your soup bowl? Eh? You get it? The hair from an engineer's beard? A non-commissioned officer's? A Drum-Major's? Eh, Woyzeck? But you've got a good woman. Not like the others.

WOYZECK. Yes sir. What do you mean, sir?

CAPTAIN. What a face the man's making. Well, perhaps not in the soup, but if you run around the corner, maybe you can still find a pair of lips. A pair of lips, Woyzeck! I too have felt the love itch, Woyzeck. Why, you're white as chalk.

WOYZECK. Captain, I'm just a poor devil, and I have nothing else in the world. Captain, if you're joking . . .

CAPTAIN. Joking? Joking with you, Woyzeck?

DOCTOR. Your pulse, Woyzeck, your pulse. Short, hard, jerky, irregular.

WOYZECK. Captain, the earth is hot like hell, but to me it's ice cold, ice cold. Hell is cold. You want to bet? Impossible! God! God! Impossible!

CAPTAIN. Soldier, do you—do you want a couple of bullets in your head? You keep stabbing at me with those eyes, but I'm trying to help you, because you're a good man, Woyzeck, a good man.

DOCTOR. Facial muscles rigid, tense, occasionally jumpy. Disposition excitable, tense.

WOYZECK. I'm going. Anything can happen. God! Anything can happen. It's nice weather, Captain. A fine, clear, gray sky. A man could almost want to hammer a nail up there and hang himself on it. Just on account of that little dash between yes, and yes again, and no. Yes and no, Captain? Is no yes's fault? Or yes no's? I'll think it over.

He leaves, taking long steps, slowly at first, then faster and faster.

DOCTOR. A phenomenon. *Calling after him.* Woyzeck, a raise!

CAPTAIN. These people make me dizzy. So fast. You know, a good man takes care of himself. A good man doesn't have courage. Only a mongrel bitch has courage. I joined the army to show myself that I have no courage.

10   MARIE'S ROOM

MARIE, WOYZECK.

WOYZECK, *staring straight at her and shaking his head.* Hm! I can't see it. I can't see it. You should be able to. You should be able to hold it in your fist.

MARIE, *frightened.* What is it, Franz? You're raving, Franz.

WOYZECK. A sin, so big, and so wide. It should stink, until the angels are smoked out of heaven. You have a red mouth, Marie. No blisters on it? Marie, you're as beautiful as sin—but can mortal sin be so beautiful?

MARIE. Franz, you're talking like you had a fever.

WOYZECK. Hell! Did he stand there? Like this? Like this?

MARIE. The world is old and the day is long, so lots of people can stand in the same place, one after the other.

WOYZECK. I saw him!

MARIE. There's a lot you can see if you have two eyes, you're not blind, and the sun is shining.

WOYZECK. You whore!

He goes for her.

MARIE. Just touch me, Franz! I'd rather have a knife in my ribs

than your hands on me. At ten, my father didn't dare touch
me. I only had to look at him.

WOYZECK. Bitch! No, it should show on you. Each one of us is
a precipice. You get dizzy when you look down. — There
should be! She's innocence itself. All right, innocence. You
bear the mark on you. Do I know it though? Do I know it?
Who does?

11 THE GUARD HOUSE*

WOYZECK, ANDRES.

ANDRES, *singing.*

> *Our hostess has a merry maid,*
> *She sits in the garden night and day,*
> *She sits within her garden.*

WOYZECK. Andres!

ANDRES. Huh?

WOYZECK. Nice weather.

ANDRES. Sunny Sunday weather. Music outside town, the
bitches already there, the men sweating. Great stuff.

WOYZECK, *restless.* Dancing, Andres! They're dancing!

ANDRES. At the Horse and the Star.

WOYZECK. Dancing! Dancing!

ANDRES. I don't care.

> *She sits within her garden,*
> *Till twelve o'clock has chimed away,*
> *And the infantry comes mar-arching.*

WOYZECK. Andres, I can't calm down.

ANDRES. Fool!

WOYZECK. I've got to get out. It keeps turning in front of my

* Where the sentries congregate.

eyes. Dancing! Dancing! Her hands will be hot. Damn her, Andres!

ANDRES. What do you want?

WOYZECK. I've got to go, got to see for myself.

ANDRES. You lunatic. On account of that bitch?

WOYZECK. I've got to get out, it's so hot in here.

12 AN INN

The windows open. Dancing. Benches in front of the house. Apprentices.

FIRST APPRENTICE.

This little shirt I'm wearing is not mine,
And my soul it stinks of brandy wine.

SECOND APPRENTICE. Hey, brother, let me knock a hole in your nature for friendship's sake. Forward! I'll knock a hole in his nature. I'm just as big a man, you now, and I'll slaughter every flea on his body.

FIRST APPRENTICE. "*And my soul, my soul, it stinks of brandy wine.*" Even money falls into decay. Forget me not, how beautiful the world is! Brother, I could fill a rain barrel with tears. I wish our noses were bottles, so we could pour them down each other's throat.

OTHERS, *in chorus.*

A hunter from the Rhine
Was riding through the forest fine.
Hallee, hallo, how merry are the hunting men,
Roaming the fields so free.
A hunting life for me.

WOYZECK *posts himself by the window. Marie and the* DRUM-MAJOR *dance by, without noticing him.*

WOYZECK. Him and her! Damn it to hell!

MARIE, *dancing by.* Don't stop! Don't stop!

WOYZECK, *choking*. Don't stop!

He jumps up and falls back on the bench.

Don't stop! Don't stop!

Pounding his hands.

Turn around! Roll on! Why doesn't God blow out the sun so they can all roll on top of each other in filth? Male and Female! Man and Beast! They'll do it in broad daylight! They'll do it on your hands, like flies! Women! That woman is hot, hot! Don't stop!

He jumps up.

That bastard! Look how he's feeling her up—all over her body! He's, he's got her—like I did at first.

He slumps down, bewildered.

ANDRES. What are you doing here?

WOYZECK. What time is it?

ANDRES. Almost ten.

WOYZECK. I thought it was later. It should go faster.

ANDRES. Why?

WOYZECK. So it'd be over.

ANDRES. What?

WOYZECK. The fun.

ANDRES. What are you sitting by the door for?

WOYZECK. It's fine here. Some people don't know they're near the door until they're dragged out, feet first.

ANDRES. Come on with us.

WOYZECK. It's fine here.

ANDRES. You're drunk.

He leaves with the others.

WOYZECK. Not enough.

FISRT APPRENTICE, *preaching from a table*. Nevertheless, consider the wanderer who standeth leaning by the stream of time, answereth himself with the wisdom of God, and asketh: What is Man? What is Man? Yea, verily I say unto you, On what would the farmer, the cooper, the cobbler, and the doctor live—if God had not created Man? How would the tailor live—if God had not planted a sense of modesty in men? How would the soldier live—if God had not equipped him with the urge to slaughter himself? Therefore, doubt not, everything is sweet and lovely. Yet everything on earth is evil, even money falls into decay! In conclusion, my beloved, let us now piss over the Cross, so that somewhere a Jew will die.

In the middle of the general howling WOYZECK *wakes up.*

FOOL. It smells.

WOYZECK. Yes, it smells! She had a red, red mouth. Is that what you smell?

FOOL. I smell blood.

WOYZECK. Blood! Everything's going red before my eyes. Like they were all rolling on top of each other in a sea of it!

13   AN OPEN FIELD

WOYZECK. Don't stop! Don't stop! Hish! Hash! That's the way the flutes and fiddles go. Don't stop! Don't stop! No more music! Who's talking under there?
He stretches out on the ground.
What? What are you saying? Louder! Louder! Stab, stab the bitch of a goat-wolf dead? Stab, stab the bitch of a goat-wolf dead! Should I? Must I? Is it out there, too? Is the wind saying it, too? The words don't stop! Don't stop! Stab her dead! Dead!

14   A ROOM IN THE BARRACKS

Night. ANDRES *and* WOYZECK *in one bed.*

WOYZECK, *softly.* Andres!

ANDRES, *murmurs in his sleep.*

WOYZECK, *shaking* ANDRES. Hey, Andres! Andres!

ANDRES. What do you want?

WOYZECK. I can't sleep. When I close my eyes, everything turns around and I hear the fiddles saying: Don't stop! Don't stop! Then it comes out of the wall, too. Don't you hear anything?

ANDRES. Sure. Let them dance. A man gets tired. God bless us all. Amen.

WOYZECK. It keeps saying: Stab! Stab! And it pulls my eyes open, like a knife. A big, thick knife, lying on a counter in a dark narrow street, with an old man sitting behind it. That's the knife I keep seeing in front of my eyes.

ANDRES. You ought to drink some schnaps with a powder in it. That cuts the fever.

WOYZECK. Don't stop! Don't stop!

ANDRES. Go to sleep, you fool!
He goes to sleep.

15 THE COURTYARD AT THE DOCTOR'S

STUDENTS *and* WOYZECK *below, the* DOCTOR *at the garret window.*

DOCTOR. Gentlemen, I am on the roof like David when he beheld Bathsheba, but I behold only the Parisian panties of the boarding-school girls, drying in the garden. Gentlemen, we have come to the important problem of the relation between the object and the subject. Now, if we select just one of the creatures in which appears the highest organic self-affirmation of the Divine Spirit, and explore its relation to space, earth, and the planetary constellations . . . Gentlemen, if I throw this cat out the window, how will this organism react with respect to its center of gravity —its *centrum gravitationis*—and its own instincts? Hey, Woyzeck!

Roaring.
Woyzeck!

WOYZECK, *picking up the cat.* Doctor, she's biting me!

DOCTOR. Numbskull! He handles the beast as tenderly as his grandmother.
He comes down.

WOYZECK. Doctor, I've got the shakes.

DOCTOR, *quite delighted.* Oh, fine, fine, Woyzeck!
Rubs his hands. Takes the cat.
What is this, gentlemen? A new species of chicken lice? A fine species.
He takes out a magnifying glass. The cat gets away.
Gentlemen, that animal has no scientific instincts! However, here's something better for you to examine. Just look at this man. For three months, he's eaten nothing but peas. Note the result. Just feel him! What an irregular pulse. And those eyes!

WOYZECK. Everything's getting black, Doctor.
He sits down.

DOCTOR. Courage, Woyzeck! A couple of days and it will be over. Feel that pulse, gentlemen, feel it.
The students fumble over his pulse, temples, and chest.
Incidentally, Woyzeck, wiggle your ears for the gentlemen. I've been intending to show you this. He does it with two muscles. Come on, snap into it!

WOYZECK. Doctor! Oh!

DOCTOR. You brute, do I have to wiggle your ears for you? Are you going to behave like that cat? Well, gentlemen, here's a case of evolution into a donkey, which is frequently the consequence of being brought up by women. How much of your hair has your sentimental old mother been pulling out for souvenirs? It's gotten quite thin the last couple of days. Yes, gentlemen, it's those peas!

16 THE BARRACKS YARD

WOYZECK. Heard nothing?

ANDRES. He is still in there with a pal.

WOYZECK. He said something.

ANDRES. How do you know? What do you want me to say? Well, he laughed, and he said: A luscious piece! What thighs! And red hot!

WOYZECK, *quite coldly.* So that's what he said? What was I dreaming last night? Something about a knife? What crazy dreams you can have.

ANDRES. Where you going, pal?

WOYZECK. Getting wine for my Captain. You know, Andres, she was one girl in a thousand.

ANDRES. Who was?

WOYZECK. Never mind. So long.

17 THE INN

DRUM-MAJOR. WOYZECK. PEOPLE.

DRUM-MAJOR. I'm a real man!
Pounds his chest.
A real man, see? Anyone looking for something? Anyone who isn't drunk as the Lord better let me alone or I'll smash his nose up his arsehole for him. I'll——
To Woyzeck.
Hey, you lout, get drunk! I wish the whole world was schnaps, schnaps. That guy better start drinking.

WOYZECK *whistles.*

DRUM-MAJOR. You lout! You want me to yank your tongue out of your throat and wrap it round your ribs?

They wrestle. WOYZECK *loses.*
You want me to leave you enough wind for an old lady's
fart? Do you?

WOYZECK *sits on a bench, trembling and exhausted.*

DRUM-MAJOR. The bastard can whistle himself blue in the face.

Brandy is the drink for me
Brandy keeps your fancy free.

SOMEONE. He sure got his.

ANDRES. He's bleeding.

WOYZECK. One thing after the other.

18   PAWNSHOP

WOYZECK. *The* JEW.

WOYZECK. The pistol's too much.

JEW. So, are you buying or not buying? Make up your mind?

WOYZECK. How much was the knife?

JEW. It's good and sharp. Going to cut your throat with it?
Make up your mind. I'm giving it to you cheap as anybody.
You can die cheap, but not for nothing.

WOYZECK. It'll cut more than bread . . .

JEW. Two groschen.

WOYZECK. Here!
Goes out.

JEW. Here! Like it was nothing. And it's good money! The pig!

19   MARIE'S ROOM

FOOL, *stretched out, telling fairy tales on his fingers.* This
one has a golden crown. He's Our Lord the King. Tomorrow

I'll bring Her Royal Highness the Queen her child. . . . Pork
Sausage says, "Come on, Liverwurst . . ."

MARIE, *leafing through the bible.* "And no guile is found in
his mouth." Lord God, Lord God, don't look at me!

Leafs again.

"And the scribes and the Pharisees brought unto him a
woman taken in adultery, and set her in the midst . . . And
Jesus said unto her, 'Neither do I condemn thee; go, and
sin no more.'" Lord God, Lord God, I can't—Lord God,
give me the strength to pray!

The child cuddles up to her.

The child stabs me to the heart.

To the FOOL.

Karl! Strutting in the sun!

The FOOL *takes the child and becomes quiet.*

Franz hasn't been here yesterday or today. It's getting hot
in here.

She opens the window.

"And stood at his feet weeping, and began to wash his
feet with tears, and did wipe them with the hairs of her
head, and kissed his feet, and annointed them with oint-
ment."

Beats her breast.

Everything's dead. Saviour, Saviour! If only I could annoint
Thy feet!

20 BARRACKS

ANDRES. WOYZECK *rummaging through his belongings.*

WOYZECK. This jacket isn't regular issue, Andres. You might
be able to use it, Andres.

ANDRES, *quite rigid, keeps saying.* Sure.

WOYZECK. This cross was my sister's. The little ring, too.

ANDRES. Sure.

WOYZECK. I've also got a Holy picture, with two hearts, pure gold—it was in my mother's Bible, and it said:

> Lord, like thy body, red and sore,
> So let my heart be, evermore.

My mother can't feel much any more, only when the sun shines on her hands. That doesn't matter.

ANDRES. Sure.

WOYZECK *pulls out a document*. Private Friedrich Johann Franz Woyzeck, Rifleman, 2nd Regiment, 2nd Battalion, Company Four. Born Feast of the Annunciation, July 20th. I'm thirty years, seven months, and twelve days old.

ANDRES. Franz, why don't you go on sick-call? You poor guy, you ought to get some schnaps with a powder in it. It'd kill the fever.

WOYZECK. Yes, Andres. When the carpenter puts that wooden box together, you never know whose head is going to lie in it.

21   THE STREET

MARIE, *with little girls, in front of the door*. OLD WOMAN. *Later* WOYZECK.

GIRLS.
> The sun shines bright at Candlemas.
> The corn is in full bloom.
> They danced across the meadow grass,
> They danced it two by two.
> The flutes, they marched ahead,
> The fiddles in the rear,
> Their stockings were the reddest red . . .

FIRST GIRL. Aw, that's no good.

SECOND GIRL. You always want to do something different.

FIRST GIRL. Marie, you sing for us.

MARIE. I can't.

FIRST GIRL. Why not?

MARIE. Because.

SECOND GIRL. But why because?

THIRD GIRL. Grandma, tell a story.

GRANDMOTHER. All right, you little crabs. Once upon a time there was a poor little girl who had no father or mother because everyone was dead and there was no one left in the whole world. Everyone was dead, and she went off and kept looking for someone night and day. And since there was no one on earth, she thought she'd go to heaven. The moon looked out at her so friendly, but when she finally got to it, it was just a piece of rotted wood. So she went on to the sun, and when she got there, it was just a dried up sunflower. And when she got to the stars, they were just little gold flies stuck up there as if they'd been caught in a spider web. And when she thought she'd go back to earth, it was just an upside down pot. And she was all alone. And so she sat down and cried. And she's still sitting there, all alone.

WOYZECK *appears*. Marie!

MARIE, *frightened*. What?

WOYZECK. Marie, it's time to go.

MARIE. Where to?

WOYZECK. You think I know?

22   A WOODLAND PATH BY A POND

MARIE *and* WOYZECK.

MARIE. The town's that way. It's dark.

WOYZECK. You're not going. Come on, sit down.

MARIE. But I have to go.

WOYZECK. Your feet will get sore running.

MARIE. You're so changed.

WOYZECK. Do you know how long it's been, Marie?

MARIE. Two years, Pentecost.

WOYZECK. Do you know how long it will last?

MARIE. I have to go and get supper.

WOYZECK. You're not freezing, Marie? No, you're warm. You've got hot lips. Hot! A hot whore's breath! And I'd still give heaven to kiss them again. Are you freezing? When your bones are cold, you don't freeze anymore. You won't freeze in the morning dew.

MARIE. What are you saying?

WOYZECK. Nothing.
Silence.

MARIE. The moon's rising. It's red.

WOYZECK. Like a sword with blood on it!

MARIE. What are you going to do, Franz? You're so pale.
He raises the knife.
Franz, stop! For Heaven's sake! Help! Help!

WOYZECK, *stabbing madly.* Take that, and that! Why can't you die? There! There! Ha! She's still twitching. Still can't? Still twitching?
Stabs again.
Now are you dead? Dead! Dead!
He drops the knife and runs away.

23   THE INN

WOYZECK. Dance, everyone dance! Don't stop! Sweat and stink! He'll get all of you in the end.
Sings:
Oh, daughter, darling daughter,
You thought it no harm
When you hung around with stable boys
And the coachmen in the barn.

He dances.

Whew, Käthe! Sit down. I'm hot, hot!

He takes off his coat.

That's the way it goes. The devil takes one and lets the other get away. Käthe, you're hot. How come? You'll cool off now too, Käthe. Be reasonable. Can't you sing something?

KÄTHE *sings.*

> To Swabia I'll never go,
> And dresses wear down to my toe.
> For dresses long and pointed shoes
> A servant girl should never choose.

WOYZECK. No, no shoes. You can get into Hell without shoes.

KÄTHE *sings.*

> No, no, my love, that was not right.
> Take back your gold, sleep single tonight.

WOYZECK. That's true. I don't want to get any blood on me.

KÄTHE. But what's that on your hand?

WOYZECK. On me? Me?

KÄTHE. Red! Blood!

People gather round.

WOYZECK. Blood? Blood?

INNKEEPER. Ugh! Blood!

WOYZECK. I think, I cut myself. There, on my right hand.

INNKEEPER. How come it's on your elbow?

WOYZECK. I wiped it off.

INNKEEPER. Wiped your right hand on your right elbow? You have talent!

FOOL. And the Giant said: I smell, I smell. What do I smell? A man, a man who's bound for Hell! Pah! it stinks already!

WOYZECK. What the devil do you all want? What business is it of yours? Out of my way, or the first one who . . . Hell,

do you think I did away with someone? Am I a murderer?
What are you gaping at? Gawk at yourselves! Get out of
my way!

He runs off.

24   AT THE POND

WOYZECK *alone.*

WOYZECK. The knife? Where's the knife? I left it here. It'll
give me away. Nearer. Nearer yet. What place is this?
What's that I hear? Something moving! No, it's quiet. Over
there. Marie? Ha, Marie! You're quiet. Everything's quiet!
What are you so white for, Marie? What's that red string
around your neck? Who did your sins earn that necklace
from? You were black with them, black! Did I bleach you
white again? Why is your black hair hanging so wild? Didn't
you braid your long braids today? Here's something! Cold
and wet, and still. The knife! the knife! Got it? Get rid of it!

He runs into the water.

There! Down it goes.

He throws the knife in.

It dives down into the water like a stone. The moon's like
a sword with blood on it! Is the whole world going to gab
about it? No, it's lying too close. When they're swimming....

He goes into the pond and throws it further.

There, that's it! But, in the summer, when they're diving
for mussels? Bah! it'll be rusty. Who'd recognize it—I should
have broken it. Am I still bloody? I better wash up. There's
a spot and there's another.

Goes deeper into the water.

Time passes. People come.

FIRST PERSON. Wait up!

SECOND PERSON. You hear? Shh! Over there!

FIRST PERSON. Ugh! Over there. What a sound!

SECOND PERSON. It's the water, calling. It's been a long time
since anyone was drowned. Let's go, it's not a pleasant
thing to hear.

FIRST PERSON. Ugh! There it is again! Like a man, dying.

SECOND. It's eerie. So foggy, that gray mist everywhere, and
the bugs humming like broken bells. Let's go!

FIRST. Wait! It's too clear, too loud. It's up there. Come on!

25 THE STREET

CHILDREN.

FIRST CHILD. Let's go look at Marie!

SECOND CHILD. What for?

FIRST CHILD. Don't you know? Everybody's gone out there.
To Marie's Child.
Hey, your mother's dead.

MARIE'S CHILD, *playing horsey.* Giddyap, giddyap!

SECOND CHILD. Where is she?

FIRST CHILD. On the path to the pond.

SECOND CHILD. Hurry up! Let's get there before they bring
her back.

MARIE'S CHILD. Giddyap, giddyap!

26 AT THE POND

COURT CLERK. DOCTOR. JUDGE.

POLICEMAN. A real murder, a first-rate murder, a beautiful
murder. As beautiful a little murder as you could ask for.
It's a long time since we had one like this.

CAVALLERIA RUSTICANA

Scenes from the Life of the People
by

GIOVANNI VERGA

English version by
Eric Bentley

Characters

TURIDDU MACCA
MASTER ALFIO
LOLA, *his wife*
SANTUZZA
MOTHER NUNZIA, *mother of Turiddu*
UNCLE BRASI, *stableman*
AUNT CAMILLA, *his wife*
AUNT FILOMENA
PIPPUZZA

The time: 1880
The place: Southeastern Sicily

Cavalleria Rusticana means *Rustic Chivalry*. The first word of the title is accented on the fourth syllable which is pronounced *ee*.

1

*On stage, we see a small irregular village square. On the
left at back, a tree-lined avenue leading to the small
village church; also the wall of an orchard, marking the
boundary of the square. On the right, a path between
hedges of prickly pear, merging with the fields in the distance. In the foreground on the right,* MOTHER NUNZIA'S
*tavern with a branch over the entrance; a bench with eggs,
bread, and greens displayed on it; and, on the other side, a
bench against the wall. The tavern forms a corner with a
narrow street which passes into the interior of the village.
On the other corner the barracks of the* carabinieri *or police
—two floors, insignia over the door. Further away, following
the same line,* UNCLE BRASI'S *livery stables with an ample*
tettoia *in front, a* tettoia *being a straw roof propped against
the wall and looking like an awning. In the foreground on
the left, a terrace with an arbor. Then a narrow street.
Finally,* AUNT FILOMENA'S *little house.*

UNCLE BRASI *crosses the stage from the left with a bundle
of hay on his head; he puts it down under the* tettoia. AUNT
CAMILLA *on the terrace, folding the washing. Women along
the avenue on their way to church. A peasant is sitting under
the* tettoia, *his chin in his hands, humming a song. The
bells sound for Mass.* AUNT FILOMENA *comes out of* MOTHER
NUNZIA'S *tavern carrying things under her apron.*

CAMILLA. You been shopping, Aunt Filomena?

FILOMENA. At Easter, Mother Camilla? Lord save us!
She goes into the house.

CAMILLA, *to* SANTUZZA, *who enters by the first path on the
left, excited, her face hidden in her shawl.* Hey, Santuzza!
Going to confession?

SANTUZZA *raises her head in* CAMILLA'S *direction but passes
on without reply.*

35

BRASI, *to* CAMILLA *from the door of the livery stable.* Go back
in there and mind your business, you old gossip!

CAMILLA *goes back in the house. To a* carabiniere *who is
leaning on the balustrade of the terrace of the barracks.*

She's forever getting in my hair! What a wife!

To the peasant under the tettoia.

Come here, Peppi!

Takes him off into the stable.

SANTUZZA, *at the tavern door.* Mother Nunzia!

NUNZIA, *coming out.* Why, Santuzza! . . . What is it?

The carabiniere *goes back indoors.*

SANTUZZA. Don't worry, I'm going. Right away. Just tell me . . .
is your son Turiddu in?

NUNZIA. You have the gall to ask me that? *You* looking for
Turiddu *here?* No, he's *not.*

SANTUZZA. Lord have mercy!

NUNZIA. And I want no part in all these carryings-on, understand?

SANTUZZA, *drawing her shawl aside.* You can see the state I'm
in, Mother Nunzia. Couldn't you be like Our Lord with
Mary Magdalene? Where is your son Turiddu? Please tell
me!

NUNZIA. He's gone to Francofonte. For the wine.

AUNT FILOMENA *appears in the doorway of her house, her
hands on her stomach.*

SANTUZZA. It's not true! He was here last night. He was seen
here at two in the morning.

NUNZIA. What?—He didn't . . . come home last night. . . . Come
inside, Santuzza.

SANTUZZA. No, Mother Nunzia. I cannot enter your house.

BRASI, *from the* tettoia. It's Holy Easter, Aunt Filomena! The
time when girls make peace with their mothers-in-law! Shall
you and I kiss and make up?

FILOMENA. Be quiet, you heathen!
She goes back in the house.

NUNZIA, *to* SANTUZZA. Speak then. What has happened to my son?

SANTUZZA. Not so loud, Mother Nunzia, please!

PIPPUZZA, *from the little street on the right at the back, with a basket over her arm.* Want any eggs, Mother Nunzia?

NUNZIA. At three for two soldi, all right? Look, Pippuzza, I've got plenty already.

PIPPUZZA. All right, sure. I'll eat them myself, with the kids. We'll celebrate Holy Easter.
She is leaving.

BRASI. Haven't you been to confession, Mother Nunzia?

NUNZIA. Very well. Seeing it's Holy Easter. A soldo apiece. I'll take a dozen, and you can throw in one extra for luck. Put them with the others—over there. . . . Hey, don't break them, careful! Here's the money. A whole fistful of it, just look!

BRASI. Listen, Pippuzza, I think you and I can do business too. Come to my house. This way.
He takes her into the first little street on the left.

NUNZIA, *to* SANTUZZA. Speak then! What do you know of my son?

SANTUZZA. I know nothing of your son.

NUNZIA. Where was he last night—not coming home?

SANTUZZA, *bursting into tears with her face in her shawl.* Oh, Mother Nunzia, it's driving a nail through my heart!

NUNZIA. Then you know where Turiddu was?

ALFIO, *from the first little street on the right, with a flask in his hand.* Some wine, Mother Nunzia. Do you have any of the good at six soldi?

NUNZIA. I'll go see. My son Turiddu was bringing some over today from Francofonte.

ALFIO. Your son Turiddu is still here. I saw him this morning. Doesn't he wear the red cap of a *bersagliere?**

AUNT CAMILLA *again appears on the terrace.*

SANTUZZA. *taking the flask from* MASTER ALFIO's *hand and passing it to* MOTHER NUNZIA. Meanwhile, go see if there's any left.

MOTHER NUNZIA *goes back in the tavern.*

ALFIO. Quite one of the family now, aren't you, Miss Santa?

CAMILLA. Coming to all the Easter festivities with your wife Lola, Master Alfio?

ALFIO. As many as I can take in, Aunt Camilla.

FILOMENA, *from the doorway, her shawl on her arm, to* AUNT CAMILLA. You coming to Holy Mass?

BRASI, *running up from the left.* She's coming, she's coming! Master Alfio, hi! Can you take a load over to Militello for me?

ALFIO. Sure, if tomorrow's all right, Uncle Brasi. Today I've come to spend Easter at home.

FILOMENA, *reciting.*
At carnival time you all may roam
Christmas and Easter you spend at home!

CAMILLA, *to* MASTER ALFIO. And your wife, that only gets to see you at Christmas and Easter, what does *she* have to say?

ALFIO. Guess I don't rightly know, Aunt Camilla. It's my job, that's all. A carter's job is carting—all over the place—here today, there tomorrow.

NUNZIA, *returning with the flask full. Her shawl is folded; she leaves it on the table with the greens.* Better than that other, Master Alfio. I know you're going to think so—it'll bring you long life and happiness! Eighteen soldi.

* Later, the *bersagliere's* "feather" is referred to. This famous regiment of sharpshooters wore black cocks' plumes with their full dress uniform, a red fez (here translated as cap) with their undress uniform. As already mentioned in the dialogue, the *carabinieri* also sport feathers.

FILOMENA. It's not right, what you said, Master Alfio. With a young wife at home . . .

ALFIO. I wear my cap in my own way!

He strikes himself on his breast pocket.

You think *I* can't judge what's right—for her—and other people—for that matter?

Two carabinieri with their plumed caps on come out of the barracks and leave by the avenue.

I look after *my* affairs! Myself! Without assistance from our friends with the feather in their caps! And everybody in town knows it, thanks be to God!

The bells for Holy Mass ring a second time.

FILOMENA, *crossing herself.* May the day not soon come!

She locks the door, puts her shawl round her head, and makes for the church.

CAMILLA. I'm coming, Aunt Filomena, I'm coming too!

Leaves the terrace.

FILOMENA, *to* MASTER ALFIO. You'd better go and tell your wife the bell's ringing for Holy Mass, you heathen.

ALFIO. Got to run and groom the horses. I'll tell her afterwards, don't worry. I'm a Christian, aren't I?

NUNZIA, *to* MASTER ALFIO. Eighteen soldi.

ALFIO. So I'll do it, now don't be a pest. Let me count the money.

CAMILLA, *from the first little street on the left, with her shawl on her head, goes and gives her husband the key.* Here's the key, anyhow. And don't you turn up when the service is nearly over like you usually do!

She goes off, toward the church, with AUNT FILOMENA. UNCLE BRASI *goes back into the stable. One after another, people cross the square on their way to church.*

ALFIO *to* MOTHER NUNZIO . . . sixteen, seventeen, eighteen. And may it bring you health and happiness!

He moves off in the direction he came from.

NUNZIA. Just a minute. Where was it you saw my son Turiddu, Master Alfio?

SANTUZZA, *plucking her by the dress, softly*. Don't tell him anything, please don't tell him anything!

ALFIO, *turning*. Near my place it was. Around dawn. I was just getting back. He was running like he was in a hurry. Didn't notice me. Want me to send him to you if I see him?

NUNZIA. No. No.

ALFIO *leaves*.

To SANTUZZA.

What were you signalling me to hush up for?

SANTUZZA *does not reply. She bows her head*.

NUNZIA. Eh? What's got into your head?

SANTUZZA, *hiding her face in her apron, bursting into tears*. Oh, Mother Nunzia!

NUNZIA, *stunned*. Mrs. Lola? ... Master Alfio's wife?

SANTUZZA. What shall I do? He's leaving me—

NUNZIA. No, no. What are you telling me? It's impossible, you're mistaken, Master Alfio's mistaken too for that matter ... Lots of fellows wear the red cap of a *bersagliere* ...

SANTUZZA. Master Alfio was not mistaken. It was he, Turiddu.

NUNZIA. How can you know that?

SANTUZZA. I know. Turiddu ... before he served in the army ... he used to talk with Mrs. Lola.

NUNZIA. What of that? When he came home, he found her good and married to Master Alfio di Licodiano. He had to resign himself to his lot, didn't he?

SANTUZZA. She didn't. She didn't resign herself to any lot.

NUNZIA. How do you know she didn't?

SANTUZZA. I know this. Every time she saw him pass my door, she'd come out and make those eyes, the little heathen. And she'd try and start up a conversation. "What are you doing in these parts, Neighbor Turiddu? Things like this are the will o' God, they say. Now let me be! I belong to my husband!" The will o' God was a temptation to him. When he first took to singing under my window, it was just to spite another girl who'd taken another man. Old love is never forgot, they say, and it's true. But me, when I heard him sing, this Christian soul, I thought my heart had jumped right out of my chest. I was crazy, oh yes! But how could I say no? He pleaded with me. "Open up, Santuzza, you love me, don't you?" How could I say no? I said, "Listen, Neighbor Turiddu, first I want you to take an oath before God." He took it. But afterwards, when she found out about it— oh, she's wicked, that girl!—she was jealous, mortally jealous, and she made her mind up to rob me of him. She changed Turiddu right around.

With a gesture.

He denies it because he feels sorry for me, but really— really he doesn't love me any more! And now—with me in this condition—when my brothers find out they'll kill me with their own hands! As to that, I don't care. . . . If Turiddu didn't love this other girl, I'd die content. Last night he came in and said, "Good-bye, I got an errand to do." His face was very sweet. Lord God, with a face like that, how can you harbor in your heart the treachery of Judas? Later in the evening, a neighbor came over to do some spinning. She said she'd seen Turiddu back home there . . . at Mrs. Lola's door.

NUNZIA, *crossing herself.* Mother of God! What are you telling me on the holy day that it is?

SANTUZZA. Think what kind of day dawned for me this morning.

NUNZIA. Listen, Santuzza, you must throw yourself at the feet of the Crucified!

SANTUZZA. No. No, I can't. I can't go to church—now.

NUNZIA, *unfolding her shawl and putting it on her head.* And I must go too. I wouldn't like to miss it.

SANTUZZA. You go, Mother Nunzia, and I'll keep an eye on your store.

Pause.

Don't be afraid. I'm not a thief as well!

NUNZIA. What are you going to do, Santuzza?

SANTUZZA. I don't know, Mother Nunzia. Wait for him here, I guess,

She points at the bench beside the door.

like a beggar on the doorstep.

NUNZIA. Here? At my place?

SANTUZZA. Don't worry, Mother Nunzia, I won't go inside. But don't drive me from your door. You'll be praying to the Lord; He's merciful, you be merciful too, Mother Nunzia. Leave me here. Please! By the souls of our dead, I beg, let me talk to him—this last time!

NUNZIA *makes for the church, grumbling.* Lord God above, *You* do something!

BRASI, *running out of the stable.* Hold on a minute, Mother Nunzia! We shopkeepers should stick together—even if we do arrive last!

But MOTHER NUNZIA *has gone.*

To SANTUZZA.

Ah! Not going to service—even today, Miss Santa? Would you like for us to recite the rosary together?

SANTUZZA. Leave me alone.

BRASI. Eh! I won't eat you, what the devil? . . . . As if we didn't all know . . .

SANTUZZA. Leave me alone!

PIPPUZZA, *from the first path on the left, out of breath.* Shall I be in time for service, Uncle Brasi?

BRASI. If you run, you will.

PIPPUZZA *runs.*

See? I'm like the bell-ringer that calls everyone else to church
and then stays outside himself.

Looks toward the path at the back on the right.

Ah! I see why you wanted to be left alone. Here comes that
Simple Simon . . . Now *I'm* going too . . .

He goes off towards the church.

2

TURIDDU MACCA *in haste from the path at the back on the
right, and* SANTUZZA, *who jumps to her feet on seeing him.*

TURIDDU. Santuzza! You here? What——?

SANTUZZA. I was waiting for you.

TURIDDU. Where's my mother?

SANTUZZA. She's gone to church.

TURIDDU. Then you go too. I'll keep an eye on the store.

SANTUZZA. No. I'm not going to church.

TURIDDU. At Easter?

SANTUZZA. You know I can't.

TURIDDU. Then what do you want to do?

SANTUZZA. I want to talk to you.

TURIDDU. Here? In the middle of the street?

SANTUZZA. It doesn't matter to me.

TURIDDU. Think of all the people that can see!

SANTUZZA. It doesn't matter to me.

TURIDDU. Hey, what's wrong with you?

SANTUZZA. Tell me where you've just come from.

TURIDDU. Ho, ho! what does *this* signify?

SANTUZZA. Where were you last night?

TURIDDU. Ah! I must say where I was?

SANTUZZA. Why do you get angry if I ask where you were? You can't tell me?

TURIDDU. At Francofonte, if you want to know. Francofonte.

SANTUZZA. It's not true. Last night—at two in the morning—you were here!

TURIDDU. I was where it pleased me to be!

SANTUZZA, *letting her shawl fall from her shoulders*. Turiddu, Turiddu, why do you treat me so? Won't you look me in the face? Can't you see I'm dying a thousand deaths!

TURIDDU. That's your fault. You've been getting ideas. You've been telling tales about me to all and sundry. You've been prying into my affairs like I was a little boy and didn't have the right to do what I want!

SANTUZZA. No, no, I didn't ask, they told me, they told me just now they'd seen you at dawn at Mrs. Lola's door.

TURIDDU. Who said that?

SANTUZZA. Master Alfio, her husband.

TURIDDU. Him! Ha! So this is the love you bear me! You go and pour fleas in Master Alfio's ear! You risk getting me killed!

SANTUZZA, *falling on her knees, her hands joined*. Oh, Turiddu, how can you say that?

TURIDDU. Get up! Get up, and don't make such a song and dance! Get up or I'll go.

SANTUZZA, *slowly rising*. You'll go, Turiddu? You'll leave me now like Our Lady of the Sorrows?

TURIDDU. What do you expect me to do if you don't believe what I say any more? What the others tell you, though, that's a different matter, you believe *that*! I tell you again, not one word of it is true. Master Alfio was mistaken. I had an errand to do. Look, you chose the wrong time for getting this notion into your head—her husband's in town, you said so yourself. So it's impossible, don't you see?

SANTUZZA. Her husband didn't get in till this morning.

TURIDDU. Ah! You know everything, don't you? Don't miss a thing. You're spying on me, missy! I've got no rights any more!

SANTUZZA. Oh, you have, Turiddu, you have. You have the right to slaughter me like a lamb with your own hands. Or, if you wish, I will lick your hands like a dog.

TURIDDU. Well then?

SANTUZZA. But not Lola, you understand? That girl wants to damn my eternal soul.

TURIDDU. Leave Lola out of this. She has a home of her own.

SANTUZZA. Why can't she leave me alone? Why must she rob me of you when I've nothing else in the world?

TURIDDU. Mind you don't make a mistake!

SANTUZZA. I'm making no mistake. Weren't you *always* running after her—even before you went in the army?

TURIDDU. Water under the bridge. Mrs. Lola is married now, with a home of her own.

SANTUZZA. What difference does that make? Don't you still love her—even if she *is* married? And hasn't she robbed me of you out of jealousy? And don't I go on feeling the fire in my blood—for you, my betrayer?

TURIDDU. Oh, shut up!

SANTUZZA. I won't shut up! I have the rabies in my heart! What shall I do if you desert me?

TURIDDU. I won't desert you—if only you'll stop trying to stand me up against the wall! I keep telling you, I claim the right to do what it pleases me to do. I'm not used to having any chain around *my* neck, thank God!

SANTUZZA. What do you mean by that?

TURIDDU. I mean you're crazy—with this groundless jealousy of yours.

SANTUZZA. Is it my fault? Look what's become of me. Oh yes, Mrs. Lola is better than me, with her neck and hands all laden with gold. Her husband doesn't let her want for anything. He makes her look like the Madonna on the altar, that heathen girl!

TURIDDU. Oh, leave her alone.

SANTUZZA. You're not defending her?

TURIDDU. No, I'm not. What does it matter to me if her husband makes her look like the Madonna on the altar? What matters to me is not passing for a man who hasn't got the right to do what it pleases him to do. I say no to that!

3

MRS. LOLA *from the first path on the right.* TURIDDU *and* SANTUZZA.

LOLA. Oh, Neighbor Turiddu! Did my husband go into the church, do you know?

TURIDDU. I don't know, Mrs. Lola. I only just got here.

LOLA. He says to me, "I'll be going to the blacksmith's for the bay horse, the one with the shoe missing, see you in church right afterwards." Are you listening to the service from out here? And making conversation too?

TURIDDU. Miss Santa was just telling me—

SANTUZZA. I was telling him today is a great day and the Lord above sees all things.

LOLA. And you're not going to church, Miss Santa, how about that?

SANTUZZA. "He that hath a clean conscience, let him go and worship."

LOLA. I thank the Lord, I kiss the ground.

She bends down and touches the ground with the ends of her fingers, which she then raises to her lips.

SANTUZZA. I'm glad to hear it, Mrs. Lola. For sometimes they say of a man, "He planteth his feet on the ground, but is not worthy to put his lips to it."

TURIDDU. Let you and me be going, Mrs. Lola. We've nothing to do here.

LOLA. Don't you put yourself out on my account, Neighbor Turiddu. I've no wish to interrupt. My feet know the path they're taking.

TURIDDU. We've nothing to do here, I say.

SANTUZZA, *pulling him by the coat.* But we have! We hadn't finished talking—

LOLA. Health and happiness, Neighbor Turiddu. You stay and manage your affairs, I'll go and manage mine.

She goes off towards the church.

4

TURIDDU *and* SANTUZZA.

TURIDDU, *furious.* Ah! See what you've done?

SANTUZZA. Yes, I see.

TURIDDU. You did it on purpose then?

SANTUZZA. Yes, I did it on purpose.

TURIDDU, *crying out.* Ah! Blood of Judas!

SANTUZZA, *suddenly.* Kill me!

TURIDDU. So you did it on purpose! You did it on purpose!

SANTUZZA. Kill me! I don't care. Come on!

TURIDDU. No. That's not what I want either.

He starts to go

SANTUZZA. You're leaving me?

TURIDDU. Yes. It's what you deserve.

The bell rings for the Elevation of the Host.

SANTUZZA. Don't leave me Turiddu! Don't you hear that bell?

TURIDDU. I'll not be led by the nose, understand?

SANTUZZA. You can walk on me, I told you that, you can trample on my face. But not her, not her!

TURIDDU. Oh, let's have done! I'm going now—I'll cut this scene short!

SANTUZZA. Where are you going to?

TURIDDU. Where it pleases me to go—to Holy Mass.

SANTUZZA. No. You can't go showing Mrs. Lola you've left me out here, left me for her, you can't go showing her I'm nothing to you!

TURIDDU. You're crazy!

SANTUZZA. Don't go, Turiddu! It's a sin, Turiddu, and in the church too, don't go! Don't insult me again, letting that girl see everything!

TURIDDU. But it's you! *You're* trying to insult *me!* You're trying to show the world I have no rights, I can't move backwards or forwards, you have me tied to your apron strings!

SANTUZZA. That's what *she* says! What should you care? Unless you want me to die—die of despair!

TURIDDU. Ah, you're crazy!

SANTUZZA. Yes! Yes, I am! I'm crazy! Don't leave me—when I'm crazy like this!

TURIDDU, *tearing himself away.* Have done, I say! Damnation!

SANTUZZA. Turiddu, by the God descending now in the consecrated Host, do not leave me for Lola!

TURIDDU *goes.*

Ah!

Pause.

Bad luck to you, this Easter day!

5

MASTER ALFIO *in haste from the path at the back on the right, and* SANTUZZA *center stage.*

SANTUZZA. It's the Lord Himself that sends you, Master Alfio!

ALFIO. How far along is the Holy Mass, Miss Santa?

SANTUZZA. You're late. But your wife's there in your place, with Turiddu Macca.

ALFIO. What do you mean?

SANTUZZA. She goes around all laden with gold, I'm telling you, like the Madonna on the altar, she's a credit to you, Master Alfio, she upholds the family honor . . .

ALFIO. Oh? And what's it matter to you?

SANTUZZA. It's for you it matters to me. While you're roaming the wide world and buying her lovely presents—you load her with jewels and gold, and she loads you with something else, Master Alfio.

ALFIO. What's that you're saying, Miss Santa?

SANTUZZA. I'm saying, oh yes, you earn a pretty penny all right, but rain or shine you're off and away, leaving your young wife to adorn your house for you, and she adorns it, oh yes, she adorns it with——!

ALFIO. In the name of God, Miss Santa! You got yourself drunk good and early this Easter morning. I'll make the wine come out through your nose for you!

SANTUZZA. I am not drunk, Master Alfio. I speak in good earnest.

ALFIO. All right. If it be truth, what you tell me, I thank you
for it, I kiss your hands like the soul of my mother had
come back from the graveyard on the hill. But if you're
lying, Miss Santa, by the souls of my dead, I won't leave
you any eyes to weep with, Miss Santa, you or your whole
infamous family, I swear it!

SANTUZZA. I can't weep, Master Alfio. These eyes didn't weep
—even when they saw Turiddu Macca—who has robbed
me of my honor—on his way to Mrs. Lola your wife!

ALFIO, *turning and, all of a sudden, calm.* If it is so, it is so.
And I thank you, neighbor.

SANTUZZA. No, no, don't thank me, I'm wicked!

ALFIO. You're not the wicked one, Miss Santa, the wicked
ones are those that plunge this knife in your heart and
mine! And now, to split open their hearts, split them open
with a real knife poisoned in garlic, that would be nothing!
If you see my wife looking for me, tell her I've gone home
to get a present for her good neighbor Turiddu.
He goes off, by the first path on the right.
*The people are beginning to return from church and to
disperse to left and right.* TURIDDU MACCA, MRS. LOLA,
AUNT CAMILLA, MOTHER NUNZIA, AUNT FILOMENA *come
forward, paying no attention to* SANTUZZA *who stays near
the path at the back on the right, muffled in her shawl.
Only* UNCLE BRASI, *coming last, notices her.*

BRASI. Going to church, Miss Santa, when's there's nobody
there?

SANTUZZA. Uncle Brasi, I'm in mortal sin!

6

UNCLE BRASI *goes back for a moment into the stable.* AUNT
CAMILLA *makes for her house,* AUNT FILOMENA *puts the
key in the lock.* MOTHER NUNZIA *goes into the tavern to
take off her shawl.*

TURIDDU, *to Mrs. Lola who is also making for home.* Mrs. Lola! *She stops.*
Why are you going off like this—without a word?

LOLA. I'm going home. I'm worried—about my husband. I didn't see him in church.

TURIDDU. Don't give it a thought. He'll be along. Drink a drop of wine with me, let's all be drinking some wine, health, long life, and a Happy Easter, hey, friends, neighbors, Aunt Camilla, and you Aunt Filomena, Aunt Filomena!

FILOMENA. Coming, coming!
She goes into the house to leave her shawl; returns at once.

LOLA. I thank you, neighbor Turiddu. But I'm not thirsty.

TURIDDU. Oh come, that's an insult, neighbor. . . . Eh, you're not angry with me?

LOLA. And what reason would I have to be angry with you, Neighbor Turiddu?

TURIDDU. That's what *I* say! What reason would you have to be angry with me? I've not done anything to you, have I? Anyhow, Easter Day will wash away any wrongs we've been doing each other. Let's send for your husband Master Alfio. Let's have *him* drink with us.

BRASI, *drawing near.* Fun and festivity!

CAMILLA. Oh sure, if there's anything like that,
Indicating LOLA *and* TURIDDU.
trust you to be around.
She folds her shawl, puts it over her arm.

TURIDDU, *calling into the interior of the tavern.* Hey, Mother! You still have some of the good?

NUNZIA *appears, grumbling.* The good indeed! You should've been bringing it over from Francofonte today!

TURIDDU. Oh, come on, Mother, today is Easter! Now don't *you* start making a long face at me! I'll explain later. Our friends are waiting!

FILOMENA. Oh, Mother Nunzia, there ain't much profit in what you'll sell today!

TURIDDU. But I'm paying! With my own money!

MOTHER NUNZIA *goes in again.*

BRASI. "He who has it, spends it."

LOLA. We can just see you—when you were a soldier—in those places—over there—gallivanting around and flirting with all the girls! You've had experience, we can see that!

TURIDDU. Girls? What girls? Why, my heart was always right here—in my own village.

CAMILLA. Tell it to the dead!

TURIDDU. Now, Aunt Camilla, upon my word! I know they say the *bersaglieri* are like honey, the women stick to them. What a little feather *will* do! "This way, dark and handsome," says one. The other just looks and looks and looks at you. . . . None of this applies to me, you understand? Out of sight, out of mind.

LOLA. Oh, these men! Who can believe 'em?

TURIDDU. And, oh, these women! They swear a thousand oaths, and then—when a poor guy goes away and leaves his heart behind him, and his head too, and can't even eat, and thinks all the time of just one thing—all of a sudden comes the news like a shot from a gun: "Know what? She's getting married!" Kinda like having a stroke.

FILOMENA. They say, "Marriages and Bishoprics are made in Heaven."

LOLA. You believe that? You believe they think all the time of just one thing—when they're away with all the other girls? You believe they don't even give 'em a look? You don't believe they're soon ready to console themselves with the first pretty skirt they see?

TURIDDU. Now, pardon me——

NUNZIA, *returning with jug and glass.* What there's left of it! Course, it's *his* fault!

CAMILLA. It's all right, we'll have a lot of fun!

BRASI. It's just the time for a drink, you're right!

TURIDDU. I said it—and my word's my bond. You won't drink with us, Mother?

NUNZIA. No. I don't care to.
Goes back in the house, grumbling.

TURIDDU. She's mad about something. I kinda think I know what, too. . . . God bless the oldsters, I say, they just don't care to recall what they did when they were youngsters! Your health, Mrs. Lola! And yours, Aunt Camilla! Drink up, Uncle Brasi! Begone dull care, say I!

7

MASTER ALFIO *from the right*, TURIDDU, UNCLE BRASI, MRS. LOLA, AUNT CAMILLA, *and* AUNT FILOMENA.

ALFIO. Good health to all present!

TURIDDU. Come here, Master Alfio. You've a drop of wine to drink here. We're drinking each other's health.
He fills his glass.

ALFIO, *pushes the glass away with the back of his hand.* Thank you very much, neighbor Turiddu, but I don't want your wine. It makes me feel sick.

TURIDDU. As you please.
He throws his wine to the ground and puts his glass on the table. They stand looking into each other's eyes.

BRASI, *pretending someone is calling him from the stable.* Coming, coming!

TURIDDU. Is there any small favor I can do for you, Neighbor?

ALFIO. None, Neighbor. What I have to say you know.

TURIDDU. I am here. At your service.

UNCLE BRASI *makes a sign from under the tettoia for his wife to go into the house; she does so.*

LOLA. But what do you mean?

ALFIO, *paying no heed to his wife, putting her aside with his arm.* If you wish to come out for a moment, we can discuss this matter more freely.

TURIDDU. Wait for me at the end of the village street. I'm going in to get what is necessary. I'll be back.
They embrace and kiss. TURIDDU *bites* MASTER ALFIO *lightly on the ear.*

ALFIO. Ah! That means you have given me your word! You are a man, Neighbor Turiddu!

LOLA. Mother of God, where are you going, Master Alfio?

ALFIO. Not very far. And what is it to you? Better for you if I never came back.

FILOMENA, *going away, stammering.* Jesu Maria, Jesu Maria . . .

TURIDDU, *calling Master Alfio to one side.* Listen, Master Alfio, as God's in Heaven, I know I'm in the wrong, and I'd let myself be slaughtered without a word, but I have Miss Santa on my conscience, I'd be dropping her over the precipice. So, as God's in Heaven, I'm going to kill you, Master Alfio, I'll kill you like a dog! I won't leave that girl on the streets.

ALFIO. Very good. Act in your own interest, Neighbor Turiddu.
He goes off, along the path at the back on the right.

8

LOLA. Neighbor Turiddu! You're not leaving me—like this?

TURIDDU. I'll have nothing to do with you. It's over between us. Didn't you see us kiss and embrace for life and death— your husband and me? Mother Nunzia!

NUNZIA, *appearing*. What is it now?

TURIDDU. I've got an errand to do, Mother, I can't please myself.
Give me the key of the gate, will you, so I can leave by
the orchard and save time? And, Mother, embrace me,
will you—like when I left for the army and you thought
I'd never come back again? It's Easter today!

NUNZIA. What is it you're saying, Turiddu?

TURIDDU. Oh, it's just the wine talking, I've had a drop too
much, and I'm taking a little walk to cool my brains?
Anyhow . . . Santuzza . . . she has no one in all the world,
you take care of her, will you, Mother?
He goes off, into the house.

9

MOTHER NUNZIA *in amazement*; MRS. LOLA *in agitation*;
AUNT CAMILLA *peeping round the corner*; AUNT FILOMENA
in the doorway; UNCLE BRASI *near the tettoia.*

NUNZIA. What does it mean?

BRASI, *approaching, attentive*. Go home, Mrs. Lola, go back
home!

LOLA, *in a terrible state*. Why? Why must I go home?

BRASI. It's not good you should be here right now, in the
public square! If you want someone to go with you . . .
Camilla, you stay with Mother Nunzia . . .

FILOMENA, *drawing near*. Jesu Maria, Jesu Maria . . .

NUNZIA. But where's he gone, my son?

CAMILLA, *now at her husband's ear*. What's all this?

BRASI, *in an undertone*. Didn't you see him, silly? He bit into
his ear. That means I kill you or you kill me.

CAMILLA. Our Lady of Danger, help us!

NUNZIA, *more and more overcome.* But where's he gone, my son Turiddu? What does it all mean?

LOLA. It means we have bad luck, this Easter day! And the wine we've been drinking will turn to poison, Mother Nunzia!

PIPPUZZA *runs up from the rear, shouting.* They've killed Neighbor Turiddu! They've killed Neighbor Turiddu!

All run towards the rear, talking and shouting, MOTHER NUNZIA *with her hands in her hair, quite beside herself. Two* carabinieri *cross the stage, running.*

WOMAN OF PARIS

A Comedy in Three Acts
by

HENRY BECQUE

English version by
Jacques Barzun

Characters

CLOTILDE
LAFONT
DU MESNIL
SIMPSON
ADELE

The Time: The eighteen-eighties
The Place: Paris

TRANSLATOR'S NOTE In the reading aloud or stage production of Becque's play in English, it is advisable that no attempt be made to give the proper names their French pronunciation—if for no other reason than that two of the persons referred to are named Simpson and yet are not foreigners. The names of the other principals may be anglicized as follows: Doomeny (accent on first syllable) and Lafont (accent on second syllable, sounded like "font"). As for Beaulieu, it is pronounced Bolio in Canada and the example is worth following; Mercier becomes Mur-cyay; and the two women's Christian names are most readily intelligible if vowels and consonants are allowed their usual English pronunciation.

ACT ONE

A fashionably furnished drawing-room. At center, double folding doors. To the left, a second pair of doors. Right, a window. On each side, additional doors—a double door on the right, a single on the left, which is also farther downstage. Against the wall, right, a secretary desk; left, a small table with a blotting-pad. Other furniture, chairs, mirrors, flowers, etc.

When the curtain rises, the stage is empty. CLOTILDE, *dressed to go out, with hat and gloves on, enters center, hurriedly, with a letter in her hand. She goes to the table and conceals it beneath a writing case, at the same time drawing a bunch of keys from her pocket and going to the secretary desk. At that point,* LAFONT *appears. She pretends to lock the desk.* LAFONT *puts down his hat, goes towards her, upset and controlling himself with difficulty.*

LAFONT. Open the desk and give me that letter.

CLOTILDE. No.
  Pause.

LAFONT. Open the desk and give me that letter.

CLOTILDE. I shan't.
  Longer pause.

LAFONT. Where have you been?

CLOTILDE. Ah! Something else, now.

LAFONT. Yes, it is something else. I'm asking you where you've been.

CLOTILDE. I shall tell you. I wish you could see yourself now, with the face you're making. You don't look handsome, my dear. I like you better with your usual face. Heavens! What

59

are we coming to if you lose your head over a wretched little note that anybody at all may have written me.

LAFONT. Open the desk and give me that letter.

CLOTILDE. You shall have it. . . . But you can see that scenes like these, if often repeated, would soon alienate me from you. I warn you, I won't stand a cross-examination every time I set foot outside the house.

LAFONT. Where have you been?

CLOTILDE. Try to be logical, at least. Is it likely that I'm leaving someone and find a note from him when I get home?

LAFONT. Open the desk and give me that letter.

CLOTILDE. You're joking, aren't you?

LAFONT. Do I look like it?

CLOTILDE. You suspect me, then?

LAFONT. That's more likely.
He points to the desk.

CLOTILDE. You really want it? You demand it? You issue orders? Very well.
Slowly, with affectation, she draws out of her pocket first a handkerchief, next a small engagement book, then the keys. She replaces the handkerchief and the book, and throws the keys across the room.
Open it yourself.
She turns her back. He stands motionless, undecided.
Go on, pick them up and open it. You've begun, go through with it. Be a man at least.
He makes up his mind, goes to the keys, stoops down.
Be careful! Consider what you're going to do. If you touch those keys with so much as your fingertips—your fingertips —I shan't be the one to regret it: you will.

LAFONT *picks up the keys.* Take back your keys.
Pause; she takes off her hat and gloves.

CLOTILDE. It's getting worse, you know.

LAFONT. What is getting worse?

CLOTILDE. The disease is gaining.

LAFONT. What disease?

CLOTILDE. I had already noticed that you were watching my comings and goings and I laughed at the trouble you were taking—so fruitlessly. I couldn't say anything, then. It was jealousy, but a pleasant sort of jealousy, which flatters the vanity of a woman, which amuses her. Now you've come to that other, stupid, crude, brutal jealousy which wounds us deeply and which we never forgive twice. Will you ever do this again?

LAFONT. Clotilde!

CLOTILDE. Will you?

LAFONT. No.

CLOTILDE. Good.

LAFONT. Clotilde!

CLOTILDE. What is it, my dear?

LAFONT. You love me?

CLOTILDE. Less than yesterday.

LAFONT. You want me to be happy?

CLOTILDE. I think I have proved it often enough.

LAFONT. I'm worried about all these young men you meet, who hang about you.

CLOTILDE. You're silly to worry. I talk with this one and that, and once gone I don't even know which I was talking to.

LAFONT. You don't recall anyone you might have encouraged—inadvertently—who might have felt entitled to address you?

CLOTILDE. No one.

LAFONT, *piteously*. Open the desk and give me that letter.

CLOTILDE. Again! That letter is from my friend, Mme. Doyen Beaulieu,

LAFONT *starts.*

the most virtuous of women—under her flighty appearances. I know what Pauline says in it and I shall tell you as soon as you've stopped asking me.

LAFONT. Clotilde!

CLOTILDE. What now?

LAFONT. Do you feel sensible?

CLOTILDE. More than ever.

LAFONT. Your head is cool?

CLOTILDE. My head is cool—and my heart also.

LAFONT. Think of me, Clotilde, and think of yourself. Reflect that a mistake is easily made and can never be mended. Don't give in to that taste for adventures which makes so many victims nowadays. Resist it, Clotilde, resist it. As long as you stay faithful to me, you remain worthy and respectable. If you should deceive me. . . .

She stops him by getting up and going towards the center door.

CLOTILDE. Careful! Here comes my husband!

Enter DU MESNIL.

DU MESNIL. I thought I heard Lafont's voice! My! But you do talk and gossip and argue when you're together! An earthquake wouldn't stop you!

CLOTILDE *to* DU MESNIL *alone.* So, you were back?

DU MESNIL. Yes, I was back.

CLOTILDE. You've been home a good while?

DU MESNIL. A little while.

CLOTILDE. It seems to me that when one of your friends is here you could at least show yourself and entertain him.

DU MESNIL. I was finishing a piece of work.

CLOTILDE. What did your uncle say?

DU MESNIL. I didn't find him in.

CLOTILDE. He's not easily found.

DU MESNIL. He left word that I should drop in later today.

CLOTILDE. Do you want me to go with you?

DU MESNIL. You'd only be in the way.

CLOTILDE. Thanks.

DU MESNIL *going to* LAFONT. How are things with you?

LAFONT. Fairly well. What about you?

DU MESNIL. Well, I don't feel very lively right now.

LAFONT. What's the matter?

DU MESNIL. I work a great deal and my health suffers.

LAFONT. Take a rest.

DU MESNIL. That takes time—and money.

LAFONT. Money—yes, but you're earning a good deal.

DU MESNIL. I get it with one hand and spend it with the other.

LAFONT. That'd be fun, I should think.

DU MESNIL. Fun—when one's a bachelor.

CLOTILDE. Aren't you done complaining? Do you suppose you're entertaining Mr. Lafont or pleasing me? Why the lamentation? Your appetite is good, you sleep well; I don't know of any husband more pampered than you are. You work! Of course you do! Everybody does. If I were you, I'd work four times as much and say forty times as little about it.

DU MESNIL. She's a wonder, my wife! You don't know, my dear fellow, what a household like this is like, with expenses going up every year and tastes getting more expensive every day.

CLOTILDE. You keep on?

DU MESNIL. Let me talk a little. I didn't stop the two of you a while ago. Why don't you sit down and do your sewing since you are so industrious. Take a look at the children's pants, it won't do any harm; the poor things are always exposed to the air.

CLOTILDE. I spoil them too much.

DU MESNIL. But you don't mend them enough.

CLOTILDE. That's the maid's job.

DU MESNIL. We lodge as modestly as possible. I pay a great deal to live in a prison. Servants are no longer contented with wages, they want salaries. We dine out often, it's true, almost every day; but my wife, naturally, wants to dress like all the other women, and what's saved on the one hand is spent with the other. . . . The only advantage is that one gets better meals.

CLOTILDE. Well, you enjoy that.

DU MESNIL. I don't deny it. I'd rather have a good dinner outside than a bad one at home.

CLOTILDE. That's enough now, let's talk of more entertaining things.

DU MESNIL. You're a bachelor, my dear Lafont; well, take my advice and stay one.

LAFONT. Do you agree with that, Mrs. Du Mesnil?

CLOTILDE. Marry or not, as you please.
She moves away.

DU MESNIL. Will you be more agreeable than my wife and listen to me?

LAFONT. With pleasure—

DU MESNIL. Some people just now are making efforts in my behalf, efforts worth the trouble.

LAFONT. Tell me the whole story.

DU MESNIL. It's my uncle, my uncle John, who's a member
of the Institute and who has long been dissatisfied with
my position. He wants me in the Finance Ministry. He has
friends there, most of them know me. They have made up
their minds to find me a certain post.

LAFONT. That would be just the thing for you. You could do
your own work and you wouldn't depend on anybody.

DU MESNIL. At the same time, my work is going pretty well,
now. The learned societies think well of me. Not an ap-
propriation that I don't pass on. I'm very much in demand
by the "Monitor of Agricultural Interests" in the pages of
which I explode a bombshell once in a while. It spreads my
name. I take on everything that comes my way. But my
uncle does not approve. He thinks at my age, with wife and
children, my place should be secure.

LAFONT. He's right.

DU MESNIL. Perhaps he is right. I'm not a statistician, I'm not
an economist, I'm a . . . something apart. Let me tell you,
between ourselves, that my little work called "Moral Considerations on the Budget" has been widely noticed. Such
books are only for the few and don't sell like novels; but
nevertheless, to date, one hundred and nineteen copies have
been sold—or one hundred and eighteen—there's one copy
missing; it may have been stolen. I see ahead of me a grand
opening for my activities, a field of specialization to exploit.

LAFONT. Try to get your Finance job first: it's a surer thing;
afterwards you can do what you want. I'll try, by the way,
to help the thing along. I know someone . . .

DU MESNIL. Please don't. My uncle has taken the lead and he
wants to be the one to push it through. It seems to me that
when a member of the Institute of Political Science consents
to ask a favor, when he asks that favor for his nephew—
when that nephew happens to be somebody, the government can only grant it, don't you agree?

LAFONT. Positions are not always open.

DU MESNIL. I happen to know of one that will be very soon.

LAFONT. Tell me, is it certain that the post you've been promised is in Paris?

DU MESNIL. In Paris, of course. My wife couldn't stand it in
the country.

CLOTILDE, *during these last words, has been sitting at the
small table from which she has picked up her letter to show
it behind her husband's back to* LAFONT, *with a taunting
look and gesture. The end of the business should coincide
with* DU MESNIL'S *last speech.*

CLOTILDE, *getting up.* Adolph, read this letter.

DU MESNIL, *turning around.* What does it say?

CLOTILDE. Open it and you'll see.
Gives him the letter.
It's from Pauline.

DU MESNIL. "My dearest, you will receive, if you have not already done so, an invitation to Mrs. Simpson's ball for the
25th. Your request was in good hands, and your self-respect
in no wise suffered. I mentioned your name; it was taken
up with many agreeable comments; you were said to be
extremely pretty, and that it would be charming to have
you. You are now among the intimates of the house. I feel
sure you will like Mrs. Simpson immensely. You shall tell
me how old you think her; I shall tell you how old she is.
Which does not prevent her, in decolleté and with all her
jewels on, from getting away with it; the ex-beauty Mrs.
Simpson still creates an illusion. What shoulders and eyes,
and a way of smiling like no one else! And what kindliness!
Nothing shocks her; she understands every weakness; there
is no indiscretion, however great, which does not seem to
her either interesting or excusable. She is a true aristocrat."

DU MESNIL, *exchanging with* LAFONT *a look of displeasure; both
nod disapproval* "What kindliness!" "Nothing shocks her!"
"She understands every weakness." "There is no indiscretion, however great. . . ." I don't think I care very much for
Pauline's letter.

LAFONT. Your friend, Mrs. Du Mesnil, seems a rather—irrespon-
sible person.

DU MESNIL. You see, you see! I've heard of Mrs. Simpson. There are rather shady stories about her.

LAFONT. Mrs. Simpson has a deplorable reputation.

DU MESNIL. You hear that, don't you? I'll not take you into such a house.

LAFONT. I assure you it's not at all your set, you don't belong with women of dubious reputation.

DU MESNIL. Well, aren't you struck by the fact that Lafont and I are of the same mind?

CLOTILDE. Very well, we'll do as you wish. If we don't go to Mrs. Simpson's we'll go elsewhere, that's all. But in the future, I wish that before you discuss certain things you'd wait until we are alone. I'm not in the habit of taking advice from strangers.
She turns from them abruptly.

DU MESNIL. What are you talking about? Lafont a stranger!
To LAFONT.
So you two have had a tiff?

LAFONT. It's you, ever since you've been here, who have got on her nerves for no reason.

DU MESNIL *to* CLOTILDE. I'm going.

CLOTILDE *drily.* Good luck to you.

DU MESNIL. What are you doing today?

CLOTILDE. What I please.

DU MESNIL. Where are we dining tonight?

CLOTILDE. I haven't the slightest idea.

DU MESNIL. Lord! What answers.

CLOTILDE. As if I should put myself out for a man who is quarrelsome and disagreeable.

DU MESNIL. So you want very much to go to this ball?

CLOTILDE. The ball has nothing to do with it. I'd already forgotten it. I'm no longer in my 'teens to worry about a dance
more or less. But you—you complain, you lecture, you abuse
your wife without the least consideration for her. If someone
overheard you he would have a very false idea of our home-
life.

DU MESNIL. You mustn't take me seriously, stupid! Do you
suppose there are many husbands like me? I growl for a
second, but when you've made up your mind, I do things
your way after all. Who is master here?

She smiles.

I'm very intent about this appointment, which would be
a big thing for us, and which ought to interest you more
than a ball. Seriously, Clotilde, do you think I'll get it?

CLOTILDE. We shall see.

DU MESNIL. I have good claims and plenty of merit on my
side, haven't I?

CLOTILDE. Merit—what good is that?

DU MESNIL. I'm backed by able men.

CLOTILDE. What if they have no influence?

DU MESNIL. But don't you think the support of the Institute
will swing it?

CLOTILDE. You don't want me to take a hand in it—I think
you're wrong.

DU MESNIL. What could you do?

CLOTILDE. Oh, a thousand things that are no trouble to a
woman, which she can do as she goes her usual rounds.
I'd put all my friends on the warpath; Pauline first, she
admires you so much. She wishes her husband were like
you. Pauline, who is very close to Mrs. Simpson, would have
interested her in our affairs. You make me smile when you
don't want to go to Mrs. Simpson's. A lot she cares about
our company. Every day, everyone in Paris who counts
is at her house. She always has two or three cabinet mem-

bers at her table, and you could have dined with them.
You would have expounded your ideas to them, quietly,
on a footing of equality, while you smoked those large
cigars you are so fond of. And the day that your able men
at the Institute come to tell you, "We're very sorry, the
appointment was given to someone else," you'll say, "I
know it, I have it in my pocket." That's how business is
done!

DU MESNIL. You may be right. Listen, let's not do anything
rash. If after a while things don't go right for my uncle and
his friends, we'll try your method.

CLOTILDE. Whenever you like—you know that's my motto with
you.

They laugh.

DU MESNIL. I'm going to see Uncle. Shall I take Lafont with
me or are you keeping him?

CLOTILDE. I'll keep him. He irritates me but he amuses me. His
nose always makes me laugh.

They laugh.

DU MESNIL. You don't treat him right, you know. He is always
so kind and obliging.

CLOTILDE, *whispering.* I wouldn't want a man with a nose like
that to kiss me.

They laugh.

DU MESNIL. Well, good-bye.

To LAFONT.

You'd better stay here if I'm as disagreeable as my wife
says. You don't know what it is to have a wife and children.
You love them a great deal, you don't find time to think
of anything else, and you couldn't get along without them—
but just the same, every once in a while, you wish them
all to the devil.

Exit.

CLOTILDE. Don't you see, now, how careful you must be? If
my husband had come in one minute sooner, I was lost.

LAFONT. You made a fool of me.

CLOTILDE. How so?

LAFONT. With that letter. It would have been so easy to show it to me in the beginning.

CLOTILDE. I thought you wouldn't like it and I was right. Besides, it was a trap I set for you. I wanted to find out just how far you would go.

LAFONT. For the next time?

CLOTILDE. For the next time, precisely. My! how stupid you are, my dear, how unlucky in your suppositions! Look here, I'm going to set your mind at ease, though you hardly deserve it: my husband opens all my letters—all, without exception. I have always preferred it so. Now let's sit down and talk a while, and, please, let's talk without getting angry. My husband on one side, then you—it's a bit too much in one day. Can you give me any reason for acting the way you do? What does this absurd jealousy mean and what is it coming to? It took you all of a sudden—without warning—around January 15.

He looks at her; she smiles.

I have a reason for remembering that date.

LAFONT. What reason?

CLOTILDE. I have one, that's enough. Are you going to take me up on every word now? Go ahead, talk, I'm listening.

LAFONT. Where have you been?

CLOTILDE, *laughing.* That's right. I beg your pardon, my dear. I forgot you had asked me that question several times and I hadn't answered. I had an appointment—don't start—with my milliner, where one meets very few gentlemen, I assure you. You allow me to go to my milliner once in a while, don't you? Now do what I ask and tell me just what you reproach me with. I always find it difficult to discover anything wrong in the way I treat you.

LAFONT. I hardly see you any more.

CLOTILDE. Boo! What are you doing now? Aren't I here? It's your own fault if you waste the time quarreling when we might spend it more agreeably.

LAFONT. I waited for you all this week—last week too—and the week before that also.

CLOTILDE. Nonsense!— why not say all last year? And even if it were true, even if I hadn't kept my promises, not once, but a hundred times, is that any reason to imagine all sorts of horrible things? Am I always free to do what I want? Don't I depend on everyone here?
Touching his arm.
I'm married, you know, you don't seem to realize it. . . . But there's something else on your mind. I want to hear about it.

LAFONT. It seems to me that our relation no longer interests you . . . that you want novelty . . . and may have found it . . . that we're at the inevitable stage where . . . prevarication enters in, and the shabby tricks and little indignities.

CLOTILDE. I don't quite know when all those pretty things begin. You doubtless know more about them than I do, I'm asking you for facts—something clear and positive that I can refute with one word. As for what goes on in your imagination, what can I possibly say? It doesn't strike me as very jolly, your imagination, nor filled with very rosy memories.

LAFONT. That date—January 15—that you remember so well.

CLOTILDE, *more attentive*. Well, what about that date?

LAFONT. It struck me too.

CLOTILDE. Tell the truth—it didn't strike you. I'm sorry I bothered you with it. It means something to me and can mean whatever to you.

LAFONT. I've observed a number of things since.

CLOTILDE. What?

LAFONT. I've taken note.

CLOTILDE. Of what?

LAFONT. Oh, nothing. They're just nuances. But, after all, nuances . . . You mustn't trifle with nuances.

CLOTILDE. Let's have a look at these nuances.

LAFONT. You've changed a good deal, my dear Clotilde, without noticing it. You make fun of me, for one thing, which is not nice. I find you absent-minded, very often, and then also very much embarrassed. I see you're hiding something from me and I'm afraid to ask you questions. Sometimes you contradict yourself.

CLOTILDE. You amaze me.

LAFONT. You tell me about people of an altogether different set from yours, whom you've come to know overnight. How do you do it? Nowadays it's you who tell me all the scandals —hitherto I've had the pleasure of telling them to you. Even your politics have changed.

CLOTILDE. What a child you are! And here I am, listening to you solemnly. My politics! You mean I'm reactionary? I haven't changed. Yes, as to that, you're quite right, I'm a good, staunch reactionary. I love order, quiet, well-established principles. I want the churches to be open if I feel like going into one. I want the shops also open and full of pretty things, so that I may look at them even if I can't buy. But even if my politics were changed, it seems to me that you should be the last to complain. *You* have changed with the times, you are a liberal; it's the fashion today; it doesn't commit you, every party is full of liberals. You're a free-thinker, too. I do believe you could get along with a mistress who had no religion. Horrors!—What did my husband talk to you about?

LAFONT. About a position he would like to get an~~~~ may get.

CLOTILDE. Were you interested?

LAFONT. Very much.

CLOTILDE. You say "very much" just as you would say "not at all." How did you find my husband?

LAFONT. Pretty well.

CLOTILDE. Doesn't he seem to you worried and worn out?

LAFONT. No.

CLOTILDE. Enough of that. I don't know why I should talk to you about Adolph—for all the affection you bear him! No matter. This is my point—you know my husband's expecting a position, expecting it from the government. No matter what government is in power, when one wants something, one must apply to it. Do you suppose, then, that I would go around criticizing the present order just when we're expecting favors? A man would do that. Men are such chatterboxes, they're so clumsy and ungrateful. Women, never! Shall I tell you, my friend, you've acted on a very low scheme. You thought that if you voiced suspicion at random you might find out something—but you won't . . . because there is nothing to find out. I shan't forget it, though. Meanwhile you must be good, patient, trusting. You must be content with what you get and not try for the impossible. You must realize I'm not free, that I have a house to manage, friends to entertain—. Pleasure comes after. Keep in mind also that the slightest outburst might compromise me, and if my husband heard of it, destroy me entirely. I do not want—do you hear?—I do not want ever again to find you, as I found you today, planted in front of my door, gesticulating and ready to eat up everything when I'm peacefully returning from my dressmaker's. *He raises his head sharply.* Well, what's biting you now?

LAFONT. Where have you been?

CLOTILDE. I've just told you.

LAFONT. Is it your milliner or your dressmaker?

CLOTILDE. Why?

LAFONT. Answer me. Is it your milliner or your dressmaker?

CLOTILDE. I went to both, are you satisfied? Now it's time for you to get up and go.

LAFONT. No.

CLOTILDE. Yes.

LAFONT. Later.

CLOTILDE. Right now.

LAFONT. Are you busy, or in a hurry?

CLOTILDE. I've nothing to do, I'm in no hurry.

LAFONT. Let me stay then.

CLOTILDE. I can't. If my husband came back and found you still here he might be annoyed. Be reasonable and say good-bye. You'll talk less next time.

LAFONT. Clotilde?

CLOTILDE. What now?

LAFONT. I'm going home.

CLOTILDE. Go ahead, I'm not keeping you.

LAFONT. You know what time it is?

CLOTILDE. Approximately.

LAFONT. The day's not over.

CLOTILDE. It isn't dawn either.

LAFONT. All you have to do is put on your hat.

CLOTILDE. I thought we were coming to that. I should have been surprised if all your fussing had ended up otherwise.

LAFONT. Put on your hat, won't you?

CLOTILDE. All right. It's the one good idea you've had. It's only fair I should take advantage of it. Go on first.

LAFONT. You're coming after.

CLOTILDE. Right after.

LAFONT. In a minute?

CLOTILDE. One minute. But go on, go.

LAFONT. Till then.

CLOTILDE. Till then.

Exit LAFONT, CLOTILDE *rings.*

ADELE. Did you ring, madam?

CLOTILDE. Adele, please bring me my wrapper and slippers.
I'm not going out again.

ACT TWO

Same as Act One.

CLOTILDE, *dressed, ready to go out, looking at herself in a
mirror.* Do I look all right, Adele?

ADELE. Yes, madam.

CLOTILDE. Do I look quite right?

ADELE. Quite, madam.

CLOTILDE. What time is it?

ADELE. Almost three, madam.

CLOTILDE. Is everything on the table?

ADELE. Everything that madam usually takes—keys, address
book, powder box. . . .

CLOTILDE. Let me have them.

ADELE, *knowingly.* Madam will not return today.

CLOTILDE. Possibly not.

ADELE. Probably not.

CLOTILDE. How so?

ADELE. I believe the master dines with the economists. He wouldn't miss it for the world.

CLOTILDE. Well?

ADELE. I've noticed madam always spends the day with a schoolmate whom the master never sees.

CLOTILDE. So you've been eavesdropping.

ADELE. No, I haven't, madam; I've just caught a word here and there—I told madam that my brother—

CLOTILDE. I know all about your brother! You want to go out; all right, go!

ADELE. Thank you, madam.

Going out.

Madam wishes for nothing else?

CLOTILDE. No. Don't let the cook leave. Mr. Du Mesnil might want something when he comes in to dress.

ADELE. Yes, madam. Does madam not want me to call a cab for her?

CLOTILDE. No thanks. I'll find one on my way.

ADELE. Good-by, madam, pleasant time, ma'am.

following CLOTILDE *out.*

Bell rings.

Someone rang, madam.

CLOTILDE. Yes, I heard it.

Coming back.

Three o'clock! He hasn't seen me for quite a while. He knows today is the economists' dinner. I should have expected some such performance.

ADELE. What is madam going to do?

CLOTILDE. Go to the door, Adele. I am at home to no one.

ADELE. If it were Mr. Lafont, madam?

CLOTILDE. I said "to no one." I make no exception for Mr. Lafont or anyone else.

ADELE. Very good, madam.

CLOTILDE. Leave the door open so I can hear what it is. If it should be business for my husband, ask the person to sit down and I'll come out.

ADELE. I understand, madam.

Third ring.

My! What impatience, and how useless!

Exit.

CLOTILDE. I should have hurried. I'd be gone by now and wouldn't have been bothered.

Goes to center door which she holds ajar.

It's he all right. He couldn't miss such a fine opportunity. . . . Talk on, my friend, talk. . . . That's right, question the servant. He's asking Adele where I am. He insists. What's this, she's letting him in? He's walking in, as I live, he's walking in!

Coming back.

Is he going to take a siesta here? Ah, these men! How they hang on to us when we no longer care for them!

CLOTILDE *hides behind door at right.*

LAFONT. All right, my girl, all right.

ADELE. But why don't you believe me, sir? You can see that no one's home.

LAFONT. I shall wait.

ADELE. Wait for whom? Both the master and the mistress have just gone out.

LAFONT, *hesitating.* Together?

ADELE. No, sir, not together. Mr. Du Mesnil went his way, madam hers.

LAFONT. Did he say when he would be back?

ADELE. I know only that madam will not be home for dinner. She's dining out.

LAFONT, *hesitating.* With Mr. Du Mesnil?

ADELE. No, sir, they are dining separately.

LAFONT. Well, you can go back to your work. I'm going to write a note here at the desk.

ADELE. As you wish, sir, this isn't my house. I can't show you the door.

Exit.

LAFONT. I came in and I don't know why I came in; it's just another blunder on my part, that's what it is. I must take hold of myself, make up my mind to a necessary break. In Paris, you can't keep a mistress who is halfway respectable. Damn it, it can't be done! The more respectable she is, the less chance you have of keeping her. I'll have an explanation with Clotilde, and a bloody one! It'll be kinder on my part, then I'll leave her for good. I fret, run, pursue, look for her this way when she's gadding the other way, what's the use? What more can I find out? She's the mistress of that fellow Mercier, it's as clear as day. Since when? What good will it do me to know? Yes, why fuss? Ah, why—I don't know. Perhaps she doesn't love him—that's one consolation. But what am I going to do? If Adolph were here, at least we could have spent the rest of the day together. Really, when I'm blue and Clotilde has upset me, there's nobody like her husband to set me up again. I feel less lonely. Adolph's position cheers me a lot. It's not so good as mine. It certainly is not. Clotilde, after all, doesn't owe me anything, but she's certainly cheating him atrociously. I can judge her conduct pretty severely when I put myself in her husband's shoes—what a mess! Here I am, suddenly alone, without a friend, sick at heart about an unconscionably vulgar situation into which I am sinking deeper and deeper. What a life we men lead! Either bachelors or cuckolds—what a choice!

CLOTILDE. Here goes. I'll come out and at least find out what he wants.

LAFONT. What? You here!

CLOTILDE. What's so strange about my being here? The queer thing is *your* being here, especially when I'm not at home and you are told so in unmistakable language. That's how grateful you are for my kindness. You can't think of enough things to do to make yourself unpleasant, and every time, I'm weak enough to forgive you.

LAFONT. It's your own fault.

CLOTILDE. Oh, let's not start all over again, please! No scenes today, not today. I shan't *let* you make any, by the way. Had you any reason, may I ask, for coming, any pretext—some dreadful discovery that you couldn't keep to yourself any longer?

LAFONT. I confess I feared you were ill.

CLOTILDE. How charming of you! You've seen me, you're re-assured—now
Showing him the door, with a flip of her hands.
take wing.

LAFONT. You're going out?

CLOTILDE. Don't I look as if I were going out? I'm not in the habit of going about the house with my hat on.

LAFONT. In a hurry?

CLOTILDE. I'm late.

LAFONT. Shall we make up our minds?

CLOTILDE. What does that mean?

LAFONT. I thought we might dine out—if I'm still your old schoolmate.

CLOTILDE. There isn't any schoolmate any more—neither you nor anyone else. I've come to the conclusion that these escapades in restaurants were full of danger. They involve me in lies that are revolting. I don't want to go on. Don't you think I am right?

LAFONT. Don't ask me what I think.

CLOTILDE. You resent what I've just said?

LAFONT. I'm ready for anything now.

CLOTILDE. That's a good way to be. Then you'll never be disappointed.
Pause.

LAFONT. Please sit down and let's have a friendly chat.

CLOTILDE. I can't spare the time—to chat. Some other time, tomorrow, if you wish.

LAFONT. Tomorrow I'll expect you and something else will prevent—at the last minute—

CLOTILDE. Tomorrow won't do? Very well, that suits me. I'm never in a hurry to find myself with discontented and disagreeable people.

LAFONT. It's loving you that makes me so.

CLOTILDE, *disgusted.* Then love is a nuisance.

LAFONT. That's right—complain now! It's easy to see you're not in my place. I despair and mope while you're gadding about.

CLOTILDE. Gadding about! What sort of language is that! Admitting just for argument that I've grown a little cooler toward you, do you suppose a woman is won back by behaving as you do and by nagging her all the time? You accomplish just the opposite—you annoy her, bore her, and put notions into her head that she would never have thought of.
Going near him with a show of tenderness.
Take a little trip. Yes, take a little trip. Go away for—six months. It isn't long. Separation just now would do you worlds of good, and you'd come back all the more attractive. Don't be afraid about me. I'm not a woman who forgets easily. You'll find me just the same as ever. Will you go? No, you won't go. You can't go away for six months when your mistress asks you to—even though she'd regard it as a real proof of your attachment.

LAFONT. Where are you going?

CLOTILDE. That's all you can find to say to me?

LAFONT. Where are you going?

CLOTILDE. I was sure you'd ask me that question. I've been waiting for it ever since you came in.

LAFONT. Does it embarrass you?

CLOTILDE. Not in the least. You'll be a great deal wiser, of course, when I tell you where I'm going. What is to prevent my saying "I'm going there," and then going somewhere else?

LAFONT. I'll follow you.

CLOTILDE. Go ahead: follow me! Much good it's done you so far. But take care. I have a weakness for you, a great weakness. I make allowances for everything—the state you get into and the moments we've spent together, but don't feel free to abuse the privilege.
Emphatically.
I do whatever I like and it's nobody's business but my husband's.

LAFONT. You're deceiving me.

CLOTILDE. Me? Who with? Tell me who—who—who? You know, vague suspicions aren't enough. To accuse a woman you must have proofs. And when proofs exist and the woman is guilty, a man of the world knows what he's supposed to do—he leaves her or shuts up.

LAFONT. Clotilde!

CLOTILDE. Who! Tell me his name, if you're so sure of him. I'd be glad to know this Don Juan. Perhaps I pester him with my attentions, or he doesn't suspect his own good luck. You're forcing me to tell you something I'd always wanted to keep from you, I've made a sad mistake. I had a husband, children, a charming home. I wanted something more. I wanted everything. I dreamed like all other women of an ideal existence, in which I could fulfill my duties without sacrificing my heart. I wanted heaven and earth! And you've managed to demonstrate to me that it's impossible. I don't know what might have happened with someone else, certainly nothing worse. What's done is done. I don't blame you for it; but it's been the first and last time.

She puts her handkerchief to her eyes.

LAFONT. You are unhappy?

CLOTILDE, *going to a chair*. It's nothing. It will pass.

LAFONT. I've been horrid!

CLOTILDE. Quite.

LAFONT. I'm going.

CLOTILDE. It's the best thing you could do.
He goes away and comes back.

LAFONT. Please forget that one word I said beyond what I meant. I don't believe that you're deceiving me. You are too good and too sincere; at heart you appreciate the fondness I feel for you. I thought our usual little celebration still held; I was beside myself when you said no. Where are you going? Paying calls, visiting a friend? Is it such fun or so absolutely necessary? Why don't you call it off? Write that your husband is ill and that you must stay with him. It's so easy; do as I say. Give me back my evening, which has been mine for so long and which you always kept free for me.

CLOTILDE. Even if I would, I couldn't.

LAFONT. Why not?

CLOTILDE. I am being called for in a carriage to take me to the park.

LAFONT. But you were going out.

CLOTILDE. No, I wasn't. I was waiting.

LAFONT. Mrs. Simpson?

CLOTILDE. Mrs. Simpson, precisely. I'm dining with her. What a strange man you are. You take everything the wrong way, even what ought to reassure you.

LAFONT. Mrs. Simpson!

CLOTILDE. That's right. I was forgetting that Mrs. Simpson is not on your calling list, and that you wanted to forbid me her house. A charming house, beautifully appointed, and irreproachable. There may be trifling love affairs going on—I don't know—but that's like everywhere else.

LAFONT. Mrs. Simpson, as you very well know, has the worst of reputations.

CLOTILDE. So much the worse for those who made it so. When a man has been intimate with a woman she ought to be sacred for him—yes, sacred! Remember that principle and let it be your guide on occasion. I am very much perturbed, I assure you. I wonder what we're headed for and what you still have in mind. The gravest offence a man may do to a woman, you committed today toward me. What next? What else is there you can do? Violence, I suppose. I trust you will keep your self-control and stop short of blows. Think it over, my friend. It would be better to break off right now than wait and come to blows. Come now, I'm dismissing you in earnest this time; your mind is at rest, isn't it? Whatever loathing Mrs. Simpson may arouse in you, you'd rather have me be with her than. . . . We'll talk over the idea of your trip again; and I may bring you around to my point of view.

LAFONT. Tomorrow?

CLOTILDE. Ah, tomorrow. You've come back to that. You're willing to wait for me tomorrow? Well and good. I'll keep my word. But do watch yourself. You're calm enough now, don't go upsetting yourself when you're on the other side of the door. You have no luck with stairways. I promise you, if before tomorrow I run into you—at the Park or elsewhere—if I catch sight of the tip of your classic nose anywhere—you'll never see me again!

LAFONT. Till tomorrow, then?

CLOTILDE. Yes, tomorrow.

He goes out quickly.

Well, he wasn't so bad. Fairly sensible. When he gets angry, it's amusing enough, but I couldn't stand his tears.

At the window.

Better make sure before I go down that he won't follow me. He looks pretty sad, with his head hanging, poor fellow! I'll surely drop in to see him tomorrow. What! He's coming back! Hoho, into the house opposite. The devil! He's going to lie in wait and keep me here till he drops from sheer fatigue! I must show him he's been seen, or I'll never get rid of him.

DU MESNIL *enters from rear, with a look of ill humor and discouragmeent; throws his hat on the table angrily.*

Now the other one! Adolph! Adolph! What are you doing? Adolph, please answer me!

DU MESNIL. Let me alone for a bit, please!

CLOTILDE. What's the matter? What sort of face is this to come home with? I'd never seen that one before.

DU MESNIL. Don't annoy me more than I am already, will you, I'm not in a mood to trifle or listen to your nonsense. (*Pause.*)

CLOTILDE, *in a new tone.* What is the matter?

DU MESNIL. You'll find out soon enough.

CLOTILDE. So It's serious?

DU MESNIL. Very serious.

CLOTILDE. You're cross?

DU MESNIL. I have good reason to be.

CLOTILDE. You're cross—with me?

DU MESNIL. It has nothing to do with you. You were leaving—well, run along. Where are you going, anyway?

CLOTILDE. Shopping.

DU MESNIL. Yes, do. Buy yourself trinkets and things. It's most appropriate.

CLOTILDE. I'm getting tired of this. I shan't budge a step until you've told me what it is.

Bruskly takes off her hat.

I don't go out when my husband is worrying and I don't know what he's worrying about.

Sits down.

If he makes me wait to tell me, I wait.

DU MESNIL, *getting up and going to her.* You're a dear.

CLOTILDE. Speak up, you goose.

DU MESNIL. We're done for.

CLOTILDE. What about?—How?

DU MESNIL. What about?—About the position.

CLOTILDE. Is that it? You, a man, get into such a state and upset me about a little thing that didn't come through. It didn't, that's all. That's the definition of business, something goes through, something else doesn't. Make use of one, forget the other. Perhaps you thought I was going to complain and reproach you. Never, dear, never in the world. Come now, brace up; drop that hangdog look. What would you do, if you ran into a real calamity? If you lost me, for example? And now, tell me who was right? A fine sponsor, your uncle! Nothing suits him. Your position, your writings, your wife—nothing. And when he goes out for something you can be sure it'll be a fizzle. How did he ever get into the Institute, I wonder? If he were married, I could guess, but . . . tell me just what happened. You've told me everything and I don't know a thing as yet.

DU MESNIL. I don't know any more than you do.

CLOTILDE. Well, but is the thing settled?

DU MESNIL. Almost.

CLOTILDE. Only almost? What do you mean, almost? Has the appointment been made or not?

DU MESNIL. Not yet.

CLOTILDE. Then nothing is settled?

DU MESNIL. The appointment is going to be made and I've been given to understand that I shan't get it.

CLOTILDE. That's better. Now we're gettig to the point. Who's getting it?

DU MESNIL. A very—ordinary fellow!

CLOTILDE. Of course!—Married?

DU MESNIL. What has that got to do with it?

CLOTILDE. Tell me anyway.

DU MESNIL. Yes, married.

CLOTILDE. Young wife?

DU MESNIL. About your age.

CLOTILDE. Pretty?

DU MESNIL. Attractive.

CLOTILDE. Easy-going?

DU MESNIL. So they say.

CLOTILDE. The hussy!

DU MESNIL. I get you.

CLOTILDE. It's about time.

DU MESNIL. But you're wrong. They don't do things that way in the Treasury Department.

CLOTILDE. At any rate, nobody's been appointed—neither you nor anyone else—and you lost heart too soon, as usual.

DU MESNIL. All right, have it your way. But what are we to do?

CLOTILDE, *reflecting.* Get out of the way.
She sits at the table and writes.

DU MESNIL. But tell me—

CLOTILDE. Don't bother me.

DU MESNIL. But let's consult first.

CLOTILDE. No need. I'm writing to Lulu, asking her for an appointment; she'll know it's something important.

DU MESNIL. Lulu? Who the devil's Lulu?

CLOTILDE. Lulu is Mrs. Simpson. We call her Lulu ever since she played that part in a comedy, and she likes it.

DU MESNIL. Go to it—write to Lulu, but if she succeeds where a member of the Institute has failed, I'll be delighted personally but I shall be sorry for France.

CLOTILDE. Never mind that. France doesn't worry about you, don't you worry about France.

Getting up.

What are you doing in the next few minutes?

DU MESNIL. I want to lock myself in for a week and see nobody.

CLOTILDE. I won't have it. I don't want you to make yourself sick over something that may still come out all right. Take this letter to Mrs. Simpson's, it'll get you out into the fresh air. And from there you can go and see your uncle.

DU MESNIL. Why should I? A perfectly useless old fogy—you said so yourself. I'll write to him and tell him I'm fed up with his advice and that he may bestow his influence elsewhere.

CLOTILDE. I won't have that, either. Everyone knows your uncle has been behind this affair. Now, whoever makes it succeed, we shall owe the position to your uncle, do you understand? I don't suppose you want it said that we get favors through Mrs. Simpson and her friends.

DU MESNIL. Right again. I'll take your letter and see the uncle. But the economists will have to do without me tonight.

CLOTILDE. I won't have it. Why change your habits? That dinner is no chore for you. You generally come back late, quite gay, and with stories that give me an insight into the nature of your conversation. You're among men, and you say a lot of silly things, but you have a good time and you're right. Don't pass it up, there's little enough to be had in this world. You'll be with people you like, and I'll drop in on my little friend who'd miss me awfully if I didn't.

DU MESNIL. All right. I won't insist. But I feel pretty low and I would rather stay with you.

CLOTILDE. Thanks, but you'll have plenty of opportunities again.

DU MESNIL. Good-bye; where's the letter?

CLOTILDE. Here.

He goes, sheepishly.

And brace up a bit, a little cheerfulness in your face if you can manage it. Let's not take others into our confidence when we have trouble: it never helps.

DU MESNIL, *coming back*. What shall I say to uncle?

CLOTILDE. Whatever you wish.

DU MESNIL. So really you're packing me off to this dinner? I'm going there in the worst of moods.

CLOTILDE. The mood will change when you get some food.

DU MESNIL. Yes. I'm going to gorge.

Exit.

CLOTILDE. Talk of Madame Bovary! Bring up women to be quiet and respectable! Let a woman stay at home and her house will prosper—not so I can notice it! What would he have done if I hadn't been here? Not to mention the fact that decent folk have all the luck and are welcome everywhere. Yes, yes! Every time there's something to be given out—a position, a favor, a medal—anything, important or unimportant, and there are two applicants, one a modest and deserving fellow, not very strong on pull, the other a clever humbug with nothing to recommend him but his social graces, it's the humbug who gets it and the good fellow who gets—left. . . . Now perhaps I'll get out before nightfall. I hope Mr. Lafont will have got tired of waiting. He won't complain, anyway, if I get the start of him, I'm off.

She goes rapidly to the back door, which opens slowly in.
LAFONT *appears hesitantly.*

This is too much!

She comes back, furious.

LAFONT You're angry with me for coming back? This is what
happened. I was leaving, I swear to you. I didn't want to
think of you until tomorrow. I saw your husband coming
home. What as I to do? I should have liked to shake his
hand; but perhaps you did not want him to know of my
visit. You always say that I care for nothing and disregard
everything, though really I spend my life saving appearances
with Adolph. In fact, I quickly retraced my steps and hid
in a doorway to let him go by. He did come home, didn't
he? I'm not making up anything? Afterwards, it is true,
I was weak. I shouldn't have stayed. I told myself: Clotilde
has been expecting Mrs. Simpson but she doesn't seem to
be calling for her very promptly. What if her plans had
changed? Clotilde might be glad to see me. You can't reproach me for so—so humble and tender a thought? Your
husband came out again, which left things—as they were.
So I looked once more to see if Mrs. Simpson was coming,
I didn't see her, I came up. Oh, I came trembling, I assure
you; I might have gone down again

Laughing.

if it had not been for one of those little coincidences that
are so funny: your husband had left the front door open.
I say, Clotilde, it's all quite simple and natural; you mustn't
be angry for so slight a thing. Say something. You won't
answer? One word? Only one?

Going away.

Till tomorrow?

Coming back.

Till tomorrow?

Impatiently.

You won't say one word?

Going away.

You won't say one word? I am very much hurt, if you must

know. You've been treating me for some time past with
too little consideration.

Coming back.

You're resolved not to answer me?

Going away.

As you wish. Let it be over and done with. You don't love
me any more; I'm in your way; I have no joy of your friendship and I could be happy elsewhere. Let us part.

Coming back and holding out his hand.

But let's part like sensible people. Shall I tell you? You're
not waiting for anybody. You're going to see your lover; it's
with him you're dining. You can't deny it: I know. I did
not want to mention it before. It's Ernest Mercier.

LAFONT. Alfred?

CLOTILDE. Alfred.

CLOTILDE. Alfred Mercier.

LAFONT. 28 Madeleine Street?

CLOTILDE. 28 Madeleine Boulevard.

LAFONT, *upset.* Clotilde! Is this a joke or is it the truth you're
confessing?—It's the truth, isn't it? Ah! Clotilde! Clotilde!
What have you done!

Stopping.

You should have deceived me without telling me, delicately,
so that I would not notice it. This time it is the end. Good-by.

Sobbing.

Good-bye? Good-bye!

Exit.

CLOTILDE. That's about enough. I've been indulgent and
always ready to explain—or at least once in a while; but
every day, twice a day, no! It surely would be pleasant,
wouldn't it, living with a passion like that, which doesn't
give you time to breathe. And what's more, always hovering
on the brink of scandal! It's come to the point where I'm
never safe from him except when my husband's at home.

ACT THREE

Same as Acts One and Two. The double door, right, is wide open. The table has been set in the middle of the room to serve the coffee.

CLOTILDE, *near the table.* Mr. Simpson.

SIMPSON, *seated and finishing his coffee.* Yes, Mrs. Du Mesnil?

CLOTILDE. Please make yourself at home, as you would at your mother's. Just help yourself.

SIMPSON. Yes, Mrs. Du Mesnil.

CLOTILDE, *to Adèle.* Give this cup to Mr. Du Mesnil. Then you may go.

ADELE. Madam will not need me any more?

CLOTILDE. No.

ADELE. I had told madam that my brother—

CLOTILDE. Please go; you may talk of that later.

ADELE, *sourly.* Very well, madam.
Exit with cup.

CLOTILDE, *half aloud, going to him.* So it's true? You're leaving Paris for good?

SIMPSON. Yes, it's true.

CLOTILDE. This very day?

SIMPSON. I'm taking the seven o'clock train, which will drop me at home about midnight.

CLOTILDE. Your trunks are packed?

SIMPSON. My man is putting in the last things now.

CLOTILDE. There's nothing you would like to have me do?

SIMPSON. I have so little time left I should be afraid to put you to any trouble.

CLOTILDE. As you wish.

She turns away from him. He rises to put his cup on the table.

What does your mother think of this sudden resolution?

SIMPSON. My mother's delighted to see me go. It's partly on her account that I'm leaving earlier than usual. She wants me to overhaul her old place and supervise the repairs. I want to do it so that she won't be able to recognize Ginger-bread—that's the name of it—when she comes down.

CLOTILDE. If your mother approves, I have nothing more to say.

SIMPSON. You like Paris too well; you won't admit that one can be bored in Paris or that one can live somewhere else.

CLOTILDE. I don't think any such thing. Only I think that a man of your age, and in your position does not quit the capital so easily, especially if he is held back by any the slightest attachment. The season is not nearly over; the weather's atrocious; no one dreams of leaving except you. You must have some reason.

SIMPSON. If I had one it would be rather a reason for staying.

CLOTILDE. Then why are you leaving?

SIMPSON. I'm bored. I'm annoyed and humiliated. I feel like a pauper in your capital. What does that wretched flat of mine look like? I'm ashamed to live in it. It's even worse when people call on me. My mother has always refused to set me up decently. She'd rather have me travel. I spend a lot of money without getting either pleasure or happiness from it. Down there, at Gingerbread, the scene is different. I lead a great life. I'm somebody in the country. People take off their hats when I go by, I have everything I miss here—my horses, my dogs, my guns. You know I have a magnificent collection of shotguns that I'm always eager to go back to and see properly cared for. Paris is fun, to be sure, and perhaps I'd like it as much as anybody else, if I could live in it so as to satisfy my self-respect.

CLOTILDE. It's my fault. I haven't known how to console and keep you. To part as we're doing, as if with a light heart, after only four months—well, I hope it won't have seemed too long for you.

SIMPSON. It's five months.

CLOTILDE. Are you sure?

SIMPSON. Let's see: January 15, February 15, March 15—

CLOTILDE. You are right. Let's call it five months and say no more about it.

Pause.

SIMPSON, *going to her.* You should come down to Gingerbread later on, when my mother will be there with some of her friends.

CLOTILDE. Don't count on me. My husband cannot easily get away.

SIMPSON. You could come by yourself.

CLOTILDE. He wouldn't like that.

SIMPSON. Your friend Mrs. Beaulieu will be there. Those considerations don't seem to bother her.

CLOTILDE. Oh, it's different with Pauline. She has an independent income, in the first place; it enables her to do what she wants. Then her husband has wronged her dreadfully and she takes advantage of it; she's right!

SIMPSON. She has a good time of it, hasn't she?

CLOTILDE. That I don't know. We're very close, Pauline and I, but we don't discuss everything.

SIMPSON. But it's through her that you came to know my mother?

CLOTILDE. Yet Pauline never knew why I wanted to know your mother. What made you think Mrs. Beaulieu didn't behave altogether—regularly? Have you heard anything about her?

SIMPSON. I happen to know of her infatuation for one of my friends.

CLOTILDE. What's his name?

SIMPSON. Hector de Godefroy.

CLOTILDE. It's a lie.

SIMPSON. You mean it's not quite a secret.

CLOTILDE. You should know that Mrs. Beaulieu has been living for years with a charming young man who adores her and never leaves her side.

SIMPSON. What's his name?

CLOTILDE, *hesitating, then smiling.* Alfred Mercier.

SIMPSON. Yes, but Mrs. Beaulieu has suddenly gone crazy, I don't know why, about my friend Hector, and she doesn't spend a day without seeing him.

CLOTILDE. Who told you that?

SIMPSON. Mrs. Beaulieu herself. She's not at all shy about such things.

CLOTILDE. What a child Pauline is! Why couldn't she keep it to herself!

SIMPSON, *going away from her.* That's another thing I like about leaving Paris. One buries a deal of stories that aren't very pretty.

CLOTILDE. Is it about my friend you're saying this?

SIMPSON. Well, she can take her share of it.

CLOTILDE. Pauline has suffered a great deal, you know.

SIMPSON. She doesn't show many traces of it now.

CLOTILDE. Perhaps you made love to her?

SIMPSON. It never occurred to me.

CLOTILDE. But Mrs. Beaulieu is simply adorable.

SIMPSON. I don't like to be merged with the common herd.

CLOTILDE. Still, it's bound to happen to you more or less.

SIMPSON. The ladies wouldn't like to hear you admit it.

CLOTILDE. What did I give away? That we're weak, fickle, guilty, if you like; that we always let ourselves be led astray; that we meet oafs who don't love us as they should, or, worse, ungrateful wretches who have respect and affection only for themselves. . . . You may be right after all. The best thing would be to have nothing to do with either kind; to blind one's eyes and stop one's ears, to upbraid oneself and say, "Here is your place, stick to it." Perhaps life wouldn't be very thrilling or amusing, but one would avoid many worries, many disillusions, many regrets.

SIMPSON. What is the matter?

CLOTILDE. Don't—!

SIMPSON. You're in tears!

CLOTILDE. Real ones, I may say.

SIMPSON. Why do you weep, my dear?

CLOTILDE. Who knows? There is a bit of everything in a woman's tears.

SIMPSON. I should be sorry if my leaving—

CLOTILDE. No; don't make yourself out worse than you are. We met, grew fond, separated—it's something that happens every day. But you men, who are so accommodating when you want to obtain our good graces, are terribly harsh when we have granted them. Come! I must call my husband. He'd leave us here together until tomorrow, with his trusting faith and sublime ignorance of all our follies.

Holding out her hand.

Say farewell, now. Keep a happy memory of these five months, that's all I ask. Keep it to yourself, though—you must—and I know you will. It is thanks to you that we succeeded in obtaining what we desired, but your help came after my wrongdoing, and was not strictly needed. If some

time you want to drop in and say how do you do, you know
the house; you've done everything you should to be a welcome guest here.

SIMPSON. You are charming.

CLOTILDE. I know it.
Going to the door on the right.
I say, Adolph, haven't you smoked your fill? You can finish
your paper later, Adolph, do you hear? Mr. Simpson is
getting his hat. Hurry up if you want to go down with him.
Coming back.
My husband will be in immediately.
Enter DU MESNIL.

DU MESNIL. I'm behaving like a boor, leaving you alone like this.

SIMPSON. It's perfectly all right.

DU MESNIL. I've got into the habit of napping for an instant
after lunch. That's the only time I really feel at home.

SIMPSON. Are you ready?

DU MESNIL. At your service.

SIMPSON. Let's go then.

DU MESNIL. Excuse me while I say a word to my wife?

SIMPSON. Certainly.

DU MESNIL, *whispers to* CLOTILDE. Should I thank this young
man?

CLOTILDE. No, we had him to lunch, that's enough.

DU MESNIL. We're greatly obliged to his friend in the Government.

CLOTILDE. His mother did everything—after I wrote to her, you
remember, in your presence.

DU MESNIL. I didn't know Mrs. Simpson had a son that old;
what do you think of him?

CLOTILDE. He's distinguished looking.

DU MESNIL. Grand airs about him, eh?

CLOTILDE. I don't dislike it.

DU MESNIL. What was he saying to you?

CLOTILDE. That I was perfect.

DU MESNIL. Morally?

CLOTILDE. Personally, too.

DU MESNIL. I suppose I'm a trusting soul to have left you together.

CLOTILDE. He's leaving tonight.

DU MESNIL. Yes, but he can come back.

CLOTILDE. He's still not the one to make me forget my duty. *She turns away.*

SIMPSON, *joining her.* You'll forgive me, Mrs. Du Mesnil, for running off so hurriedly.

CLOTILDE. I know your time is short; you said so, and I wouldn't dare keep you.

SIMPSON. I seem to regret Paris, already, even before I leave it.

CLOTILDE. Oh, you'll forget it quite easily.

SIMPSON. My mother will doubtless see you soon and give me news of you.

CLOTILDE. We shall also inquire about you.

SIMPSON. Remember that you are expected at Gingerbread.

CLOTILDE. It's not likely that you'll see me there.

SIMPSON. Oh, I won't give up so easily. If any occasion brings me to Paris—if need be, I shall make one—I'll try again to persuade you.

CLOTILDE. Don't come to invite me, come to see me.

SIMPSON. Good-bye, then, until the near future.

CLOTILDE. Good-bye, until then.

DU MESNIL. What was I telling you?

CLOTILDE. And what did I tell you? Never mind him and attend to your business.

He goes out.

A silly episode! None of the young men today is worth the trouble one takes about them. They are dry, full of pretensions, believe in nothing. They love to pose and that's about all. I had thought that Mr. Simpson, having been educated by his mother, could become seriously attached to a woman. I shouldn't complain about him anyway, I suppose. He's always been very well-bred and obliging—he's a bit dull on the subject of his shotguns—but it serves me right: I had what I needed, an excellent friend, a second husband, you might say; I mistreated him in every possible way, and he got tired of it, that's natural enough. Who knows? He may think me angrier than I really am; men know so little about us. We've a weakness, it is true, for those who charm us, but we always come back to those who love us.

Bell rings.

ADELE. Mr. Lafont, madam.

CLOTILDE. Well, why do you take that astonished air to announce Mr. Lafont?

ADELE. Is madam going to receive him?

CLOTILDE. Why, certainly.

ADELE. Very well, madam.

CLOTILDE. You can go out, if you wish to.

ADELE. Thank you, ma'am.

LAFONT, *much moved, enters slowly.* How do you do?

CLOTILDE, *with a calculated inflection.* How do you do, dear friend?

LAFONT. How are you?

CLOTILDE. Quiet, very quiet, and you?

LAFONT. Pretty bad—very bad. Am I in your way?

CLOTILDE. Not in the least.

LAFONT. You were perhaps going out?

CLOTILDE. No. I scarcely go out nowadays. Where should I go?

LAFONT. You had guests for lunch?

CLOTILDE. Guests? No—a guest.

LAFONT. A friend?

CLOTILDE. An acquaintance.

LAFONT. Do I know him?

CLOTILDE, *puzzling*. My husband told me his name, but I've mislaid it!

LAFONT. I just saw them leave together.

CLOTILDE. Really? You were there under my window? Had I known I would have shown myself for an instant. It was very sweet of you. At least you didn't forget me right away.

LAFONT. Who was that gentleman?

CLOTILDE. A stranger, I tell you, a very casual acquaintance. You can't possibly take umbrage at his being here. My husband introduced him this morning and tonight he will have left town.

LAFONT. You're speaking the truth?

CLOTILDE. Why should I lie to you? You, at least, don't change. That's one thing I must say in your favor. Come here and sit in the easy chair and try to stay there if you can. Don't let me see you move, pace or jump about as formerly. I have memories of you that are so much pleasanter.

LAFONT. Clotilde!

CLOTILDE. There is no longer any such person.

LAFONT. My dear!

CLOTILDE. Let's be calm, please; don't let us wander off so soon.

LAFONT. I do regret, you may be sure, that ridiculous scene which you could so easily have prevented. Look at me, Alfred Mercier!

She laughs.

Ah, but you know, I had been jealous of that fellow Mercier for so long. All my suspicions pointed to him. Mrs. Beaulieu will be grateful for your discretion.

CLOTILDE. That may be. What have you been doing since I saw you last?

LAFONT. I've thought about you.

CLOTILDE. That's easily said. What else?

LAFONT. What else? I've lived as usual.

CLOTILDE. You didn't go on a trip?

LAFONT. I had the opportunity, but I didn't have the heart.

CLOTILDE. Have the ladies been kind to you? Have you been well looked after?

LAFONT. I refuse to answer that.

CLOTILDE. Why? It may be that previously an infidelity on your part would have wounded me—deeply; but what was forbidden to you then is allowed now. As if I didn't know you, and as if you were the sort of man to deny yourself consolations! You weren't always very lovable, you know, nor very jolly, nor very trusting, but still——

LAFONT. Still?

CLOTILDE. Let us not talk of those things.

LAFONT. I am much too miserable, I assure you, to be thinking of consolations. And besides, if it is fated that I should lose you forever, I shall never try to replace you by someone from a circle I no longer frequent.

CLOTILDE. That's wrong. You should frequent at least the ladies of that circle. They enjoy freedom. You don't have to handle them with kid gloves. They love scenes, tears, and battles. Which you won't find with us. We can only give a peaceful, quiet affection, sincere and . . . disinterested.

LAFONT. That is what I want. That is what we all want.

CLOTILDE. Then, my friend, you should have taken care and not risked losing what you had, merely for the pleasure of being headstrong.

LAFONT. Clotilde?

CLOTILDE. What is it, my dear?

LAFONT. Give me your hand.

CLOTILDE. No.

LAFONT. Can't you give me your hand?

CLOTILDE. We'll see. And don't put on that look or I shall send you home.

LAFONT. Give me your hand.

CLOTILDE. Well, there it is. Now you want the other, I suppose.

LAFONT. You're so—frigid.

CLOTILDE. What do you mean, frigid? I let you sit down near me, I let you kiss my hand—you didn't think I was going to fall on your neck as soon as you entered, did you?

LAFONT. I am here as a culprit. I agree with all your reproaches but I think you deserve some yourself.

CLOTILDE. None.

LAFONT. Was it my fault or yours that our relations suddenly changed? No man was happier than I until the day you turned your own life topsy-turvy.

CLOTILDE. What do you mean—I turned my life topsy-turvy? Only you could have done that—would have done it—if I hadn't stopped you in time.

LAFONT. You may be right. I don't know why I harp on what happened. Let bygones be bygones.

CLOTILDE. Bygones! You're incorrigible. I receive you, I listen to you, I believe that you sincerely regret your inexplicable behavior. I tell myself that later, if you reform sincerely, it might not be impossible for me to forgive you—and you begin again, baiting me with that evil streak in you that I detest and have never been able to eradicate. Nothing happened, do you hear—nothing, nothing, nothing—absolutely nothing. Please move away.

LAFONT. Why?

CLOTILDE. Please move. I want to get up.

LAFONT. No.

CLOTILDE. Yes.

LAFONT. Let us stay as we are.

CLOTILDE. Let me get up for a moment. You're not leaving yet.

LAFONT. Let us be.

CLOTILDE. How stubborn you are!

LAFONT. You're not upset?

CLOTILDE. I'm nervous and agitated.

LAFONT. All the more reason.

CLOTILDE. I beg your pardon?

LAFONT. I'm trying hard to keep cool.

CLOTILDE. Don't lose your temper. I'll stay put.

LAFONT. So you were thinking of forgiving me a little.

CLOTILDE. I said so and I was wrong.

LAFONT. Let's go back to our good old ways.

CLOTILDE. What's the use? You'll never be happy with me, and I'll never have a quiet moment with you. You refuse to understand my position.

LAFONT. What position?

CLOTILDE. My position. Haven't I a husband on whom I am wholly dependent and who must find me at home whenever he wishes? It's the least I can do for him, you must admit. And that's another fault of yours which you would correct if you really understood me.

LAFONT. What have I done now?

CLOTILDE. You don't like my husband.

LAFONT. Of course I do, I do!

CLOTILDE. But you don't, I tell you. You don't like Adolph. I can see it in many ways. Perhaps your temperaments don't jibe, or perhaps it's due to the situation.

LAFONT. That is very unfair to me. Your husband—why, your husband never had but two friends in the world.

CLOTILDE. Two?

LAFONT. Yes, two.

CLOTILDE. Who?

LAFONT. You and me.

They laugh.

Let's leave the others out. Come, Clotilde, be honest! Don't you think that you suited me?

CLOTILDE. As for that, yes. I do believe I suit your taste.

LAFONT. Now, a devotion like mine is not met with every day. Do you ever think of that?

CLOTILDE. Certainly. It is precisely because I valued it that I was considerate and used to put up with all your storming.

LAFONT. I am very gentle, usually, very tender.

CLOTILDE. I don't deny it. You know extremely well how to please when you want to, and you find very pretty things to say that are very agreeable to hear . . . *you're* not the one to talk to a woman about shotguns.

LAFONT. What does that mean?

CLOTILDE. Nothing. A story I was told, not worth repeating.

LAFONT, *coming nearer*. Tell me you forgive me.

CLOTILDE, *softly*. Yes. Now be good.

LAFONT. You forgive me—altogether?

CLOTILDE. Altogether—don't pester me. I'll come to see you.

LAFONT. Soon?

CLOTILDE. Whenever you wish. Only take care. I'm not my own mistress here.

LAFONT. Clotilde!

CLOTILDE. You love me?

LAFONT. I adore you.

CLOTILDE, *getting up*. Dear me! How many wasted words to get to where we were before.

LAFONT *joining her*. Do you regret it?

CLOTILDE. Not yet.

LAFONT. I was feeling rather blue when I came here. I shall leave in a better mood.

CLOTILDE. Well, I hope you've learned a lesson: Namely, no more scenes, and no more of those appalling suspicions that disgust a woman and that are so useless. When something goes wrong or annoys you, tell me; I'm always ready to listen to reason. Now, I'm going to tell you something that will rather please you.

LAFONT. I'm all ears.

CLOTILDE. I think my friendship with Mrs. Simpson is about over.

LAFONT. Nonsense!

CLOTILDE. I mean it!

LAFONT. She has offended you?

CLOTILDE. On the contrary, I feel nothing but gratitude for her.

It is not so much that I don't want to see Mrs. Simpson, it's her house that I think it wiser to avoid.

LAFONT. What did I tell you in the first place?

CLOTILDE. You're cleverer than I, that's all.

LAFONT. I know another person whose company is not good for you, and whom you ought to drop.

CLOTILDE. You're going to say something stupid, I can see it coming. That person is . . ?

LAFONT. Mrs. Beaulieu.

CLOTILDE. Pauline? I, drop Pauline? I should indeed like to know why, tell me why?

LAFONT. It seems to me—

CLOTILDE. It seems to you—what?

LAFONT. Mr. Mercier!

CLOTILDE. What about Mr. Mercier?

LAFONT. Well, I know all about him and you doubtless know too.

CLOTILDE. Yes, I do know. What of it?

LAFONT. You don't defend Mrs. Beaulieu, I trust?

CLOTILDE. I say, do you know what you're saying? Are you going to blame Pauline for doing for Mr. Mercier what I am doing for you?

LAFONT. It isn't the same thing.

CLOTILDE. Are you sure? Where is the difference?

LAFONT. I can see one.

CLOTILDE. What is it? Let's hear it. Oh, you're all alike, you men. For your sake, we can allow ourselves everything, but you object when others benefit. Rather than meddle in Pauline's business, you should be thinking of my husband who has complained every day that you didn't come around any more, and who'll ask you for an account of yourself.

LAFONT, *pointing to the door.* Is it Adolph we just heard?

CLOTILDE. Yes, it's Adolph. Have you thought of what you're going to tell him?

LAFONT. No.

CLOTILDE. The idea makes you laugh? So much the worse for you, my dear. You'll have to extricate yourself as best you can.
Enter DU MESNIL.

DU MESNIL. What, is that you?

LA FONT, *embarrassed.* Hello, old man.

DU MESNIL. Hello. Why haven't we seen you these many—

LAFONT, *again.* How are you?

DU MESNIL. Splendid. You don't answer my question. What happened to you that you dropped out of sight like a plummet?

CLOTILDE. Don't torment him. He's had great troubles. Isn't that so, Mr. Lafont?

LAFONT. Yes, Mrs. Du Mesnil.

DU MESNIL. What sort of troubles?

CLOTILDE. Shall I tell my husband?

LAFONT. Just as you wish.

DU MESNIL. Come, out with it.

CLOTILDE. He was jealous.

DU MESNIL. Jealous! What? You still jealous at your age?
To CLOTILDE.
And who the devil was he jealous of? Some woman who doesn't belong to him, I suppose! These bachelors, they never deny themselves anything, and they're jealous into the bargain. Shall I tell you the opinion of a famous economist on jealousy? Jealousy is just the fact of being deprived.

Nothing more. If you were married you wouldn't feel deprived and you wouldn't be jealous. Isn't that true, Clotilde?

CLOTILDE. Come, now, that's enough.

DU MESNIL. Jealous! Have you told him?

CLOTILDE. Told him what?

DU MESNIL. That I'd been appointed.

CLOTILDE. Mr. Lafont was the first to congratulate you by letter.

DU MESNIL. Of course, I'd forgotten. He wrote to me! Instead of coming to see me.

To LAFONT, *but looking at* CLOTILDE.

It's my uncle, my good old uncle, who swung the thing.

CLOTILDE. Everybody knows it's your uncle, you don't need to shout it from the housetops.

DU MESNIL. Well, it's better to be a government official than to be jealous, eh?

To CLOTILDE.

Poor fellow, he's not completely recovered. His nose doesn't look right. By the bye, did she or did she not deceive you?

LAFONT. Why don't you leave me alone?

DU MESNIL. Surely you can tell that much to an old friend.

CLOTILDE. My husband's asking you a question, why don't you answer it?

LAFONT. What do you expect me to say? Is there any man, any one man, who could swear that his mistress never deceived him? Mine says she hasn't. She couldn't very well say she had. We've had a reconciliation. No doubt that's what we both wanted.

CLOTILDE. Indeed! It's too bad the lady is not present to hear you; she would know what opinion you have of her and of all other women. Trust us, Mr. Lafont, trust us—that's the only system that works with us.

DU MESNIL. It's always been mine, hasn't it, dear?

THE
THREEPENNY OPERA

A Play with Songs in Three Acts
based on John Gay's
The Beggar's Opera
by

BERTOLT BRECHT

English Version by
Eric Bentley and Desmond Vesey

Characters

The Time: *Not too long ago*
The Place: *London*

PROLOGUE

THE BALLAD OF MACKIE THE KNIFE

Market day in Soho. Beggars are begging, thieves thieving, whores whoring.* A street singer is singing a ballad.

And the shark, he has his teeth and
Always keeps them in his face
And MacHeath, he has a knife but
Keeps it in a diff'rent place

By the River Thames' green waters
People suddenly fall down
And 'tis neither plague nor chol'ra
But 'tis said: MacHeath's in town!

When the shark bites through his victim
There is crimson 'midst the green
But MacHeath, he has his gloves on
And the blood is never seen

It was such a lovely Sunday
But the body, it was dead
And a man slipped round the corner
It was Mackie, people said

Solly Silverstein has vanished
Likewise other rich young men
And MacHeath has all their money
Try and prove it, if you can

PEACHUM *with his wife and daughter walk slowly across the stage.*

Jenny Towler was discovered
With a knife stuck in her breast
And MacHeath strolls down the dockside
Knows no more than all the rest

*The economical director will make do with his Gang (of six), his Family (of seven), and his Five Beggars.

Where is Alphonse Glite the coachman?
Controversy sure is rife
Maybe someone has the answer
But it's not MacHeath the Knife

Seven children and their grandpa
In the fire near Old Soho
In the crowd MacHeath is watching
Doesn't ask and doesn't know

And the widow, not yet twenty,
She whose name has gone the rounds
Woke up and was violated
Mac collected forty pounds

There is a burst of laughter from the whores. A man steps out from among them, walks quickly across the stage, and out.

GINNY JENNY, *from among the whores.* Look! That was Mackie the Knife!

ACT ONE

1 IN ORDER TO COMBAT THE INCREASING
HARD-HEARTEDNESS OF MEN, MR. J. J. PEA-
CHUM, MERCHANT, HAS OPENED A SHOP
WHERE THE POOREST OF THE POOR MAY AC-
QUIRE AN APPEARANCE THAT WILL TOUCH
THE STONIEST OF HEARTS.

The wardrobe room of MR. PEACHUM's *establishment for
beggars.* MR. PEACHUM *sings his* MORNING HYMN.

Wake up, you old Image of Gawd!
Get on with your sinful existence!
Continue to perpetrate fraud
The Lord will reward your persistence

Double-cross your old mother, you turd!
And sell your young wife in her bed!
You think G.O.D.'s just a word?
He'll show you as soon as you're dead

PEACHUM, *to the audience.* My business is arousing human
pity, and I've got to find something new. It's just too hard,
that's all. There are a few things, of course, that'll shake a
man up, a few, but the trouble is, when they've been used
for a while, they don't work any more. Human beings have
a frightful capacity for, um, anesthetizing themselves at
will. So it happens, for instance, that a man who sees
another man on the corner with only a stump for an arm,
will be so shocked—the first time—that he'll give him six-
pence. But the second time it'll only be a threepenny bit.
And if he sees him a third time, he'll hand him over to the
police and not bat an eyelash. It's the same with these
spiritual weapons.

A large board comes down from the flies bearing the inscription: IT IS MORE BLESSED TO GIVE THAN TO RECEIVE.

What's the use of such sayings—be they never so fine, be they never so convincing—painted on boards that are positively alluring—if they get used up so quick? There are four or five sayings in the bible that go straight to the heart. But when they're used up? Take that one there: GIVE AND IT SHALL BE GIVEN UNTO YOU. Finished in three weeks. Something new—the market demands something new! Sure, I can fall back on the bible again, but how often? *There is a knock. Peachum opens the door, and a young man named* FILCH *comes in.*

FILCH. Peachum & Co.?

PEACHUM. Peachum.

FILCH. Then you're the owner of the firm called "The Beggars' Friend"? Wise saws, eh? What capital! I suppose you've got a whole library of such things? Something new! Fellows like us—we'd never get an idea like that. And not being properly educated, how could we make a good business of it if we did?

PEACHUM. Your name?

FILCH. Well, you see, Mr. Peachum, I've had bad luck ever since I was a boy. My mother was a drunkard, my father was a gambler. From an early age I had to fend for myself. And without the loving hand of a mother to guide me I sank deeper and deeper into the morass of the great city. I never knew a father's care or the blessings of a happy home. So now you see me . . .

PEACHUM. So now I see you . . .

FILCH, *confused.* . . . see me . . . completely destitute, a prey to my own desires.

PEACHUM. Like a wreck on the high seas, and so on. Tell me, wreck, in which district do you recite this nursery rhyme?

FILCH. What do you mean, Mr. Peachum?

PEACHUM. You deliver this speech in public?

FILCH. Well, you see, Mr. Peachum, there was a little incident yesterday in Highland Street. I was standing quietly and miserably at the corner, hat in hand, intending no harm . . .

PEACHUM, *turning over the pages of a notebook.* Highland Street. Yes. This is the one. You're the crawling blackleg that Honey and Sam caught redhanded. You had the impertinence to solicit passers-by in District 10. We let it go at a good beating, we took it you didn't know where God lives. But if you let yourself be seen there again, we shall have to use the saw. Understand? The saw.

FILCH. Please, Mr. Peachum, please! What can I do, Mr. Peachum? The two gentlemen beat me black and blue, and then gave me your business card. If I was to take off my coat, you'd think you was looking at a haddock.

PEACHUM. My young friend, if you don't look like a flounder, my people were a sight too easy with you. This young sprout comes along and imagines that if he sticks out his paws, he'll be all set for a steak dinner. What would you say if someone took the best fish out of *your* pond?

FILCH. But you see, Mr. Peachum—I haven't got a pond.

PEACHUM. Well, licenses are only supplied to professionals.
Points in businesslike way to a large map of London.
London is divided into fourteen districts. Every one wishing to ply the trade of begging in any of them must get a license from Jonathan Jeremiah Peachum and Company. *Anybody* could come along—"a prey to his own desires"!

FILCH. A few shillings stand between me and total ruin, Mr. Peachum . . .

PEACHUM. One pound.

FILCH. Mr. Peachum!
He points beseechingly at a poster which reads: SHUT NOT YOUR EARS TO MISERY. PEACHUM *points to a curtain in front of a show-case, on which is written:* GIVE AND IT SHALL BE GIVEN UNTO YOU.

Ten shillings.

PEACHUM. And fifty per cent of the weekly takings. Including outfit, seventy per cent.

FILCH. And what does the outfit consist of?

PEACHUM. The Firm decides that.

FILCH. Well, what district can I start on?

PEACHUM. Baker Street. That'll be cheaper too. It's only fifty per cent there, including outfit.
He pays.

FILCH. Thank you.

PEACHUM. Your name?

FILCH. Charles Filch.

PEACHUM. Correct.
Writes
Mrs. Peachum!
MRS. PEACHUM *enters*
This is Filch. Number 314. Baker Street District. I'll enter it myself. Of course, you would want to start now, just before the Coronation—the chance of a lifetime to earn a little money. Outfit C for you.
He draws back the linen curtain in front of a show-case in which are standing five wax models.

FILCH. What's that?

PEACHUM. These are the five types of misery best adapted to touching the human heart. The sight of them induces that unnatural state of mind in which a man is willing to give money away. Outfit A: Victim of Modern Traffic Development. The Cheerful Cripple, always good-tempered, always carefree.
He demonstrates it.
Effect heightened by a mutilated arm. Outfit B: Victim of

the Art of War. The Troublesome Twitcher, annoys pedestrians, his job is to create disgust.

He demonstrates it.

Modified by medals. Outfit C: Victim of the Industrial Boom. The Pitiable Blind, or the High School of the Art of Begging.

PEACHUM *displays him, advancing unsteadily towards* FILCH. *At the moment when he bumps into* FILCH, *the latter screams with horror.* PEACHUM *stops, gazes at him in astonishment, and suddenly roars.*

He feels *pity! Pity! You'll* never make a beggar—not in a hundred years. A creature like you is only fit to be begged *from!* Then it's outfit D! Celia, you've been drinking again, you're cockeyed! Number 136 has been complaining about his neck-rag. How often must I tell you a gentleman will *not* have filthy clothing next to his skin. Number 136 has paid for a brand new costume. Stains—the only thing about it that could awaken pity—it needs *stains!* Iron in some candle wax! I always have to do everything myself.

To FILCH.

Undress and put this on. Keep it in condition!

FILCH. And what happens to *my* things?

PEACHUM. Property of the Firm. Outfit E: Young man who's seen better days, preferably one who "never thought he would come to this."

FILCH. Why can't *I* have the better days outfit?

PEACHUM. Nobody believes in a man's real misery, my lad. If you've got the stomach-ache and *say* so, it only sounds repulsive. Put these things on.

FILCH. Aren't they rather dirty?

PEACHUM *gives him a piercing glance.*

I'm sorry, Mr. Peachum, I didn't mean it.

MRS. PEACHUM. Hurry up, my man. I'm not going to hold your trousers till Christmas.

FILCH, *suddenly, with great determination.* And I'm not going to take my shoes off! I'd rather chuck the whole thing. They're the only present I had from my poor mother, and never, never, however low I may have fallen . . .

MRS. PEACHUM. Don't talk rot. You've got dirty feet.

FILCH. You expect me to wash them? In the middle of winter?

MRS. PEACHUM *leads him behind a folding screen, then sits down left and begins ironing candle grease into a suit.*

PEACHUM. Where's your daughter?

MRS. PEACHUM. Polly? Upstairs.

PEACHUM. Was that man here again yesterday? The one that comes when I'm out?

MRS. PEACHUM. Don't be suspicious, Jonathan! There isn't a finer gentleman alive, and the Captain takes quite an interest in our Polly.

PEACHUM. *Does* he?

MRS. PEACHUM. And if I'm any judge, Polly is fond of him too.

PEACHUM. There you go, Celia! Throwing my daughter about as if I were a millionaire! So she's going to marry! And do you think our miserable business would last another week if the filthy customers had only *our* legs to look at? A husband! *He'd* soon have us in his clutches. Do you think your daughter would be any better than you at keeping her mouth shut in bed?

MRS. PEACHUM. A nice opinion of your daughter you've got!

PEACHUM. The worst! She's nothing but a lump of sensuality.

MRS. PEACHUM. Well, she doesn't get that from you!

PEACHUM. Marry! My daughter should be to me what bread is to the starving.
He thumbs through the Bible.
That's in here somewhere. Marriage is a nasty business, I'll beat the marriage out of her.

MRS. PEACHUM. Jonathan, you're just ignorant.

PEACHUM. Ignorant! What's his name, this gentleman?

MRS. PEACHUM. People just call him "the Captain."

PEACHUM. So you haven't asked him his name! Ve-ery nice!

MRS. PEACHUM. We wouldn't be so ill-bred as to ask for a birth certificate; him being such a gentleman, inviting us to the Octopus for a little dance.

PEACHUM. *Where!?*

MRS. PEACHUM. To the Octopus. For a little dance.

PEACHUM. Captain? Octopus Hotel? I see——!

MRS. PEACHUM. The Captain never touched me and my daughter except with kid gloves on.

PEACHUM. Kid gloves!

MRS. PEACHUM. Now I come to think, he always has gloves on—white kid gloves.

PEACHUM. Ah! White kid gloves and a stick with an ivory handle and spats on his patent leather shoes and an ingratiating personality and a scar . . .

MRS. PEACHUM. On his neck. How do *you* know?
FILCH *comes out from behind the screen.*

FILCH. Mr. Peachum, could you give me a few tips? I like to have a system and not go at things haphazard.

MRS. PEACHUM. He wants a system!

PEACHUM. He can systematically be an idiot. Come back this evening at six and you'll be given the necessaries. Now, get out!

FILCH. Thank you, Mr. Peachum, thank you very much.
Exit FILCH.

PEACHUM. Fifty per cent! And now I'll tell you who this gentleman with the kid gloves is—he's Mackie the Knife!

He runs up the stairs into POLLY's *bedroom.*

MRS. PEACHUM. Lord save us! Mackie the Knife! Jesus, Mary, and Joseph! Polly! Where's Polly?

PEACHUM *comes slowly downstairs.*

PEACHUM. Polly? Polly hasn't been home. Her bed's not touched.

MRS. PEACHUM. Then she's been having supper with that wool merchant. I'm certain of it, Jonathan.

PEACHUM. For our sake, I hope it was the wool merchant.

MR. *and* MRS. PEACHUM *step in front of the curtain and sing. Song illumination: a golden light. The organ is lit up. Three lights come down in a bar from above, and on a board is written:* THE WHEREAS-THEY SONG.

PEACHUM.

Whereas they
(Whereas they)
All should be at home now snugly in their beds
They go and play
(They go and play)
Just as if the Lord Above had poured down manna on their
* heads*

MRS. PEACHUM.

That is the moon over Soho
That is the confounded "Can you feel my heart beating"
* song*
That's the "Whither thou go'st, I shall go with thee, Johnny"
When there's love in your heart and the night is young

PEACHUM.

Whereas they
(Whereas they)
Of course should do what has a purpose and a goal
They go and play
(They go and play)
Just to make quite sure they end up in the hole

PEACHUM AND MRS. PEACHUM.

So where is their moon over Soho?

What's left of their confounded "Can you feel my heart
    beating" song?
Where now is their "Whither thou go'st, I shall go with thee,
    Johnny"?
When their love is kaputt and the night's not young?

2 DEEP IN THE HEART OF SOHO, MACKIE
THE KNIFE CELEBRATES HIS WEDDING WITH
POLLY PEACHUM, DAUGHTER OF THE KING
OF THE BEGGARS.

An empty stable.

MATTHEW, *carrying a lantern and pointing a revolver round the
    stable.* Hands up!
    MACHEATH *enters and walks across the front of the stage.*

MACHEATH. Well? Is anyone here?

MATTHEW. Not a soul. We can have the marriage here safe
    enough.

POLLY *enters in a wedding dress.* But this is a stable!

MACHEATH. Sit down on the crib for a while, Polly.
    To the audience.
    Today, in this stable, my marriage to Miss Polly Peachum
    will be celebrated, she has followed me for love and prom-
    ised to spend her life with me.

MATTHEW. A lot of people will be saying this is the riskiest thing
    you've ever done, luring Mr. Peachum's daughter out of his
    own house.

MACHEATH. Who *is* Mr. Peachum?

MATTHEW. *He'd* say he was the poorest man in London.

POLLY. Surely you're not thinking of having our marriage here?
    In a nasty, common stable? You can't invite the clergyman
    here—it isn't ours, Mac. We ought not to begin our new life
    with a burglary, Mac. This is the happiest day of our lives!

MACHEATH. Dearest, everything shall be as you wish. No stone
of this stable shall touch your little feet. Carpets and fur-
nishings are on their way at this very moment.

MATTHEW. Here it comes!

There is a sound outside of heavy wagons arriving. Enter
JACOB, ROBERT, ED, JIMMY, *and* WALTER, *carrying carpets,*
furniture, crockery, etc., and soon the stable is transformed
into an over-ornate living-room.

MACHEATH. Junk!

The five men place their presents down on the left, con-
gratulate the bride, and report to the bridegroom.

JACOB. Here's luck! At 14 Ginger Street there were some people on the second floor. We had to smoke 'em out.

ROBERT. Good luck! A copper in the Strand got in our way. We
had to beat him up, I'm afraid.

MACHEATH. Amateurs!

ED. We did what we could, but three people down west are
goners. Good luck!

MACHEATH. Amateurs and bunglers!

JIMMY. An old gentleman got something he wasn't expecting, I
don't think it's serious. Luck!

MACHEATH. My orders were: bloodshed to be avoided. The
very thought of blood makes me feel sick. *You'll* never make
businessmen. Cannibals—but never businessmen!

WALTER. Good luck! Half an hour ago, madam, that harpsichord still belonged to the Duchess of Somersetshire!

POLLY. Whatever furniture is this?

MACHEATH. How do you like it, Polly?

POLLY, *crying*. All those poor people robbed, just for a few
bits of furniture!

MACHEATH. Junk! You're right to be angry. A rosewood harpsichord—with a Renaissance sofa. That's unpardonable. And where's the table?

WALTER. A table?
They lay planks across the feeding troughs.

POLLY. Oh, Mac, I'm so unhappy. I do hope the clergyman won't come!

MATTHEW. But he will. *We* told him the way.

WALTER *pushes forward the improvised table.* A table!

MACHEATH, *seeing* POLLY *crying.* My wife is upset. And where are the other chairs? A harpsichord and no chairs! How often does it happen that I have a wedding? Shut your trap, Weeper! How often does it happen, I'm asking, that I leave anything to you? My wife will be unhappy from the start.

ED. Dear Polly . . .

MACHEATH, *knocking his hat from his head.* I'll knock your head into your chest with your "Dear Polly", you sewer rat! Whoever heard such a thing—"Dear Polly". Maybe you've slept with her?

POLLY. But Mac!

ED. I swear that . . . !

WALTER. If there's anything more you'd like, we'll go out again . . .

MACHEATH. A rosewood harpsichord and no chairs!
Laughs.
What do *you* say to that, as the bride?

POLLY. Oh well, it might be worse.

MACHEATH. Two chairs and a sofa, and the bridal pair sit on the ground!

POLLY. A fine thing that would be.

MACHEATH, *sharply.* Saw the legs off the harpsichord! Come on!

Four of the men saw the legs off the harpsichord and sing.

FOUR MEN.

> *Bill Lawton took Mary Sawyer*
> *To be his true and lawful wedded wife*
> *But when they stood before the Registrar*
> *He didn't know she lived at Temple Bar*
> *And she learnt his name for the first time in her life*
> *HO!*

WALTER. And so, miss, all's well that ends well. We have another bench.

MACHEATH. Might I now request you gentlemen to take off those rags and dress yourselves respectably? This isn't the wedding of a Nobody. And Polly, may I ask *you* to get busy with the food hamper?

POLLY. Is it the wedding breakfast? All stolen, Mac?

MACHEATH. Of course, of course.

POLLY. I'd like to know what you'd do if the Sheriff were to knock on the door.

MACHEATH. I'd show you what your husband *can* do.

MATTHEW. Not a chance of it. The police are guarding the streets. The queen's coming to town—for the coronation Friday.

POLLY. Two knives and fourteen forks! A knife for each chair!

MACHEATH. What a job of work! Haven't you any conception of *style*? Can't you tell the difference between Chippendale and Louis Quatorze?

The rest of the gang now return, wearing smart evening dress, but their behavior during the rest of the scene is not in keeping with their attire.

WALTER. We wanted to bring the most valuable things. Look at that wood!

MATTHEW. Ssst! Ssst! Permit me, Captain . . .

MACHEATH. Come here, Polly.

The two of them pose for congratulation.

MATTHEW. Permit me, Captain, on behalf of all, on the finest day of your life, the springtide of your career—its turning-point, one might say—to offer you our heartiest congratulations and . . . so forth. Well, anyway,

Shakes MACHEATH'S *hand.*

chin up, pal!

MACHEATH. Thank you. That was very nice of you, Matthew.

MATTHEW, *shaking* POLLY'S *hand, after having patted* MACHEATH *affectionately on the back*. I mean it: never let anything down that you can keep up!

Roars of laughter from the men. MACHEATH *suddenly catches hold of* MATTHEW *and jerks him to the floor.*

MACHEATH. Keep your dirty jokes for your beautiful Kitty: she's the slut for them.

POLLY. Mac, don't be common.

MATTHEW. I object to you calling Kitty a slut . . .

MACHEATH. You object, do you?

MATTHEW. And what's more, I never tell her dirty jokes—which you can't understand maybe. And *you* ought to know about sluts! You think Lucy hasn't told me the things *you've* said? I'm a kid-glove gent compared to that.

MACHEATH *gives him a look.*

JACOB. Stop it. This is a wedding!

They pull him back.

MACHEATH. A fine wedding, eh, Polly? To see these gutter-rats all round you on the day of your marriage? You didn't think your husband'd be let down by his friends.

POLLY. I think it's nice.

ROBERT. No one's letting you down. A little difference of opinion can happen any time.

To MATTHEW.

Your Kitty is all right. Now come on with your wedding present.

ALL. Come on, get on with it!

MATTHEW, *offended.* There.

POLLY. Oh! A wedding present! How sweet of you, Mr. Money Matthew! Look, Mac, what a lovely nightdress!

MATTHEW. Another dirty joke, eh, Captain?

MACHEATH. It's quite all right, Matthew my boy. Let joy be unconfined!

WALTER. What about this? Chippendale!

He uncovers an immense grandfather clock.

MACHEATH. Louis Quatorze.

POLLY. It's wonderful. I'm *so* happy. A pity we haven't a house for it, isn't it, Mac?

MACHEATH. Think of it as a beginning. Thank you, Walter. Now clear the stuff away. Food!

JACOB, *while the others are laying the table.* Of course *I've* forgotten to bring anything.

Emphatically to POLLY.

I feel embarrassed.

POLLY. Don't mention it, Mr. Crook-Finger Jacob.

JACOB. The boys throw their presents around and I stand here with nothing. Put yourself in my place. This always happens to me! I could tell you of some fixes I've been in! The other day I met Ginny Jenny, and I told her, "Now look, old pig," I said . . .

Suddenly sees MACHEATH *standing behind him and walks away without a word.*

MACHEATH. Come on.

Leads POLLY *to her seat.*

The finest food in London, Polly. Shall we start?
They all sit down to the wedding breakfast.

ED, *pointing to the service.* Lovely plates, Savoy Hotel.

JACOB. The eggs mayonnaise are from Selfridge's. We had a jar of goose liver too. But Jimmy ate it out of spite. He said he had an empty belly.

WALTER. Jacob, respectable people don't say "belly."

JIMMY. And, Ed, don't gobble your eggs today of all days!

MACHEATH. Can't someone sing something? Something delectable!

MATTHEW, *choking with laughter.* Something delectable! That's a proper word!
Under MACHEATH'S *annihilating glance, he sits down, embarrassed.*

MACHEATH, *knocking a dish out of someone's hand.* As a matter of fact, I didn't wish to start eating yet. Instead of this "on-with-the-food-and-into-the-trough" exhibition from you men, I'd been hoping for something festive. People always do something of that sort.

JACOB. What sort?

MACHEATH. Must I think of everything? I'm not asking for an opera. But you might have arranged something more than eating and telling dirty jokes.

POLLY. The salmon's great, Mac.

ED. I'll bet you've never ate salmon like it, Mac has it every day. You're in the honeypot all right. I always said Mac'll make a fine match for a girl with a yen for higher things. I said so to Lucy yesterday.

POLLY. Lucy? Who is Lucy, Mac?

JACOB, *embarrassed.* Lucy? Well, you know—
    MATTHEW *has stood up and is making furious gestures behind* POLLY *to silence* JACOB.

POLLY *sees him.* Are you wanting something? The salt? What were you going to say, Mr. Crookfinger Jacob?

JACOB. Oh nothing. Nothing at all. I'll be in trouble.

MACHEATH. What have you got in your hand, Jacob?

JACOB. A knife, Captain.

MACHEATH. And what have you got on your plate?

JACOB. A trout, Captain.

MACHEATH. I see, and with the knife, I believe, you are eating the trout. That is unheard of, Jacob. Have you ever seen such a thing, Polly? Eating fish with a knife! A person who does that is a pig, you understand, Jacob? You'll have a lot to do, Polly, before you can teach these oafs to behave like men. Do you even know what the word means: a man?

WALTER. I know the difference from a woman!

POLLY. Mr. Walter!

MACHEATH. So you don't want to sing. Nothing to brighten up the day a bit. It's to be just another damn sad, ordinary, dirty day. And is anyone standing at the door? Perhaps you'd like *me* to stand at the door, today of all days, so you can stuff yourselves here at my expense?

WALTER, *sullenly.* What do you mean, at your expense?

JIMMY. Shut up, Wally. I'll go. Who'd come here anyway?
    Exit JIMMY.

JACOB. It'd be funny if all the wedding guests were copped!

JIMMY, *bursts in.* Captain, the coppers!

WALTER. Tiger Brown!

MATTHEW. Gerr, it's the Reverend Kimball.
    The REVEREND KIMBALL *enters.*

ALL *shout.* Hello, Reverend Kimball! Hi! Welcome!

KIMBALL. So I've found you at last! In a little hut! A small thing but your own, eh, what?

He simpers.

MACHEATH. The Duke of Hampstead's.

POLLY. Oh, your reverence, I'm so happy you've come. It's the most wonderful day of my life, your reverence.

MACHEATH. I request a hymn for the Reverend Kimball.

MATTHEW. How about "Bill Lawton and Mary Sawyer?"

JACOB. That's right, "Bill Lawton."

KIMBALL. It would be pleasant to hear your voices raised in song, my men.

MATTHEW. Let's begin.

Three of the men stand up and sing, hesitating, flat and uncertain, THE WEDDING SONG FOR POORER PEOPLE.

Bill Lawton took Mary Sawyer
To be his true and lawful wedded wife
Long may they live, ho, ho, ho!
But when they stood before the Registrar
HE *didn't know she lived at Temple Bar*
And SHE *learnt his name for the first time in her life*
HO!

Do you know what your wife is up to? No!
Do you let her do what she used to do? No!
Long may they live, ho, ho, ho!
Billy Lawton said to me: "It's fine
So long as just one part of her is mine"
The swine!
HO!

MACHEATH. Is that all? Slim pickings.

MATTHEW, *choking again.* Slim pickings! A good expression!

MACHEATH. I meant—no life, no swing, nothing!

POLLY. If nobody will do anything, I'll sing a little song as best I can, and in it I'm going to imitate a girl I once saw in a threepenny bar in Soho. She was the barmaid, and you should know that everyone laughed at her, and then one day she spoke to the customers and told them the things I am going to sing to you now. So this is the little bar—you must imagine it being damn dirty!—and she stood behind it every morning and every evening. There's her slop pail and that's the cloth she used for drying the glasses. Where you are sitting sat the men who laughed at her. You can laugh, too, so that everything is just as it was; but if you can't, then you needn't.

She begins, pretending to wash glasses and muttering to herself.

Now one of you must say—you for instance Mr. Walter: *Pointing at* WALTER.
"And when is your ship coming home, Jenny?"

WALTER. And when is your ship coming home, Jenny?

POLLY. And another says—you, Mr. Money Matthew: "Do you still wash up the glasses, oh! Jenny the Pirate's Bride?"

MATTHEW. Do you still wash up the glasses, oh! Jenny the Pirate's Bride?

POLLY. Good. Now I'll begin.

Song illumination: golden light. The organ is lit up. Three lights on a bar come down from above, and on a board is written: JENNY THE PIRATE'S BRIDE.

Gentlemen, today you see me washing up the glasses
And making beds for all who stay here
And you throw me a penny and I curtsey very well
And you see my shabby apron and this dirty old hotel
And you think that I shall end my days here
But one fine night there'll be a shout down by the harbor
And you'll ask: what's the reason for that shout?
And you'll see me smiling as I wash my glasses
And you'll ask: what has she to smile about?
            For a lovely white schooner
            With fifty great cannon
            Sails in with the tide

But you'll say: go wash your glasses, my girl
And you'll throw your pennies to me
And I'll take all your pennies
And tuck the beds up tight
But no one is going to sleep in them tonight
And you still have no idea who I may be
And one fine night there'll be a roar down by the harbor
And you'll ask: what's the reason for that roar?
And you'll see me standing staring through the window
And you'll ask: now what's she grinning for?
      And the lovely white schooner
      With fifty great cannon
      Will start shooting the town

Then, gentlemen, you'll soon take that laugh off your faces
For your houses will fly in the air
And when the whole town is razed to the ground
Just one dirty old hotel will be standing safe and sound
And you'll ask: what famous person lives in there?
And all through the night there'll be shouting round the hotel
And you'll ask: why has that hotel survived?
And you'll see me step out of the front door in the morning
And you'll ask: is that where SHE once lived?
      And the lovely white schooner
      With its fifty great cannon
      Will run flags up the mast

In the morning you will see a hundred men come ashore
Who will search the shadows so still now
And they'll capture every single living person they can see
And put them in chains and bring them to me
And ask: which of these shall we kill now?
And when the sun stands at noon there'll be a hush down by the harbor
As they ask me which of these are doomed to die
And then you'll hear me saying to them: All o' them!
And when their heads fall, I shall shout: Whoopee!
      And the lovely white schooner
      With its fifty great cannon
      Will sail homeward with me

MATTHEW. Very nice!

MACHEATH. It's not nice, you fool! It's art. You did wonderfully, Polly. But it's pearls before swine. Pardon me, your reverence.

In an undertone to POLLY.

I don't approve of this play-acting, oblige me by abstaining from it in future.

Loud laughter at the table. The gang are making fun of the parson.

What have you got in your hand, your reverence?

JACOB. Two knives, Captain.

MACHEATH. And what have you got on your plate, your reverence?

KIMBALL. Salmon, I think.

MACHEATH. I see. And with the knife you're eating the salmon, is that it?

JACOB. Have you ever seen the like, eating his fish with a knife! A person who does that is nothing more than a . . .

MACHEATH. Pig. Understand me, Jacob? Pig.

JIMMY, *bursting in.* Captain! The coppers! It's the Sheriff himself!

WALTER. Brown! Tiger Brown!

MACHEATH. Tiger Brown, Chief of Police, Sheriff of London, and pillar of the Old Bailey is about to enter Captain Mac-Heath's little hut.

The gang creep away.

JACOB. Then it's the gallows for us.

BROWN *enters.*

MACHEATH. Hello, Jacky!

BROWN. Hello, Mac! Now, Mac, I've got to leave at once. Why *must* you pick on somebody's stable? Still another burglary!

MACHEATH. But Jacky, it was so convenient. Pray partake of

old Mac's wedding feast. May I introduce my wife, Polly,
née Peachum. Polly, this is Tiger Brown, isn't it, old man?
Slaps him on the back.

And these are my friends, Jacky: you may have seen them
before.

BROWN, *in embarrassment.* I'm here in my private capacity,
Mac.

MACHEATH. So are they.
He calls them. They come, one by one, hands up.
Hi, Jacob!

BROWN. That's Crook-Finger Jacob, he's a scoundrel.

MACHEATH. Here! Jimmy! Robert! Walter!

BROWN. Well, we'll forget everything for today.

MACHEATH. Hi, Ed! Matthew!

BROWN. Sit down, gentlemen, sit down.

ALL SIX MEN. Thank you, sir.

BROWN. Happy to meet the charming wife of my old friend
Mac.

POLLY. Don't mention it, sir.

MACHEATH. Sit yourself down, you old rascal, and start in on
the whiskey! Polly! Gentlemen! Today you see in your midst
a man whom the king's inscrutable wisdom has chosen to
set high over his fellow men, and who yet has remained
through fair weather and foul—my friend. Ah, Jacky, do you
remember when you were a soldier and I was a soldier and
we served together in India? Jacky, old man, shall we sing
them the Army Song?
*They sit side by side on the table. Song illumination: a
golden light. The organ is lit up. Three lights come down
from above on a bar, and on a board is written:* THE ARMY
SONG.

Johnny and Jimmy were both on the scene
And George had his promotion order
For the Army doesn't ask what a man has been:
They were all marching north to the border
  The Army's story
  Is guns and glory
  From the Cape to Cutch Behar
  When they are at a loss
  And chance to come across
  New and unruly races
  With brown or yellow faces
  They chop them into tasty bits of beafsteak tartare!

Johnny found the whiskey too warm
And Jimmy called the cold infernal
Sergeant George had to take them by the arm
And remind them that the Army is eternal
  The Army's story
  Is guns and glory etc.

Now John's a goner and Jim is dead
And Sergeant George is barmy
But blood is blood and still runs red—
They're recruiting again for the Army
  The Army's story
  Is guns and glory etc.
As they all sit there, they march in time with their feet.

MACHEATH. We were boyhood friends, and though the swirl-
ing tides of life have swept us asunder, although our professional interests are so different—some might even say,
diametrically opposed—our friendship has survived it all.
Castor and Pollux, Hector and Andromache, and so forth.
Seldom have I, the simple highwayman—well, you know
what I mean—seldom have I undertaken the smallest job
of work without giving my friend Brown a share of the pro-
ceeds (a considerable share, my good Brown) as a token and
a proof of my unswerving loyalty to him. And seldom has
the all-powerful Sheriff—take that knife out of your mouth,
Jacob—organized a raid without previously giving a little
tip to me, the friend of his youth. It's all a matter of give
and take. Do as you would be done by. The Golden Rule . . .

He takes BROWN *by the arm.*

Jacky, I'm glad you've come. That's what I call real friendship.

A pause while BROWN *sorrowfully regards a carpet.*

Genuine Persian Shirah.

BROWN. From the Oriental Carpet Company.

MACHEATH. We get all our carpets there. Do you know, I *had* to have you here today, Jacky, I hope you don't feel uncomfortable . . .

BROWN. You know, Mac, I can refuse you nothing. But I must be going. If anything should go wrong at the coronation . . .

MACHEATH. Jacky, my father-in-law is a repulsive old boor. If he were to raise a stink, are there any records in Scotland Yard that could be used against me?

BROWN. In Scotland Yard there is *nothing* against you, Mac.

MACHEATH. Of course not.

BROWN. I saw to that. And now, good-night.

MACHEATH. Aren't you all going to stand up?

BROWN, *to* POLLY. The best of luck!

Exit BROWN, *accompanied by* MACHEATH.

JACOB, *who meanwhile with* MATTHEW *and* WALTER *has been talking to* POLLY. I admit I got the wind up when I heard Tiger Brown was coming!

MATTHEW. We have our connections, don't we, Ma'am?

WALTER. Yes. Mac always has an extra iron in the fire! But we have our little irons in the fire too. Gentlemen, it's half past nine.

MATTHEW. And now—the high spot.

The other five men retire to the back left, behind a hanging carpet which conceals something. MACHEATH *enters.*

MACHEATH. What's up now?

MATTHEW. One more little surprise, Captain.

Behind the carpet they sing THE WEDDING SONG FOR POORER
PEOPLE, *but this time quite softly and full of feeling. However, when they get to the end of the first verse,* MATTHEW
*tears down the carpet and they sing on, bawling at the top
of their voices and beating time on a bed which stands behind.*

MACHEATH. Friends, I thank you.

WALTER. And now the unobtrusive departure.

The gang exeunt.

MACHEATH. And now sentiment must come into its own lest
man become a mere slave to his work. Sit down, Polly. Do
you see the moon over Soho?

Music.

POLLY. I see it, dearest. Can you feel my heart beating, belovèd?

MACHEATH. I can feel it, belovèd.

POLLY. Whither thou goest, I will go.

MACHEATH. And where thou stayest, I will stay.

Singing

And though there's no license to show your name

POLLY, *joining in.*

And on the altar, no roses fair

MACHEATH. *And though you don't know whence your wedding
dress came*

POLLY. *And no myrtles are twined in your hair*

TOGETHER.

*The platter from which you are eating your bread
Don't you keep it long, throw it down
For love lasts forever (or not so long)
In ever so many a town*

3 FOR PEACHUM, WHO KNOWS THE HARD-
NESS OF THE WORLD, THE LOSS OF HIS
DAUGHTER MEANS NOTHING SHORT OF
TOTAL RUIN.

PEACHUM'S *establishment for beggars. Right,* PEACHUM *and*
MRS. PEACHUM. *In the doorway stands* POLLY, *in hat and
coat, a small suitcase in her hand.*

MRS. PEACHUM. Married? First we hang her back and front
with dresses and hats and gloves and sunshades, and when
she's cost as much as a sailing ship to rig out, she throws
herself in the gutter like a rotten tomato. So you've gone
and got married?

*Song illumination; golden light. The organ is lit up. Three
lights come down on a bar, and on a board is written:* IN
THE BARBARA SONG POLLY TELLS HER PARENTS OF HER MAR-
RIAGE WITH MACHEATH.

*I believed—in the days of my innocence (and
I was innocent once just like you)—
The time could arrive when a man would notice me
And then I'd have to know what to do
And if he's a rich man
And if he's a nice man
And his necktie—even on weekdays—is just so
And if he knows how he should act toward a lady
I'm afraid I'll have to tell him it's: No
That's how I can hold my head up high
And a mere indiff'rence show
Oh yes, the moon shines bright the whole night long
Oh yes, the little boat will drift along
But further things won't go!
For you cannot simply stretch out on the bed
No, no, you must be cold (like winter snow)
For so much might, so much might happen
The only word to use is: No

The first man who came was a man from Kent
He was all that a man should be
The second, oh, he had three vessels in the harbor*

And the third was insane about me
And as they were rich men
And as they were nice men
And their neckties—even on weekdays—were just so
And as they sure knew how to act toward a lady
I had to say to each one: No
And so I could hold my head up high
And a mere indiff'rence show.
Oh yes, the moon shone bright the whole night long
Oh yes, the little boat would drift along
But could things further go?
No, you cannot simply stretch out on the bed
No, no, you must be cold (like winter snow)
For so much might, so much might happen
But the only word to use is: No

And yet one fine day when the sky it was blue
Came a fellow who wasn't so slow
No, he just hung up his hat upon the nail upon my door
What I did I didn't even know
And as he wasn't rich
And as he wasn't nice
And his necktie—even on Sunday—wasn't just so
And he didn't know how to act toward a lady
I simply couldn't tell him: No
And so I couldn't hold my head up high
Or a mere indiff'rence show
Oh dear, the moon shone bright the whole night long
And the little boat was tied up good and strong
And the rest I am sure you know
Yes, you've simply got to stretch out on the bed
No, you simply can't be cold (like winter snow)
Oh, so much had, just had to happen
And the word I couldn't say was: No

PEACHUM. So that's the sort she is now. A crook's trollop. Very
nice. Very pleasant.

MRS. PEACHUM. If you're immoral enough to marry at all, why
must it be a horsethief and a highway robber? It'll cost you
dear some day!

Aside.

I should have seen it coming. Even as a child she had a head
as swollen as the queen of England.

PEACHUM. So she got married.

MRS. PEACHUM. Yesterday afternoon at five o'clock.

PEACHUM. To a notorious criminal! Come to think it over, it shows great courage in the man. If I have to give my daughter away, the last support of my old age, my house will fall in and my last dog will desert me. Why, I couldn't give away the dirt under my fingernails without risking death from starvation. If the three of us can get through the winter on one log of wood, we may live to see the spring. We may.

MRS. PEACHUM. What are you thinking of? This is our reward, Jonathan. I shall go mad. Everything is going round in my head. Oh!
She faints.
A glass of Rémy Martin!

PEACHUM. There! See what you've done to your poor old mother. Quick! A crook's trollop, that's fine. The old lady has taken it to heart.
POLLY *returns with the brandy.*
The last consolation of a poor mother!

POLLY. Go on, give her two glasses. She can carry twice as much when she's not herself. That'll put her on her legs again.
During the whole of this scene she has a radiantly happy expression on her face.

MRS. PEACHUM, *revived.* Now she's showing her wicked false sympathy and solicitude!
Five beggars enter.

FIRST BEGGAR. I won't have it! What a hell of a place! This isn't a proper stump, and I won't waste my money on it.

PEACHUM. What do you want? It's as good as the others, you don't keep it clean.

FIRST BEGGAR. Then why don't I earn as much as the others? No, you can't put that over me.

Hurls the stump away.

I might as well cut off my leg, if I wanted junk like that.

PEACHUM. Well, what *do* you want? And what can *I* do about
it if people have hearts of granite. I can't give you five
stumps! In ten minutes I can make such a wreck out of a
man that a *dog* would weep if he saw him. What can I do if
people won't weep? There's another stump. But take care of
your things!

FIRST BEGGAR. This one's better.

PEACHUM *tries a mutilated arm on another beggar.* Leather is
no good, Celia. Rubber is more horrible.

To the third.

The boil is going down, and it's your last. Now we can start
over.

Examining the fourth.

Natural scars are never the same as artificial.

To the fifth.

What's the matter with you? You've been eating again. I
shall have to make an example of you.

FIFTH BEGGAR. Mr. Peachum, I haven't eaten much, my fat's
unnatural, I can't help it.

PEACHUM. Neither can I. You're dismissed.

Turning to the second beggar.

Between "giving people a shock" and "getting on their
nerves" there's a certain difference, my friend. I need artists.
Only an artist can give people *the right sort* of shock. If you'd
work properly, your public would be forced to appreciate
and applaud you. But you never think of anything. I cannot extend your engagement.

The FIVE BEGGARS *exeunt.*

POLLY. Please consider him. Is he handsome? No. But he makes
a living. He offers me an existence. He's a first class burglar
—a far-sighted and experienced highwayman. I know how
much he has saved up—I could tell you the figure. A few

more successful undertakings and we can retire to a little house in the country, just like that Mr. Shakespeare Father admires so much.

PEACHUM. Well, it's all quite simple. You're married. What do you do when you're married? Don't bother to think. You get a divorce!

POLLY. I don't know what you mean.

MRS. PEACHUM. Divorce.

POLLY. But I love him, how can I think of divorce?

MRS. PEACHUM. Polly, aren't you ashamed of yourself?

POLLY. Mother, if you've ever been in love . . .

MRS. PEACHUM. Love! Those damned books of yours have turned your head. Polly, everyone does it.

POLLY. I shall be an exception.

MRS. PEACHUM. I'll tan your bottom, you exception!

POLLY. All mothers do that, but it is no use. Love is greater than a tanned bottom!

MRS. PEACHUM. Polly, don't try my patience.

POLLY. I won't let you rob me of my love!

MRS. PEACHUM. Another word and you'll get a box on the ears.

POLLY. Love is the greatest thing in the world!

MRS. PEACHUM. The fellow has several women. When he's hanged, there'll be a half dozen widows, each with a brat in her arms. Oh, Jonathan!

PEACHUM. Hanged! How did you think of hanging? It's an idea! Go outside, Polly.
Exit POLLY. *But she stays listening outside the door.*
You're right. The idea's worth forty pounds.

MRS. PEACHUM. I know what you mean. Tell the Sheriff.

PEACHUM. Of course. Besides, this way we get him hanged free. . . . It'll be two birds with one stone. Only we've got to find out where he's hiding.

MRS. PEACHUM. I can tell you, my dear. He's with his whores.

PEACHUM. But they won't give him up.

MRS. PEACHUM. Leave it to me. Money rules the world. I'll go straight to Wapping and talk to the girls. If this fine gentleman meets one of them two hours from now, he's a goner.

POLLY *enters.* My dear Mama, you can save yourself the trouble. Before Mac would visit such women, he'd give himself up to the police. And if he went to the police, the Sheriff would offer him a cocktail and a cigar, and they'd discuss a certain business in this street where things aren't quite as they should be either. For, dear Papa, the Sheriff was very jolly at my wedding.

PEACHUM. What's the name of this Sheriff?

POLLY. You'd know him as Tiger Brown. All who fear him call him Tiger Brown. But my husband, you might like to know, calls him Jacky, his dear Jacky. They were boyhood friends.

PEACHUM. Friends are they? The Sheriff and the top criminal. They must be the only friends in this fine city.

POLLY, *poetically.* Whenever they had a cocktail together, they'd stroke each other's cheeks and say, "If you'll have another, I'll have another." And whenever one went to the men's room, the other's eyes grew moist and he'd say, "Whither thou goest, I will go." There's nothing against Mac in Scotland Yard.

PEACHUM. I see. Between Tuesday evening and Thursday morning Mr. MacHeath—a gentleman who has certainly been married several times—lured my daughter Polly Peachum from her parental home under pretense of marriage. Before the week is over this will be sufficient to bring him to the death he so richly deserves. "Mr. MacHeath, you once had white kid gloves and a stick with an ivory handle and a scar on your neck and you frequented the Octopus Hotel. All that remains is your scar, the least valuable of your distinguishing marks, and you frequent cages, and soon you won't frequent anywhere . . ."

MRS. PEACHUM. Oh, Jonathan, you'll never succeed if it's Mackie the Knife. They say he's the greatest criminal in London. He takes what he wants.

PEACHUM. Who *is* Mackie the Knife? Polly, get ready, we're going to the Sheriff of London. And *you're* going to Wapping.

MRS. PEACHUM. To his whores.

PEACHUM. For the wickedness of the world is so great you have to run your legs off to avoid having them stolen out from under you.

POLLY. And I, Papa, will be glad to shake Mr. Brown by the hand again.

All three walk to the front of the stage, and, to song illumination, sing the first finale. On a board is written: FIRST FINALE —THE UNCERTAINTY OF HUMAN CIRCUMSTANCES.

POLLY.
Is it much? O, hear my cry!
'Mid the wailing and the weeping
With a man I would be sleeping
Have I set my sights too high?

PEACHUM, *Bible in hand.*

There is a right to which man is entitled:
To call some little happiness his own
To taste some of the pleasures life can offer
Enjoying bread to eat and not a stone
That is a right to which you are entitled
But sad to say few cases are recorded
Of getting what you are entitled to
Who wouldn't claim this right if chance afforded?
But circumstances won't permit you to!

MRS. PEACHUM.

> *Gladly would I give to you*
> *All the things you ever wanted*
> *Let your dearest wish be granted*
> *Such things give us pleasure too*

PEACHUM.

> *We'd all like to be good, that's very clear*
> *Each giving to the poor in Christian love*
> *If all were good* HIS *kingdom would be near*
> *And we could bask in radiance from above*
> *We'd all like to be good, that's very clear*
> *But sad to say this Paradise comes never*
> *Supplies are scarce and man is far too low*
> *Who wouldn't choose to live in peace forever?*
> *But force of circumstance won't have it so!*

POLLY AND MRS. PEACHUM.

> *And sad to say, he states the case*
> *The world is poor and man is base*

PEACHUM.

> *Of course I state the very case*
> *The world is poor and man is base*
> *Who wouldn't like a Paradise below?*
> *But would our circumstances have it so?*
> *No, that could never be the case*
> *Your brother may be fond of you*
> *But when the food's too short for two*
> *He'll go and kick you in the bum*
> *(But Loyalty—your day will come!)*
> *But when your wife, who's fond of you,*
> *Decides your love for her won't do*
> *She'll go and kick you in the bum*
> *(But Gratitude—your day will come!)*
> *And then your child who's fond of you,*
> *If your pension's not enough for two*
> *He'll go and kick you in the bum*
> *(But Kindness—sure your day will come!)*

POLLY AND MRS. PEACHUM.

> *Yes, that's the truth about it*
> *The silly truth about it*
> *The world is poor and man is base*
> *And sad to say he states the case*

PEACHUM.

> *Of course I state the very case*
> *The world is poor and man is base*
> *We should be good—instead of low*
> *But force of circumstance won't have it so!*

ALL THREE.

> *So there is nothing we can do*
> *The world is rotten through and through!*

PEACHUM.

> *The world is poor and man is base*
> *And sad to say I state the case*

ALL THREE.

> *Yes, that's the truth about it*
> *The silly truth about it*
> *And so there's nothing we can do*
> *For the world is rotten through and through!*

ACT TWO

1 THURSDAY AFTERNOON. MACHEATH TAKES
LEAVE OF HIS WIFE BEFORE FLEEING
ACROSS HIGHGATE MOORS TO ESCAPE HIS
FATHER-IN-LAW.

The stable.

POLLY *enters.* Mac! Mac! Don't be afraid.

MACHEATH, *lying on a bed.* What's the matter? What are you looking like that for, Polly?

POLLY. I've been to see Brown, and my father was there, and they're going to catch you. My father threatened something terrible. Brown stuck up for you at first, but gave in later. He thinks you ought to disappear for a while. Mac, pack!

MACHEATH. Golly, Polly! We're going to do something quite different from packing.

POLLY. No, Mac, we can't. I'm frightened. They talked about hanging all the time.

MACHEATH. I don't like it, Polly, when you're moody! There's nothing against *me* in Scotland Yard.

POLLY. Maybe there wasn't. But now there is. Listen, I've brought the list of charges with me. I don't know whether I'll get through it, it's endless: you've killed two shopkeepers, and committed over thirty burglaries, twentythree street robberies, arsons, attempted murders, forgeries, perjuries—and all in eighteen months. You're a terrible person, Mac. And in Winchester you seduced two sisters, both under the age of consent.

MACHEATH. They told me they were twenty-one. What did Brown say?

He stands up slowly and walks along the footlights, whistling.

POLLY. He caught me up in the corridor and said he couldn't do anything more for you. Oh, Mac!

She throws her arms around his neck.

MACHEATH. If I *must* go, you'll have to take over the business.

POLLY. Don't talk of business now. I can't bear it! Mac, kiss your poor Polly and swear you'll never, never . . .

MACHEATH *interrupts her and leads her to the table where he pushes her down into a chair.*

MACHEATH. These are the account books. Listen. Here's a list of the staff.

Reads.

Crook-Finger Jacob, a year and a half in the business; let's see what he's brought in. One, two, three, four, five gold watches. Not much, but it's good, sound work.—Don't sit on my lap, I don't feel like it any more!—And here's Walter—Wally the Weeper—an unreliable dog. He's been doing business on his own account. Three weeks' grace for him, then the gallows. Simply report him to Brown.

POLLY, *sobbing.* Simply report him to Brown.

MACHEATH. Jimmy the Second, an impudent customer—profitable but impudent. Pinches sheets from under the finest female backsides in the land. Give him a rise.

POLLY. Give him a rise.

MACHEATH. Robert—call him Buzz the Saw, he hates the name —a petty thief—without a trace of genius. He won't end on the gallows, he'll come to nothing.*

POLLY. Come to nothing.

MACHEATH. Otherwise carry on as before: get up at seven, wash, take one bath a day, and so forth.

POLLY. You're right, Mac, I shall have to set my teeth and keep an eye on the business. What's yours is mine, isn't it, Mackie? But Mac, what about your rooms? Shall I give them up?

MACHEATH. No, I need them.

POLLY. But why? They only cost money.

MACHEATH. You seem to think I'm never coming back.

POLLY. What do you mean? You can take them again! Mac . . . Mac, I can't stand it any longer. I look at your lips and I don't hear what you're saying. Will you be faithful to me, Mac?

MACHEATH. Of course I shall. Do you think I don't love you? It's just that I look ahead.

POLLY. I'm so glad, Mac. Think of me when they're after you like bloodhounds . . . Oh!

At the mention of blood MACHEATH *stiffens, stands up, crosses to the right, takes off his coat and starts washing his hands.*

MACHEATH, *hurriedly*. Send all the profits to Jack Poole's banking house in Manchester. Between ourselves, it's only a question of weeks before I switch to banking exclusively. It's safer as well as more profitable. In two weeks at the

* Cf. *The Beggar's Opera*, Act I, Scene 3.

most the money must all be out of this business, and then you'll hand the whole list of names to the police. In four weeks at the most the whole lousy gang will be sitting in the Old Bailey.

POLLY. But, Mac! Can you look them in the eyes when you're going to doublecross them like this? Can you still shake them by the hand?

MACHEATH. Who? Money Matthew, Crook-Finger Jacob, Buzz the Saw, Wally the Weeper . . . those gaol-birds?
Enter the gang.
Gentlemen, I'm very glad to see you.
He shakes hands all round.

POLLY. Good-day, gentlemen.

MATTHEW. Captain, I've got the plans for the Coronation. There's days of good hard work ahead. The Archbishop of Canterbury arrives in half an hour.

MACHEATH. When?

MATTHEW. Five-thirty. We must go at once, Captain.

MACHEATH. Yes, you must go at once.

ROBERT. What do you mean: *you?*

MACHEATH. As for me, I've got to take a short trip to the country.

ROBERT. What? Are they going to nab you?

MATTHEW. A Coronation without you will be soup without a spoon.

MACHEATH. Shut your trap! I'm handing over the management of the business to my wife for a short time. Polly!
He pushes her to the front and then retires to the back, where he watches her.

POLLY. Men, I think our Captain can go away without having to worry. We shall get along fine, eh?

MATTHEW. I'll say nothing. But I don't know if a woman . . . at a time like this . . . I'm not saying anything against *you*, ma'am . . .

MACHEATH, *from the back*. What do you say, Polly?

POLLY. You've made a good start, you son of a bitch!
Screaming.
Of course you're not saying anything against me, or these men here would have had your trousers off and tanned your bottom long ago. Isn't that so, gentlemen?
A short pause, then they all clap like mad.

JACOB. She's all right!

WALTER. Bravo! Our new captain knows the answers! Hurrah for Polly!

ALL SIX. Hurrah for Polly!

MACHEATH. It's horrible I can't be in London for the Coronation. It'll be a hundred per cent business. Every house empty during the day, and at night all the best people drunk. That reminds me, Matthew—you drink too much. Last week you made it obvious that it was *you* that set fire to the children's hospital at Greenwich. If this happens again, you're sacked. Who set fire to the children's hospital?

MATTHEW. I did.

MACHEATH, *to the others*. Who set it on fire?

THE FIVE OTHERS. You did, Captain.

MACHEATH. Who did?

MATTHEW, *sullenly*. You did. The likes o' me will never come up in the world.

MACHEATH, *with a gesture of hanging*. You'll come up all right if you try to compete with me. Did you ever hear of an Oxford professor letting all his mistakes be made by an assistant? Of course not, he takes the credit for himself.

ROBERT. Ma'am, now your're in command . . . accounts settled every Thursday, ma'am.

POLLY. You're Buzz the Saw, aren't you, my man?

ROBERT. The name's Robert, ma'am.

POLLY. Buzz the Saw! I'll see you every Thursday. Every Thursday, men!
Exit gang.

MACHEATH. And now, good-bye, my love. Keep fresh, and don't forget to make up every day, just as if I were there.

POLLY. And you, Mac, promise you'll never look at another woman and that you'll leave London at once. Little Polly doesn't say this out of jealousy.

MACHEATH. But, Polly, why should *I* bother with second-hand goods? I love *you*. When it's dark enough I shall start out, get my black stallion from . . . oh, some stable or other, and before you see the moon from your window, I shall be far beyond Highgate Moors.

POLLY. Oh, Mac, don't tear my heart from my body. Stay with me! Let us be happy together!

MACHEATH. I have to tear *my* heart from *my* body: I must go. Who knows the day of my return?

POLLY. It lasted such a little while, Mac.

MACHEATH. And now is it over—forever?

POLLY. Mac, last night I had a dream. I was looking out of the window and I heard laughter in the street, and when I looked up, I saw our moon, it was quite thin, like a penny that's all worn away. Don't forget me, Mac, in the strange cities.

MACHEATH. I can never forget you, Polly. Kiss me, Polly.
She does so.

POLLY. Good-bye, Mac.

MACHEATH. Good-bye, Polly.

Music.

POLLY. And he never will come back again!

The bells begin to ring.

The Queen is now in London on her way
Where shall we be on Coronation Day?

Sings.

Sweet while it lasted, and now it is over,
Tear out your heart, say "Good-bye, my lover"
What use is my weeping (Blessed Virgin restore me!)
When 'tis plain my mother knew all this before me?

MACHEATH *sings.*

For love lasts forever (or not so long)
In ever so many a town

INTERLUDE

MRS. PEACHUM *and* GINNY JENNY *step out in front of the curtain.*

MRS. PEACHUM. So if you see Mackie the Knife, run to the
nearest copper and report him: you'll get ten shillings for it.

GINNY JENNY. But do you think we'll see him if the police are
on the job? When the hunt starts, he won't be wasting any
time with us.

MRS. PEACHUM. Let me tell you this, Jenny: if all London were
after him, MacHeath is not the man to give up his old habits.

She sings THE BALLAD OF SEXUAL SLAVERY.

Now here's a man who fights the devil's battle
The butcher, he! And all the others, cattle!
A dirty crook! No man has taken him in!
Who gets him down, that gets 'em all down? Women!
Whether he will or not, he must comply
Such is the law of sexual slavery
    He pays no heed to the Bible. He laughs at the S. P. G.
    He will persist that he's an egoist

Knows that with a woman no one can resist
So keeps them all from his vicinity
But in the day he need not feel elated
For when the night falls, he's again prostrated

MacHeath is ours: for human nature such is
That e'en the great can't keep from harlots' clutches
And they who see it swear no one takes them in—
Yet when they are corpses, who inters 'em? Women!
Whether they will or not, they must comply
Such is the law of sexual slavery
    He fastens on to the Bible. He enlists in the S. P. G.
    He's Methodist! Becomes an Anarchist!
    Has celery deleted from his midday dinner list
    The afternoon is spent in thinking patiently
    By evening he says, "I feel elevated"
    And when the night falls, he's again prostrated

2 THE CORONATION BELLS HAVE NOT YET
RUNG OUT AND MACKIE THE KNIFE IS
AMONG HIS WHORES AT WAPPING. THE
GIRLS BETRAY HIM. IT IS THURSDAY EVE-
NING.

A brothel in Wapping. An ordinary early evening. The Fam-
ily: DIANA, VIXEN, DOLLY, BETTY, OLD TRULL, COAXER,
MOLLY. *Mostly in their underclothes, they are quietly iron-*
ing, playing draughts, washing themselves: a middle-class
idyll. JENNY *sits alone on one side.* CROOK-FINGER JACOB *is*
reading the newspaper, paying not the slightest attention
to anyone. In fact, he is rather in the way.

JACOB. He won't come today.

DIANA. No?

JACOB. I don't think he'll ever come again.

DIANA. That would be a pity.

JACOB. Would it? If I know him, he's out of the city by this
time. Up and away!

Enter MACHEATH, *hangs his hat on a nail, sits on the sofa behind the table.*

MACHEATH. My coffee; please!

VIXEN, *astounded.* "My coffee, please!"
Repeats this in amazement several times.

JACOB, *horrified.* Why aren't you in Highgate?

MACHEATH. Today is Thursday. Such trifles cannot disturb my habits.
Throws his charge-sheet on the floor.
Besides, it's raining.

GINNY JENNY, *reads the charge-sheet.* "In the name of the King, Captain MacHeath is herewith charged with triple . . ."

JACOB, *snatching it from her.* Am I there too?

MACHEATH. Of course, the whole staff.

GINNY JENNY, *to another whore.* Look, here are the charges.
Pause.
Mac, give me your hand.
He holds out his hand.

DOLLY. Yes, Jenny, read his hand.
Holds forward a paraffin lamp.

MACHEATH. A rich legacy?

GINNY JENNY. No, not a rich legacy.

BETTY. Why are you looking at him like that, Jenny? It's enough to give anyone the shivers.

MACHEATH. A long journey in the near future?

GINNY JENNY. No, not a long journey.

VIXEN. What is it then?

MACHEATH. Only *good* news, please!

GINNY JENNY. I see a narrow strip of darkness there and a little

light. And then I see a large G, which means the guile of a
woman. Then I see . . .

MACHEATH. Stop. I'd like a few details about the narrow strip
of darkness and the guile: for example, the name of the
guileful woman.

GINNY JENNY. I can only see that it begins with J.

MACHEATH. Then it's wrong. It begins with P.

GINNY JENNY. Mac, when the Coronation bells ring out in West-
minster, you'll have a bad time of it.

MACHEATH. Go on.
JACOB laughs raucously.
What's the matter?
He goes across to JACOB, *and reads.*
Inaccurate, there were only three.

JACOB, *laughs.* That's just it.

MACHEATH. Nice underwear you have here.

DIANA. From the cradle to the coffin, underwear comes first.

OLD TRULL. I never use silk. The men think you're ill.
GINNY JENNY edges quietly out of the door.

COAXER, *to* GINNY JENNY. Where are you going, Jenny?

GINNY JENNY. You'll see.
Exit.

MOLLY. But plain linen puts them off.

OLD TRULL. I've had success with plain linen.

VIXEN. That's because the men feel at home with it.

MACHEATH, *to* BETTY. Have you still got the black braid?

BETTY. Yes, I've still got the black braid.

MACHEATH. And what sort of underwear do *you* have, my dear?

COAXER. I can't bring 'em to my room, my aunt hates men. And in doorways, you can't wear underwear.

JACOB laughs.

MACHEATH. Finished?

JACOB. No, I'm just at the . . . "violations."

MACHEATH, again sitting on the sofa. Where is Jenny? Ladies, before my star rose over this town . . .

VIXEN. Before my star rose over this town . . .

MACHEATH. . . . . I lived in the humblest circumstances with one of you fair ladies. And though I am Mackie the Knife now, in present happiness I shall never forget the comrades of darker days: above all Jenny that I loved the best of all the girls. Listen!

As MACHEATH sings THE BALLAD OF THE FANCY MAN, GINNY JENNY stands outside the window right and beckons to a POLICEMAN: it is CONSTABLE SMITH. Then MRS. PEACHUM joins her with CONSTABLES DARLINGTON and MERRY-WEATHER. All five stand under the street lamp and look on.

MACHEATH.
There was a time, in days now long ago
When we two lived together, I and she
And my brains told her body what to do
I protected her and she took care of me
(One can do different, but this isn't new)
And when a wooer came, I left our little bed
And had a little drink and showed myself well-bred
And when he paid, I said, "Auf Wiederseh'n!
If any time you'd care to, come again"
So six months long we lived a happy life
In that bordel where we were man and wife

Re-enter GINNY JENNY through the door: behind her CON-STABLE SMITH

GINNY JENNY.
But in that time of days so long ago
Between us there was many an angry rift
And when the cash was short he'd curse and shout

And he would say, "Now I must pawn your shift
(A shift is all right, but you can do without)
And sometimes I grew angry—all of us come to it—
And I would ask him outright how he dared to do it
And then he'd give me many a brutal biff
And it was that, I'm sure, that gave me syph

BOTH.

Those six long months we lived a happy life
In that bordel where we were man and wife

That was a time, in days now long ago

HE. *Before our simple happiness was broken*

SHE. *When every day we shared a bed for two*

HE.

For nightly, as I said, she was bespoken
(The night is usual, but the day will do too)
SHE. *And one fine day I felt a young MacHeath*

HE. *And so we worked it out: that I lay underneath*

SHE. *Because he knew an unborn child so often crushes*

HE. *(Though the child was always destined for the rushes)*

BOTH.

Too soon we ended our six months of life
In that bordel where we were man and wife

Dance. MACHEATH *picks up his swordstick; she hands him his hat; and he is still dancing when* CONSTABLE SMITH *lays a hand on his shoulder.*

SMITH. Well, now we can get going.

MACHEATH. Has this rat-hole *still* only got one exit?

SMITH *attempts to handcuff* MACHEATH. MACHEATH *thrusts himself against his chest, so that the* CONSTABLE *stumbles over backwards. Then* MACHEATH *jumps out of the window. But outside are* MRS. PEACHUM *and* CONSTABLES DARLINGTON *and* MERRYWEATHER.

MACHEATH, *calmly and very politely.* Good evening, madam.

MRS. PEACHUM. My dear Mr. MacHeath! My husband always says "The greatest heroes trip over the smallest obstacles."

MACHEATH. May I enquire how your husband is?

MRS. PEACHUM. Better—now. Well, you can take your leave of these charming ladies. Darlington! Merryweather! Take Mr. MacHeath to his new lodgings.
He is led off. MRS. PEACHUM *speaks through the window.*
The gentleman will be living at the Old Bailey. When you wish to visit him, ladies, you will always find him at home. Farewell, ladies. I knew he'd be here!
Exit MRS. PEACHUM.

GINNY JENNY. Hey, Jacob! Something's happened.

JACOB *who, on account of his intensive reading, has noticed nothing.* Where's Mac?

GINNY JENNY. The coppers were here!

JACOB. No! And here was I quietly reading! Boys, boys, boys!

3 BETRAYED BY THE WHORES, MACHEATH IS FREED FROM PRISON THROUGH THE LOVE OF ANOTHER WOMAN.

Prison in the Old Bailey. A barred cage. Enter BROWN.

BROWN. I hope my men don't catch him! Dear God, I hope he's beyond Highgate Moors thinking of his old friend Jacky! But he's light of heart, like all great men. If they should bring him in now, and he were to look at me with those faithful, friendly eyes, I couldn't stand it. Thank God, there's a moon: once he's out in the country, he'll find his way all right.
Noise outside.
What's this? Oh God, they've got him.

MACHEATH *tied with heavy ropes and guarded by* CONSTABLES SMITH, DARLINGTON, *and* MERRYWEATHER, *he enters*

proudly. Well, my minions, here we are again! Back home!
He sees BROWN *who has retreated to the farthest corner of
the cell.*

BROWN *after a long pause, under the fearful gaze of his former
friend.* Mac, I didn't do it . . . I did everything I could . . .
don't look at me like that, Mac . . . I can't bear it . . . Your
silence is terrible!

Shouts at SMITH.

Don't pull at that rope, you swine!

Exeunt SMITH, DARLINGTON, *and* MERRYWEATHER

Say something, Mac. Say something to your old friend,
Jackie! Lighten his darkness, I beseech you . . .

Rests his head against the wall and weeps.

He doesn't think me worth a word.

Exit.

MACHEATH. That miserable Brown! Evil conscience incarnate!
And such a creature is made Sheriff of London! Lucky I
didn't bawl him out. I'd intended doing something of the
sort. But then I thought a good, piercing, punishing stare
would send the shivers down his back. It worked. I looked
at him and he wept bitterly. I got that from the Bible.

Re-enter SMITH *with handcuffs.*

Well, Mr. Smith, I suppose they're the heaviest you could
find. With your permission, I should like a more comfortable
pair.

He takes out his check book.

SMITH. Certainly, Captain, We have them here at all prices.
It depends what you want to pay. From one to ten guineas.

MACHEATH. How much do none cost?

SMITH. Fifty.

MACHEATH *writes out a check.* The devil of it is, the business
with Lucy will come out. And when Brown hears what I've
done to his daughter behind his friendly back, he'll *really*
be a tiger.

SMITH. You've made your bed: lie on it.

MACHEATH. I'll bet that trollop is waiting outside. I shall have a fine time from now till the execution.

So, gentlemen, is this what you call living?
I take no pleasure in such derring-do
While yet a babe I heard my mother singing:
The life of comfort is the life for you

Song illumination: golden light. The organ is illuminated.
Three lights come down on a bar from above—and on a
board is written: THE BALLAD OF COMFORT.

You've heard about the lives of famous sages
That feed on books and never think of eating
Live in some little hut where rats are breeding?
Myself, I'd keep such lunatics in cages!
Let those who like it live the simple way
Between ourselves it rather makes me howl
From here to Babylon no beast or fowl
Would tolerate the Simple Life one day
And what is freedom—to security?
The life of comfort is the life for me

Adventurers brave, whose lives create Sensations,
Whose passion 'tis to risk their necks for Freedom
They tell the Truth in weighty publications—
God knows, all our suburbanites will read 'em—
Just look at them in their domestic station
See how they go with frigid wives to bed
Their somber thoughts five thousand years ahead
(And one ear cocked for public acclamation)
Is that what YOU *want? No, you say too:*
The life of comfort is the life for you

Yes, I myself have been steamed up about it
How marv'lous to be Great and Solitary!
But closer knowledge made me rather chary:
I told myself that I could do without it
Poverty makes you wise but it's a curse
And brav'ry brings you fame but it's a chore
And so not to be great's a bloody bore
But being great—my friends—it must be worse
Here's the solution inescapably:
The life of comfort is the life for me

Enter LUCY.

LUCY. You great slob! How can you look me in the face after all that was between us?

MACHEATH. Lucy, have you no heart? To see your own husband in this condition?

LUCY. Husband! You brute! You think I don't know about Miss Peachum? I could scratch your eyes out!

MACHEATH. Lucy, seriously, you're not jealous of Polly?

LUCY. So you're not married to her, you beast?

MACHEATH. Married! That's a good one! I go to a certain house. I talk to her. Now and then I give her a sort of kiss, and the silly bitch runs around boasting that she's married to me. Darling Lucy, I'll do anything to reassure you, if you really do believe she and I are married. What more can a gentleman say?

LUCY. Oh, Mac, I only want to become an honest woman.

MACHEATH. If you think you'll become an honest woman by marrying me—good. What more can a gentleman say?

Enter POLLY.

POLLY. Where's my husband? Oh, Mac, don't look away, you needn't be ashamed. After all, I am your wife.

LUCY. You great slob!

POLLY. Mackie in prison! Why didn't you escape across Highgate Moors? You told me you wouldn't go to those women. I knew what they'd do to you; but I didn't say anything; I believed you. Oh, Mac, think how your Polly's suffering!

LUCY. The trollop!

POLLY. Mac, who is that woman? Tell her who I am. Am I not your wife?

LUCY. You treacherous clot, have you got two wives, you monster?

POLLY. Say something, Mac. Am I not your wife? Haven't I done everything for you? Didn't you hand everything over to me? Wasn't I to tell Jacob to . . .

MACHEATH. If you two would shut your mouths for five minutes I could explain the whole thing. This is more than a man can stand.

POLLY. Yes, my love, it's clear that the wife . . .

LUCY. The wife!

POLLY. The wife has a natural priority. It's enough to drive anyone mad.

LUCY. What have you gone and picked up? This filthy piece! So that's your conquest! That's your beauty of Soho!

Song illumination: golden light. The organ is illuminated. Three lights come down on a bar from above and on a board is written: THE JEALOUSY DUET.

LUCY.
Come right out, you beauty of Soho!
Show your lovely legs for my inspection!
I too would like to see a thing of beauty
Sure there's none can rival your perfection!
You seem to have thought it was you my husband was after!

POLLY. *Did I then, did I then?*

LUCY. *And that really makes me roar with laughter!*

POLLY. *Does it then, does it then?*

LUCY. *Oh, how everyone would laugh!*

POLLY. *You think everyone would laugh?*

LUCY. *If Mac should fall for such a calf!*

POLLY. *If Mac should fall for such a calf?*

LUCY. *Ha, ha, ha, ha, ha! A man for her! No one cares a damn for her!*

POLLY. *Well, we'll soon find out the truth*

LUCY. *Yes, we'll soon find out the truth!*

TOGETHER.
>*Mackie and me, we're two birds of a feather*
>*He loves just me, we'll always stick together*
>*For you'll just have to wake up*
>*If you think we'll ever break up*
>*For a flagpole in female make up*
>*Ludicrous!*

POLLY.
>*Yes, I'm called the beauty of Soho*
>*My lovely legs are worthy of inspection*

LUCY. *You think so?*

POLLY.
>*For people like to see a thing of beauty*
>*And they say no one can rival my perfection*

LUCY. *You hussy!*

POLLY. *Hussy yourself!*
>*I knew it was always me that my husband was after*

LUCY. *Was it so? Was it so?*

POLLY. *So I can afford to roar with laughter*

LUCY. *Can you then? Can you then?*

POLLY. *And how everyone would laugh!*

LUCY. *You think everyone would laugh?*

POLLY. *If no one loved my pretty calf!*

LUCY. *If no one loved your pretty calf?*

POLLY, *to the audience.*
>*You think there's no man for me?*
>*No one cares a damn for me?*

LUCY. *Well, we'll soon find out the truth*

POLLY. *Yes, we'll soon find out the truth*

TOGETHER.

Mackie and me, we're two birds of a feather
He loves just me, we'll always stick together
For you'll just have to wake up
If you think we'll ever break up
For a flagpole in female make up
Ludicrous!

MACHEATH. And now, Lucy, be calm. This is a trick of Polly's. She wants to make trouble. They're going to hang me, and she wants to call herself my widow. Really, Polly, this is not a well-chosen moment.

POLLY. You have the heart to deny me?

MACHEATH. And you have the heart to chatter about me being married to you? Must you add to my misery?

Shakes his head reproachfully.

Polly, Polly, Polly!

LUCY. Really, Miss Peachum, you're making a show of yourself. Quite apart from the fact that it's monstrous of you to excite a poor gentleman in this condition!

POLLY. The simplest rules of deportment, my dear madam, would teach you, I believe, that a person should behave with somewhat more restraint towards a gentleman in the presence of his wife.

MACHEATH. Seriously, Polly, now you go too far.

LUCY. And if you, madam, want to start a row in the prison here, I shall have to summon a warder and show you the door. I should be sorry to have to do it, Miss Peachum.

POLLY. Mrs. MacHeath! Permit me to tell you—Miss!—these airs don't suit you in the least! My duty compels me to remain with my husband.

LUCY. What do you say to that? She won't go! She stands there and waits to be thrown out! Shall I speak more plainly?

POLLY. Shut your filthy mouth, you slut, or I'll give you a smack in the jaw, dear madam!

LUCY. I'll have you kicked out, Miss Insolence! No use mincing words with you. You don't understand delicacy.

POLLY. Delicacy! I'm compromising my own dignity! And I'm too good for that . . . I am!
She howls.

LUCY. Well, look at me, you trollop!
She has a fat stomach.
Does *that* come out of thin air?
Pause.

POLLY. Oh! I suppose you're hoping to make something out of it? You should never have let him in, fine lady!

MACHEATH. Polly!

POLLY, *sobbing.* Mac, this shouldn't have happened. I don't know *what* I shall do!
Enter MRS. PEACHUM.

MRS. PEACHUM. I knew it. She's with that man. Come here this minute, you filthy trollop. When your husband is hanged, you can hang yourself with him. A fine way to behave to your poor mother: she has to come and fetch you out of prison. So, he has two at a time—this Nero!

POLLY. Leave me alone, mama, you don't know . . .

MRS. PEACHUM. Come home this minute!

LUCY. Listen to that, your mother has to tell you how to behave.

MRS. PEACHUM. Quick march!

POLLY. Oh, Mac!
She is dragged off by MRS. PEACHUM.

MACHEATH. Lucy, your conduct was exemplary. Of course I was sorry for her. That's why I couldn't treat the silly girl as she deserved. You thought at first there was some truth in what she said? Am I right?

LUCY. Yes. dear.

MACHEATH. Had it been true, her mother would never have got me into this mess. A mother behaves like that to a seducer, not to a son-in-law.

LUCY. It makes me so happy, when you speak from the heart. I love you so much, I'd almost rather see you hanged than in the arms of another.

MACHEATH. Lucy, I should like to owe my life to you.

LUCY. It's wonderful, the way you say that. Say it again!

MACHEATH. Lucy, I should like to owe my life to you.

LUCY. Shall I escape with you, dear heart?

MACHEATH. It'll be hard to hide if we escape together. But when the search is over, I'll have you fetched by express post!

LUCY. How can I help you?

MACHEATH. Bring me my hat and stick.

LUCY goes out and returns with his hat and stick and throws them into his cell.

Lucy, the fruit of our love which you carry beneath your heart will forever bind us together.

Exit LUCY. SMITH enters and goes into the cage

SMITH. Give me that stick.

After a short chase in which SMITH, armed with a chair and crow-bar, drives MACHEATH before him, MACHEATH climbs over the bars. CONSTABLES SMITH, DARLINGTON, and MERRYWEATHER pursue him.

BROWN, *off.* Hello, Mac! Mac, please answer! It's Jacky. Mac, please be kind and answer, I can't bear it!

Enters.

Mackie! What's up? He's gone.

He sighs

Thank God!

He sits down on the bench.

Enter PEACHUM.

PEACHUM, *to* SMITH. My name is Peachum. I have come to claim the forty pounds offered for the capture of the bandit MacHeath.

Appears in front of the cage.

Hey! Is Mr. MacHeath there?

BROWN *remains silent.*

Ah! So the gentleman has gone out for a little walk? I come here to visit a criminal and whom do I find but Mr. Brown! Tiger Brown in and his friend MacHeath out.

BROWN, *groaning.* Mr. Peachum, it's not my fault.

PEACHUM. Of course not. You would never be so . . . as to get yourself into this situation . . . would you, Brown?

BROWN. Mr. Peachum, I am beside myself.

PEACHUM. I believe you. You must feel horrible, Brown.

BROWN. Yes, this helplessness is paralyzing! The men do what they like! It's terrible!

PEACHUM. Would you like to lie down a little? Shut your eyes and behave as though nothing had happened. Imagine you're lying in a lovely green meadow with little white clouds overhead. The main thing is to get this nasty affair off your mind. All that's happened, and all that *will* happen.

BROWN, *uneasily.* What do you mean?

PEACHUM. It's wonderful the way you're taking it. If I were in your position, I'd collapse, I'd go to bed and drink hot tea. I'd arrange to have a nice cool hand stroking my forehead.

BROWN. Damn you! I can't help it if a man escapes!

PEACHUM. So you don't think we shall have Mr. MacHeath back?

BROWN *shrugs his shoulders.*

Then it will be a nasty injustice, what happens to

you, Brown. Of course people will say the police shouldn't
have let him escape. No, I can't quite see that brilliant coronation procession yet.

BROWN. How do you mean?

PEACHUM. I might remind you of an historic example which,
although it aroused some excitement in its time, fourteen
hundred years before Christ, is relatively unknown to the
larger public of today. When the Egyptian king died,
Rameses the Second by the way, the chief of police of
Nineveh, and also of Cairo, was guilty of some petty injustice towards the lower classes. The results were terrible,
Brown. The coronation procession of the new queen, Semiramis, was, as the history books state, "a succession of catas-
trophes caused by the all too lively participation of the
lower classes". The historians are far too squeamish to de-
scribe what Semiramis did to her chief of police. I only
remember vaguely; but there was talk of snakes which she
nourished at his bosom.

BROWN. Really?

PEACHUM. God be with you, Brown.

Exit.

BROWN. Now only an iron hand will do it! Sergeant, a confer-
ence! Sound an alarm!

Curtain. MACHEATH *and* MRS. PEACHUM *step in front of the
curtain and sing. On a board is written:* SECOND FINALE—
THE NECESSITY OF FOUL MISDEEDS.

MACHEATH.
  *You moral gentlemen who try to lead us
  And keep us from each sin, each foul misdeed
  Your prior obligation is to feed us:
  To lead (why not?) but first of all to feed
  Yes, you who love your paunch and our morality
  Hear, mark, and learn one thing for it is late:
  Though you finagle most ingeniously
  Until you feed us, right and wrong can wait!
  Or is it only those that have the money
  Can enter in the land of milk and honey?*

VOICE OFF. What does a man live by?

MACHEATH.

What does a man live by? By grinding, sweating
Defeating, beating, cheating, eating, some other man
For he can only live by sheer forgetting
Forgetting that he ever was a man

MACHEATH, *with* CHORUS OFF.

So, gentlemen, you must concede to me
Men live by foul misdeeds exclusively!

MRS. PEACHUM.

You preach that moral rules should be decreed us
When we should lift our skirts, when we should not
Your prior obligation is to feed us
To feed comes first—then you can preach (why not?)
Yes, you who love your fun and our dependency
Hear, mark, and learn one thing for it is late:
Though you finagle most ingeniously
Until you feed us, right and wrong can wait!
Or is it only those that have the money
Can enter in the land of milk and honey?

VOICE OFF. What does a man live by?

MACHEATH.

What does a man live by? By grinding, sweating
Defeating, beating, cheating, eating, some other man
For he can only live by sheer forgetting
Forgetting that he ever was a man

MACHEATH, (*with* CHORUS OFF).

So, gentlemen, you must concede to me
Men live by foul misdeeds exclusively!

ACT THREE

1 THE SAME NIGHT PEACHUM GIRDS HIS
LOINS FOR ACTION. BY MEANS OF A DEMON-
STRATION OF MISERY HE HOPES TO DISOR-
GANIZE THE CORONATION PROCESSION.

The wardrobe-room of PEACHUM's *establishment. The* BEG-
GARS* *are painting boards with such inscriptions as* "I GAVE
MY EYE FOR MY KING", *etc.*

PEACHUM. Gentlemen, at this very hour, in our eleven branches
between Drury Lane and Wapping, there are one thousand
four hundred and thirty-two men working on such boards as
these! They will all attend the Coronation of our Queen.

MRS. PEACHUM. Come on, come on! If you won't work, you
can't beg. You're hoping to be a blind man, and you can't
even write a proper K! That's supposed to be a child's hand-
writing, not an old man's!
Roll of drums.

1ST BEGGAR. There's a guard of honor lining up! Little do they
dream that today, the grandest day of their military lives,
they'll have to deal with us!

FILCH *enters and announces.* Here come a dozen birds of night,
Mrs. Peachum. They say they're to get their money here.
Enter the FAMILY, *led by* GINNY JENNY.

GINNY JENNY. My dear madam . . .

MRS. PEACHUM. Well, well, well, so they've fallen off their
perches! I suppose you've come for the money. You'll get
nothing, understand? Nothing.

GINNY JENNY. And how are we to take that, madam?

MRS. PEACHUM. Bursting into my room in the middle of the

*Minimum: the five from Act One and a girl.

night! Coming to a respectable house at three in the morning! You should sleep off the effects of business. You look like skimmed milk.

GINNY JENNY. So we're to get no reward for having Mr. Mac-Heath arrested, madam?

MRS. PEACHUM. Quite correct. In fact, you'll get something you don't like instead.

GINNY JENNY. And why, madam?

MRS. PEACHUM. Because your wonderful Mr. MacHeath has vanished again, that's why. Now get out of my house, ladies.

GINNY JENNY. Don't you try that on us! I give you fair warning!

MRS. PEACHUM. Filch, the ladies wish to be shown the door.
FILCH *approaches the girls.* GINNY JENNY *pushes him away.*

GINNY JENNY. I'd advise you to keep your dirty mouth shut, or . . . !
Enter PEACHUM.

PEACHUM. What's the matter? I hope you haven't given them any money. Well, what's the matter, ladies? Is Mr. Mac-Heath in prison or is he not?

GINNY JENNY. Let me in peace with your Mr. MacHeath. You're not a patch on him. I had to send a gentleman away tonight because I wanted to cry on my pillow every time I thought how I had sold Mackie to you. Yes, and what do you think happened this morning? I had just cried myself to sleep when I heard a whistle, and there in the street below stood the gentleman I'd been crying for, and he asked me to throw the key down to him: he wished to forget the wrong I had done him—in my arms. He's the last gentleman left in London, ladies. And if our colleague Suky Tawdry, isn't with us now, it's because he went from me to her, to comfort her too.

PEACHUM, *to himself.* Suky Tawdry . . .

GINNY JENNY. You're not a patch on him. You're lowdown informers!

PEACHUM. Filch, run to the nearest police station and say Mr. MacHeath is staying with Miss Suky Tawdry.

Exit FILCH.

But, ladies, why are we quarreling? Your money will be paid. My dear Celia, wouldn't it be better if you went and made the ladies a nice cup of coffee?

MRS. PEACHUM. Suky Tawdry!

Sings.

Now here's a man is facing execution
The burning lime awaits his dissolution
It won't be long before the noose does him in
But what absorbs his whole attention? Women!
Though near the gallows—still he must comply
Such is the law of sexual slavery
    And now he has been sold. There's nothing left to save
    A female Judas has the money in her hand
    And now he just begins to understand:
    The charms of women lead but to the grave
    And, though his fury rages unabated,
    Before the night falls he's again prostrated

Exit MRS. PEACHUM.

PEACHUM. Come on, come on! You'd all be rotting in the sewers of Wapping if I hadn't spent sleepless nights figuring how to extract a few pence from your poverty. And I did figure something: the rich of the earth *create* misery but cannot bear to *see* it. They are weaklings and fools like you. As long as they have enough to eat and can grease their floors with butter so that even the crumbs that fall from their tables grow fat off it, they can't look with indifference on a man collapsing from hunger—although, of course, it must be in front of *their* house that he collapses.

Re-enter MRS. PEACHUM *with a tray full of coffee cups.*

MRS. PEACHUM. You can come to the shop tomorrow and fetch your money; but *after* the Coronation.

GINNY JENNY. Mrs. Peachum, you leave me speechless.

PEACHUM. Fall in! We assemble in an hour outside Buckingham Palace. Quick march!

The BEGGARS *fall in.*

FILCH (*bursts in*). The coppers! I never got as far as the station. The coppers are here!!

PEACHUM. Hide! (*To* MRS. PEACHUM. Get the orchestra ready! And when you hear me say "harmless", understand me, "harmless", play some sort of music! *There is a knocking on the door.* Now get out!

Exit MRS. PEACHUM. *The* BEGGARS, *except for a girl with the board* A VICTIM OF MILITARY DESPOTISM, *hide with their things behind the clothes racks on the right. Enter* BROWN *with Constables* SMITH, DARLINGTON, *and* MERRYWEATHER.

BROWN. And now, Mr. Beggars' Friend, action! Handcuff him, Smith. Ah, so those are a few of your charming notices.

To the girl.

"A Victim of Military Despotism"—is that you, my dear?

PEACHUM. Good morning, Brown. Slept well?

BROWN. Eh?

PEACHUM. Morning, Brown.

BROWN. Is he speaking to me? Does he know any of you? I don't think I have the pleasure of your acquaintance.

PEACHUM. Morning, Brown.

BROWN. Knock his hat off, Smith.

SMITH *does so.*

PEACHUM. Listen, Brown, since your way leads past my house —I said *past*, Brown—I can now ask you to put a certain MacHeath under lock and key.

BROWN. The man is mad. Smith, stop laughing. Tell me, Smith, how is it possible that this notorious criminal is allowed at large in London?

PEACHUM. Because he's your friend, Brown.

BROWN. Who?

PEACHUM. Mackie the Knife. Not me. I'm no criminal. I'm a poor man, Brown: you can't treat *me* badly. Listen, Brown. The worst hour of your life approaches. Would you like a cup of coffee?

To the FAMILY.

Girls, give the Sheriff a drink, that's not the way to behave. We're all friends here. We all obey the law. The law is made for the exploitation of those who do not understand it or of those who, for naked need, cannot obey it. Whoever would pick up the crumbs of this exploitation *must* obey the law.

BROWN, *blustering*. You think our judges are bribable?

PEACHUM. On the contrary, Brown, our judges are totally unbribable: no amount of money can bribe them to dispense justice.

A second roll of drums.

Departure of the troops to line the route! Departure of the poorest of the poor half an hour later!

BROWN. Quite right, Mr. Peachum. Departure of the poorest of the poor. They're departing for their winter-quarters in the Old Bailey. *To the three constables.* Well, boys, line 'em up. All the patriots you can find.

To the BEGGARS.

Ever heard of Tiger Brown? Tonight, Mr. Peachum, I have found the solution, and, I may add, I have saved a friend from death. I shall smoke out your whole nest. Then I shall lock you all up for—yes, street-begging. You warned me that you were going to bother me and the Queen with your beggars. These beggars I shall now arrest.

PEACHUM. What beggars?

BROWN. These cripples here. Smith, we'll take the patriotic gentlemen with us!

PEACHUM. Brown, I can save you from overstepping the bounds of duty. Thank God you came to me! Of course you can arrest these few people, they are harmless, harmless . . .

Music starts and plays a few introductory bars of THE SONG
OF THE FUTILITY OF ALL HUMAN ENDEAVOR.

BROWN. What's that?

PEACHUM. Music. They play pretty well, don't they? "The
Futility of All Human Endeavor". You know that song?

*Song illumination: golden light. The organ is lit up. Three
lights come down from above on a bar, and on a board is
written:* THE FUTILITY OF ALL HUMAN ENDEAVOR.

*A man lives by his head
But it does not suffice
Just try it and you'll find your head
Won't raise a pair of lice
    It'll be the same forever
    A man is never bright enough
    Bright enough to uncover
    All the tricks and bluff*

*Sure, make yourself a plan
And be a leading light
Then make yourself a second plan
And neither will come right
    It'll be the same forever
    A man just can't be bad enough
    Yet his High Endeavor
    Proves he's got the Stuff!*

*Go running after luck
But don't you run too fast
For all of us run after luck
And luck is running last
    It'll be the same forever
    Man is never meek and mild enough
    Spiritual Endeavor's
    Just another bluff*

Your plan is a stroke of genius, Brown, but im_practical_. All
you can arrest here are a few young people who have arranged a small fancy-dress ball to celebrate the Coronation
of their Queen. But when the really poor ones come—there's
not one here now, Brown—they'll come in thousands. You've
forgotten the monstrous number of the poor. If they were to
stand there in front of the Abbey, it wouldn't be a very cheer-

ful sight. They don't look very nice. Do you know what erysipelas is, Brown? Well, think of a hundred people with erysipelas on their faces. And then these mutilated creatures. At the door of the Abbey? We would rather avoid that, Brown. You say the police will make short work of us poor people. But you don't believe it. What will it look like if six hundred cripples have to be cut down with your truncheons because of the Coronation? It will look bad. It will be disgusting. Enough to make one sick. I feel ill, Brown, just to think of it. A small chair, please.

BROWN, *to* SMITH. Smith, it's blackmail. We can't do anything to this man. Such a thing never happened before!

PEACHUM. It has happened now, Brown. I'll tell you something: you can do what you like to the Queen of England but just try and tread on the toes of the poorest man in London and we'll do you brown, Brown.

BROWN. I'm to arrest Mackie the Knife? But you've got to catch your man before you can arrest him.

PEACHUM. I shall produce him for you. We'll see if there's any morality left! Jenny, where is Mr. MacHeath at the present moment?

GINNY JENNY. With Suky Tawdry, at 21 Oxford Street.

BROWN. Smith, Darlington, Merryweather, go at once to 21 Oxford Street, Suky Tawdry's flat, arrest MacHeath, and bring him to the Old Bailey.
The 3 constables click heels and leave.
In the meantime I must change into my full-dress uniform.

PEACHUM. Brown, if he's not hanged by six . . .

BROWN. Oh, Mackie, I did my best!
Exit BROWN.
A third roll of drums.

PEACHUM. Drums—the third time! A fresh plan of campaign! New destination: the Old Bailey! Quick march!
Exeunt the BEGGARS *singing.*

Since man is far from good
Just hit him on the head
And if you do it properly
He's either good or dead
        It'll be the same forever
        Man is never good enough
        So—to make him clever—
        We must treat him rough

INTERLUDE

In front of the curtain appears GINNY JENNY *with a hurdy-gurdy. She sings* THE SONG OF SOLOMON.

You saw the wise man Solomon
You know his history
So plain to him was all the earth
That in fury he cursed the hour of his birth
And saw that all was vanity
How great and wise was Solomon!
But ere night came and day did go
It all was clear to everyone:
'Twas wisdom that had brought him down so low!
How fortunate the man with none

You know Queen Cleopatra's name
Her beauty had its day
Two emperors she capturèd
And then she whored her life away
She faded, sickened, and was dead
How beautiful was Babylon!
But ere night came and day did go
It was all clear to everyone:
'Twas beauty that brought her down so low!
How fortunate were she with none

You saw the brave man Caesar too
You know what him befell
He sat, a god upon a throne,
Was murdered—as you know full well—
And just when he was greatest grown
He cried aloud: You too, my son!

But ere night came and day did go
It was all clear to everyone:
'Twas brav'ry that had brought him down so low!
How fortunate the man with none

And now you see the sensual Mack
His death he cannot flee
So long as he was rational
And stuck to highway robbery
He was a Great Professional
His heart away with him did run
And ere night comes, ere day does go
'Twill all be clear to everyone:
'Twas sensuality that brought him low!
How fortunate the man with none

2   THE BATTLE FOR POSSESSION

A room in the Old Bailey.

SMITH, *at the door.* Miss, Mrs. Polly MacHeath would like to speak to you.

LUCY. Mrs. MacHeath? Show her in.
Smith does so and leaves.

POLLY. Good morning, madam. Madam, good morning!

LUCY. What can I do for you?

POLLY. You recognize me?

LUCY. Of course.

POLLY. I've come to beg pardon for my behavior yesterday.

LUCY. That's interesting.

POLLY. I have no excuse except—my unhappiness.

LUCY. I see.

POLLY. You must forgive me. I was very upset by Mr. Mac-Heath's behavior. He shouldn't have placed us in this position, don't you agree? You can tell him so, when you see him.

LUCY. I— I— don't see him.

POLLY. You *have* seen him.

LUCY. I have *not* seen him.

POLLY. I'm sorry.

LUCY. He *is* fond of you.

POLLY. Oh no, he loves *you*, I know.

LUCY. You're very kind.

POLLY. Miss Brown, a man fears a woman who loves him too much. He neglects that woman and avoids her. I saw at first glance that he was bound to you in some way which I naturally couldn't, all at once, analyze.

LUCY. Do you mean that?

POLLY. Certainly. Of course.

LUCY. Dear Miss Peachum, we have both loved him too much!

POLLY. Perhaps that was it.
Pause.
And now, Miss Brown, I'll explain how it came about. Ten days ago I saw Mr. MacHeath for the first time in the Octopus Hotel. My mother was there. About a week later, that is, the day before yesterday, we were married. Yesterday I discovered the police wanted him for a great many crimes. And today I don't know what will happen. Twelve days ago I wouldn't have dreamed I could ever fall for a man.
Pause.

LUCY. I quite understand, Miss Peachum.

POLLY. Mrs. MacHeath.

LUCY. Mrs. MacHeath.

POLLY. And indeed, during the last few hours, I have been

thinking about this man. It's not so simple. For you see, Miss Brown, I have every reason to envy you his behavior toward you the other day. When I had to leave—coerced, I must admit, by my mother—he showed not the slightest sign of regret. But perhaps he hasn't got a heart, just a stone. What do you think, Lucy?

LUCY. Dear Miss Peachum, I am not quite sure if the fault lies entirely with Mr. MacHeath. Perhaps you should have kept to your own sort, Miss Peachum.

POLLY. Mrs. MacHeath.

LUCY. Mrs. MacHeath.

POLLY. You're right—or at least I ought to have kept everything, as my father says, "on a business basis."

LUCY. Of course.

POLLY, *weeps*. He is my only possession.

LUCY. My dear, this can happen even to the cleverest woman. But you are legally his wife, comfort yourself with that. Child, I can't bear to go on seeing you so depressed. May I offer you a little something?

POLLY. A little what?

LUCY. A little something to eat?

POLLY. Oh, yes, please! Do offer me a little something to eat!
  Exit LUCY.
  To herself.
  The silly fool!
LUCY *returns with coffee and cakes.*

LUCY. Now, that should do it.

POLLY. You give yourself too much trouble, madam.
  Pause. She eats.
  A lovely picture you have of him. When did he bring it?

LUCY. He didn't bring it.

POLLY. Didn't he give it to you right here in this room?

LUCY. He never was right here in this room.

POLLY. I see. The paths of fate are complicated!

LUCY. Don't talk bosh! You came here to spy around!

POLLY. You know where he is, don't you?

LUCY. I? Don't *you* know?

POLLY. Tell me where he is this minute!

LUCY. I haven't the slightest idea.

POLLY. Then you don't know where he is? Word of honor?

LUCY. No, I don't. Do you?

POLLY. No! This is terrible!
> POLLY *laughs and* LUCY *weeps.*
> He's run out on us!

LUCY. I can't bear it. Oh, Polly, it's so awful!

POLLY, *happily.* But at the close of this tragedy I've found a friend! Another cake?

LUCY. Oh, Polly don't be so kind to me! Oh, Polly, men aren't worth it!

POLLY. Of course not. But what can one do?

LUCY. I'll come clean. Will you be angry with me, Polly?

POLLY. What?

LUCY. It's not real.

POLLY. What isn't?

LUCY. This!
> *She points to her fat stomach.*
> I did it all for that crook!

POLLY, *laughs.* It was all a trick? Wonderful! You *are* a little fool! Listen—you want Mackie? I'll give him to you. Take him!

There is a sound of voices and steps outside.

What's that?

LUCY, *at the window.* It's Mackie! They've caught him again.

POLLY, *collapses.* Then all is over!

Enter MRS. PEACHUM.

MRS. PEACHUM. Ah, Polly, so here you are. Change your dress. Your husband's going to be hanged. I've brought your widow's weeds.

POLLY *starts to undress.*

You'll look lovely as a widow! Now give us a little smile!

3 5 A.M. FRIDAY. MACKIE THE KNIFE, WHO AGAIN WENT BACK TO HIS WHORES, HAS AGAIN BEEN BETRAYED BY THEM. HE WILL NOW BE HANGED.

The Death Cell. The bells of the City are ringing. Three constables— SMITH, DARLINGTON, *and* MERRYWEATHER—*bring* MACHEATH, *handcuffed, into the cell.*

SMITH. In here with him. The bells have rung once already.

To MACHEATH.

Try and behave like a man. I don't know how you manage to look so done up. Are you ashamed of yourself?

To the other two.

When the bells ring the third time—that'll be at six o'clock —he's to be hanged. Get everything ready. What is it, Darlington?

CONSTABLE DARLINGTON. Every street in Newgate has been jammed with people for the last fifteen minutes.

SMITH. Extraordinary! How do they know, Merryweather?

CONSTABLE MERRYWEATHER. The whole of London will know in half an hour. Those who were going to the Coronation will all come here instead. The Queen'll be driving through empty streets.

SMITH. We shall have to hurry. If we're through by six, people can be back on the Coronation route by seven. Get on with it.

Exeunt the other two constables.

MACHEATH. Hi, Smith, what's the time?

SMITH. Haven't you got eyes? Four minutes past five.

MACHEATH. Four minutes past five.

As SMITH *shuts the door of the cell from the outside,* BROWN *enters.*

BROWN, *questioning* SMITH, *with his back to the cell.* Is he there?

SMITH. You want to see him?

BROWN. No, no, no, for God's sake, manage it all yourself.

Exit BROWN.

MACHEATH, *suddenly bursting into a soft and rapid torrent of speech.* Now, Smith, I won't say a thing about bribery, never fear. I know how it is. If you let yourself be bribed, you'll have to flee the country. And you'll need enough money to live happily ever after. A thousand pounds, will that do? Don't speak! In twenty minutes I'll let you know if you can have that thousand pounds by midday. Go outside and think it over. Life is short and so is money. And I'm not sure I can raise any. But let anyone in here who wants to see me.

SMITH, *slowly.* You're talking nonsense. Mr. MacHeath.

SMITH *withdraws to the side of the stage.*

MACHEATH *sings, softly and very quickly,* THE EPISTLE TO HIS FRIENDS.

Oh hear a voice that for compassion cries
MacHeath sleeps not beneath the azure skies

Nor under poplars, 'mid the fire flies,
But in a dungeon cavernous he lies!
God grant that you may hear his final plea!
Him thickest walls surround and chains entwine
My friends, do you not ask if he be nigh?
If he is dead, go brew some maple wine
But if he still is living, O stand by!
Will you all leave your poor MacHeath to die?

MATTHEW *and* JACOB *appear in the passage.* SMITH *intercepts them on their way to* MACHEATH.

SMITH. We-e-ll! *You*

To MATTHEW.

look like a cleaned out herring!

MATTHEW. Now the Captain's away, *I* have to get the ladies pregnant—so, when they're arrested, they can plead, "Not Responsible for Their Actions."* What we need for this job is a goat. Can I speak with the Captain?

SMITH *lets them pass, then exit.*

MACHEATH. Five twenty-five. You've taken your time.

JACOB. Well, after all . . .

MACHEATH. After all, I'm going to be hanged! But I've no time for a tiff with you. Five twenty-eight. How much can you draw out of your private deposits!

MATTHEW. At five o'clock in the morning?

JACOB. Is it as bad as all that?

MACHEATH. Four hundred pounds?

JACOB. What about us? That's all we've got.

MACHEATH. Are *you* going to be hanged, or am I?

MATTHEW, *excitedly.* Did *we* sleep with Suky Tawdry or did you?

*A reference to the German law which might be cut in performance. But see *The Beggar's Opera*, Act III, Scene 3.

MACHEATH. I'll soon be sleeping somewhere else, and not with that trollop. Five thirty.

JACOB. I suppose we have to do it, Matthew.

SMITH *enters.* Mr. Brown told me to ask what you'd like for breakfast.

MACHEATH. Leave me alone!
To MATTHEW.
Will you or won't you?
To SMITH.
Asparagus.

MATTHEW. I'm not going to be shouted at!

MACHEATH, *loudly.* I'm not shouting!
Quietly.
Now, Matthew, are you going to let me be hanged?

MATTHEW. Of course not. Four hundred pounds is all that's there. I'm allowed to say that, I suppose.

MACHEATH. Five thirty-eight.

JACOB. Hurry, Matthew, or it'll be no use.

MATTHEW. If only we can get through. The streets are blocked.

MACHEATH. If you're not here by five minutes to six, you'll never see me again.
Shouts.
Never see me again . . . !

SMITH. They're off. Well, how goes it?
Makes a gesture of paying out money.

MACHEATH. Four hundred.
SMITH *walks away, shrugging his shoulders.* MACHEATH, *calling after him.*
I must speak to Brown.

SMITH, *as* DARLINGTON *enters.* You've got the soap?

CONSTABLE DARLINGTON. It's not the right sort.

SMITH. You'll set the thing up in ten minutes.

CONSTABLE DARLINGTON. But the trap isn't working.

SMITH. It *must* work, the bells have rung the second time.

CONSTABLE DARLINGTON. This is a hell of a place!

Exit DARLINGTON.

MACHEATH *sings* THE EPISTLE TO HIS FRIENDS.

O heed his suffering, O hear his sighs!
For now at last he's what you bankrupt call
O you who nothing higher recognize
Than your own filthy lucre use your eyes:
For all of you will suffer by his fall!
So hurry in a crowd and see Our Queen
Down on your knees before the throne so high!
Stampede like cattle, run like swine obscene
Tell her his teeth are fangs, his tongue is dry
Will you all leave your poor MacHeath to die?

Enter POLLY.

SMITH. I can't let you in. Your number's sixteen, it's not your turn.

POLLY. What do you mean, my number's sixteen? I am his wife. I must speak to him.

SMITH. Five minutes at the most.

POLLY. What do you mean, five minutes? This is good-by forever! Where is he?

SMITH. Can't you see him?

POLLY. Oh, yes. Thank you!

MACHEATH. Polly!

POLLY. Yes, Mackie, here I am.

MACHEATH. Yes, Polly.

POLLY. How are you? Very done up? It's too bad.

MACHEATH. Yes, and what will *you* do? What will become of you?

POLLY. Oh, the business is doing well. That's the least of our troubles. Mackie, are you nervous? Who was your father? There's so much you haven't told me. I don't understand it: you were always in such good health.

MACHEATH. Polly, can't you help me out?

POLLY. Of course.

MACHEATH. With money, I mean. I talked to the warder here . . .

POLLY, *slowly.* The money has gone to Southampton.

MACHEATH. You have none?

POLLY. No. But you know, Mac, perhaps I could speak to someone . . . maybe the Queen herself!
She breaks down.
Oh, Mackie!

SMITH, *pulling* POLLY *away.* Got your thousand pounds?

POLLY. Good luck, Mac, take care of yourself! Never forget me!
Exit POLLY. CONSTABLE MERRYWEATHER *brings on a table with a plate of asparagus on it.*

SMITH. Is the asparagus tender, Merryweather?

CONSTABLE MERRYWEATHER. Oh, very.
Exit CONSTABLE MERRYWEATHER. BROWN *enters and walks over to* SMITH.

BROWN. What does he want, Smith? I'm glad you waited with the table. We'll take it with us, so he'll see how thoughtful we are.
They both carry the table into the cell. Exit SMITH. *Pause.*
Hallo, Mack. Here's your asparagus.

MACHEATH. Don't trouble yourself, Mr. Brown, there are other people to do me the last honors.

BROWN. But Mackie!

MACHEATH. I should like the account! Forgive me if, in the meanwhile, I eat. This is my last meal.
Eats.

BROWN. Good appetite! Oh, Mac, you wound me with a searing iron!

MACHEATH. The account, sir, please! No sentimentality.

BROWN, *sighing, draws a little notebook out of a pocket.* Yes, Mac. Here is the account for the last six months.

MACHEATH, *cuttingly.* I see. So you've only come to get your money out of me.

BROWN. Mac, you know that's not true . . . !

MACHEATH. All right, I don't want you to be the loser. What do I owe you? I'm sorry, but I need a detailed statement. Life has made me mistrustful . . . And you're the one who might know why.

BROWN. Mac, when you speak like that, I can't think straight.
There is a loud banging behind.

SMITH, *off.* Very well, Darlington, that will hold.

MACHEATH. The account, Brown.

BROWN. Very well—first, there are the rewards for the arrests you made possible. Murderers. You received from the Government in all . . .

MACHEATH. Three murderers at forty pounds each makes a hundred and twenty pounds. A quarter of that for you is thirty pounds.

BROWN. Yes—yes—but I really don't know, Mac, at the last minute, as it were, if we can . . .

MACHEATH. Cut the cackle. Thirty pounds, and the one in Dover eight pounds.

BROWN. Why only eight pounds, that was . . .

MACHEATH. Do you believe me or do you not? For the last half
year you receive thirty-eight pounds.

BROWN, *sobbing loudly.* A lifetime together . . . I knew your
every thought . . .

BOTH. By just looking in your eyes.

MACHEATH. Three years in India—Johnny and Jimmy were both
on the scene—five years in London, and that's all the thanks
I get.

*In the meanwhile he shows what he will look like when
hanged.*

Here hangs MacHeath who ne'er a fly did wrong
Sold by a faithless friend of former days
He dangles from a rope a fathom long
His broken neck shows what his bottom weighs

BROWN. Mac, if you're going to treat me like this . . . ! Who
attacks my honor attacks me!
Runs angrily out of the cage.

MACHEATH. Your honor?

BROWN. Yes, my honor! Smith, begin! Let the people in!
To MACHEATH.
Excuse me.

SMITH, *entering.* Got the money yet? In one minute it'll be too
late.

MACHEATH. When the boys get back.

SMITH. They're not in sight.
Enter PEACHUM, MRS. PEACHUM, POLLY, LUCY, *the* FAMILY,
REVEREND KIMBALL, MATTHEW *and* JACOB.

GINNY JENNY. They didn't want to let us in, but I told them:
if you don't take your something heads out of my way, you'll
get to know Ginny Jenny!

PEACHUM. I am his father-in-law. Which of those present is Mr.
MacHeath?

MACHEATH *presents himself*. MacHeath.

PEACHUM *walks past the cage*. Fate, Mr. MacHeath, has decreed that you should become my son-in-law without my knowing you. The circumstances in which I meet you for the first time are tragic. Mr. MacHeath, you once had white kid gloves, a stick with an ivory handle, and a scar on your neck, and you frequented the Octopus Hotel. There remains the scar on your neck, the least valuable of your distinguishing marks, and now you frequent cages, and soon you won't frequent anywhere . . .

POLLY *walks sobbing past the cage*.

MACHEATH. What a pretty dress!

MATTHEW *and* JACOB *come past the cage*.

MATTHEW. We couldn't get through for the crowd. But we ran so fast I thought Jacob was going to have a stroke. If you don't believe us . . .

MACHEATH. What do the men say? Have they got good places?

MATTHEW. There, Captain, we knew you'd understand. But, look, we don't get a Coronation every day. The men have to earn when they can. They ask to be remembered to you.

JACOB. Kindly.

MRS. PEACHUM *walks past the cage*. Mr. MacHeath, who would have thought of this when a week ago we had a little dance together in the Octopus Hotel?

MACHEATH. Yes, a little dance.

MRS. PEACHUM. Fate is cruel.

BROWN, *to* REVEREND KIMBALL *at back*. And with this man I stood at Aserbaijan, shoulder to shoulder, under withering fire!

GINNY JENNY *comes past the cage*. Us Drury Lane girls are in a fix, no one's gone to the Coronation. They all want to see you.

MACHEATH. To see me!

SMITH. Come on! Six o'clock.

Lets him out of the cage.

MACHEATH. We will not keep the people waiting. Ladies and gentlemen, you see here the vanishing representative of a vanishing class. We artisans of the lower middle class, who work with honest jemmies on the cash boxes of small shopkeepers, are being ruined by large concerns backed by the banks. What is a picklock to a bank share? What is the burgling of a bank to the founding of a bank? What is the murder of a man to the employment of a man? Fellow citizens, I herewith take my leave of you. I thank you all for coming. Some of you have been very close to me. That Jenny should have given me up is astonishing. It is a clear proof that the world will always be the same. The concurrence of several unfortunate circumstances has brought about my fall. Good—I fall.

Song illumination: golden light. The organ is lit up. Three lights come down from above on a bar and on a board is written: A BALLAD IN WHICH MACHEATH BEGS THE FORGIVE-NESS OF ALL.

*O fellow men, who'll live when I shall die
Don't be too hard, don't give me many lashes
And when I hang from off the gallows high
Don't giggle underneath your grave moustaches
And do not rail against me 'cause I fall
Be not, as was the Court of Law, unkind
Not all of us possess a lawful mind
So, fellow men, please do not smile at all
But let my hapless life a lesson be
And pray to God that He may pardon me*

*The rain will fall in torrents from the skies
And wash the flesh I overfed before
And playful ravens will peck out my eyes
Those eyes that saw so much and wanted more
For verily I tried to climb too high
And now I'll soon be hanging 'gainst the sky
Pecked at by every raven and magpie
Like rotting fruit that on the ground doth lie
So, brothers, let my death a warning be
And pray to God that He may pardon me*

The ladies with their bosoms showing
To catch the eyes of men with yearnings
The fellows just behind them going
In hopes to steal their sinful earnings
The outlaws, bandits, whores, procurers,
Flagellant, snowbird, cannibal
The pansies selling dirty pictures
I cry them mercy one and all

But not the coppers—sons of bitches—
For every evening, every morning
The lice came creeping from their niches
And usually without a warning
Police! My epidermis itches!
But for today I'll let that fall
Pretend I love the sons of bitches
And cry them mercy one and all

Oh how I wish that I could get them
And smash them with an iron maul
But now I really must forget them
I cry them mercy one and all

SMITH. If you please, Mr. MacHeath.

MRS. PEACHUM. Polly and Lucy, stand by your husband in his last hour.

MACHEATH. Ladies, whatever may have been between us . . .

SMITH *leads him off.* Come on!

Passage to the Gallows. All exeunt then re-enter from the other side of the stage with the rest of the cast, all carrying hurricane lamps. When MACHEATH *is standing on the gallows,* PEACHUM *speaks.*

PEACHUM.
Most honored public, thus far we have come
MacHeath should now be hanged and justice done
For in the whole of Christendom
There's nothing granted free to anyone

But just in case you should have been misled
And think that we approve this execution
MacHeath will not be hanged till he be dead
For we've thought out a different solution

In order that, in opera anyway,
Mercy may prevail over justice once a year
And also since we wish you well today
The royal messenger will now appear

On a board is written: THIRD FINALE—THE ARRIVAL OF THE
MOUNTED MESSENGER.

CHORUS.
Hark, who comes! Hark, who comes!
The royal messenger riding comes!

BROWN *enters on horseback and sings recitative.* On account of
her Coronation, our gracious Queen commands that this
Captain MacHeath shall at once be released.
All cheer.

At the same time he is raised to the permanent ranks of the
nobility.
Cheers.

The castle Marmorell and a pension of ten thousand pounds
are his as long as he shall live. And to the happy couples here
the Queen presents her royal and cordial felicitations.

MACHEATH. A rescue! A rescue! I was sure of it! Where the
need is greatest, there God's help will be nearest.

POLLY. A rescue! A rescue! My dearest MacHeath has been
rescued. I am so happy.

MRS. PEACHUM. So the whole thing has a happy ending! How
calm and peaceful would our life be always if a messenger
came from the king whenever we wanted!

PEACHUM. Therefore all remain standing where you are now
and sing the chorale of the poorest of the poor, of whose
difficult life you have shown us something today. But in real
life their end is always bad. Mounted messengers from the
queen come far too seldom, and if you kick a man he kicks
you back again. Therefore never be too ready to oppose injustice.

ALL *singing to the accompaniment of the organ, they advance to the front of the stage. The words of the* VALEDICTORY HYMN *appear on a board or screen.*

Do not defend the Right with too much boldness
For Wrong is cold: its death is sure though slow
Remember all the darkness and the coldness
The world's a vale of misery and woe

ELECTRA

A Play in Two Acts
by

JEAN GIRAUDOUX

English Version
by Winifred Smith

Characters

ORESTES
THE EUMENIDES, *first as three little girls, later as fifteen-year-olds*
GARDENER
PRESIDENT OF THE COUNCIL
AGATHA, *his young wife*
AEGISTHUS
BEGGAR
CLYTEMNESTRA
ELECTRA
YOUNG MAN
CAPTAIN
NARSES' WIFE
GUESTS, SERVANTS, MAIDS, SOLDIERS

ACT ONE

SCENE 1 *A stranger,* ORESTES, *enters, escorted by three little girls, just as, from the opposite side, the gardener comes in dressed for a festival, and accompanied by guests from the village.*

FIRST LITTLE GIRL. How fine the gardener looks!

SECOND LITTLE GIRL. Of course! It's his wedding day.

THIRD LITTLE GIRL. Here it is, sir, your Agamemnon's palace!

STRANGER. What a strange façade! Is it straight?

FIRST LITTLE GIRL. No. There's no right side to it. You think you see it, but that's a mirage. Like the gardener you see coming, who wants to speak to you. He's not coming. He won't be able to say a word.

SECOND LITTLE GIRL. Or he'll bray—or meow——

GARDENER. The façade is perfectly straight, stranger. Don't listen to these liars. You are confused because the right side is built of stones from Gaul and sweat at certain seasons; that the people say the palace is weeping. The left side is built of marble from Argos, which—no one knows why—will suddenly be flooded with sunshine, even at night. Then they say the palace laughs. Right now the palace is laughing and crying at the same time.

FIRST LITTLE GIRL. So it's sure not to be mistaken.

SECOND LITTLE GIRL. It's really a widow's palace.

FIRST LITTLE GIRL. Or of childhood memories.

STRANGER. I can't remember seeing such a sensitive building anywhere.

197

GARDENER. Have you already visited the palace?

FIRST LITTLE GIRL. As a baby.

SECOND LITTLE GIRL. Twenty years ago.

THIRD LITTLE GIRL. He couldn't walk yet.

GARDENER. But he must remember if he saw it.

STRANGER. All I can remember of Agamemnon's palace is a mosaic. They set me down on a square of tigers when I was naughty and on a hexagon of flowers when I was good,— and I remember creeping from one to the other across some birds.

FIRST LITTLE GIRL. And over a beetle.

STRANGER. How do you know that, child?

GARDENER. And did your family live in Argos?

STRANGER. And I remember many, many bare feet. Not a face, faces were way up in the sky, but lots of bare feet. I tried to touch the gold rings under the edges of the skirts; some ankles were joined by chains, slaves' ankles. I remember two little feet, very white ones, the barest, the whitest. Their steps were always even, timid, measured by an invisible chain. I imagine they were Electra's. I must have kissed them, mustn't I? A baby kisses everything it touches.

SECOND LITTLE GIRL. Anyway that would have been the only kiss Electra ever had.

GARDENER. It surely would!

FIRST LITTLE GIRL. Jealous, gardener?

STRANGER. Electra still lives in the palace?

SECOND LITTLE GIRL. Still. But not much longer.

STRANGER. Is that her window, the one with jasmine?

GARDENER. No. That's the room where Atreus, the first king of Argos, killed his brother's sons.

FIRST LITTLE GIRL. The dinner when he served up their hearts took place in the room next it. I'd love to know how they tasted.

THIRD LITTLE GIRL. Did he cut them up or cook them whole?

SECOND LITTLE GIRL. And Cassandra was strangled in the sentry box.

THIRD LITTLE GIRL. They caught her in a net and stabbed her. She yelled like a crazy woman, through her veil. I'd love to have seen it.

FIRST LITTLE GIRL. That all happened in the laughing wing, as you see.

STRANGER. The one with roses?

GARDENER. Stranger, don't try to connect the windows with flowers. Im the palace gardener. I plant them at random. They're just flowers.

SECOND LITTLE GIRL. Not at all. There are flowers and flowers. Phlox doesn't suit Thyestes.

THIRD LITTLE GIRL. Nor mignonette Cassandra.

GARDENER. Oh, be quiet! The window with the roses, stranger, is the one of the rooms where our king, Agamemnon, coming back from the war, slipped into the pool, fell on his sword and killed himself.

FIRST LITTLE GIRL. He took his bath after his death. About two minutes after. That's the difference.

GARDENER. That's Electra's window.

STRANGER. Why is it so high up, almost on the roof?

GARDENER. So she can see her father's tomb.

STRANGER. Why is she there?

GARDENER. Because it's Orestes' old room, her brothers'. Her mother sent him out of the country when he was two and he's not been heard of since.

SECOND LITTLE GIRL. Listen, sisters, listen! They're talking about Orestes!

GARDENER. Will you clear out! Leave us! You're just like flies.

FIRST LITTLE GIRL. We certainly won't leave. We're with this stranger.

GARDENER. Do you know these girls?

STRANGER. I met them at the door. They followed me in.

SECOND LITTLE GIRL. We followed him because we like him.

THIRD LITTLE GIRL. Because he's a lot better looking than you are, gardener.

FIRST LITTLE GIRL. No caterpillars in his beard.

SECOND LITTLE GIRL. Nor June bugs in his nose.

THIRD LITTLE GIRL. If flowers are to smell sweet, the gardener has to smell bad.

STRANGER. Be polite, children, and tell us what you do all the time.

FIRST LITTLE GIRL. What we do is, we're not polite.

SECOND LITTLE GIRL. We lie, we slander, we insult.

FIRST LITTLE GIRL. But specially, we recite.

STRANGER. And what do you recite?

FIRST LITTLE GIRL. We never know ahead of time—we invent as we go along. But we're very, very good.

SECOND LITTLE GIRL. The king of Mycenae, whose sister-in-law we insulted, said we were very, very good.

THIRD LITTLE GIRL. We say all the bad things we can think up.

GARDENER. Don't listen to them, stranger. No one knows who they are. They've been wandering about the town for two days without friends or family. If we ask who they are, they pretend they're the little Eumenides. And the horrible thing is that they grow and get fat as you look at them. Yesterday they were years younger than today. Come here, you!

SECOND LITTLE GIRL. Is he rude, for a bridegroom!

GARDENER. Look at her! See how her eyelashes grow. Look at her bosom. I understand such things, I've seen mushrooms grow. They grow fast, like an orange.

SECOND LITTLE GIRL. Poisonous things always win out.

THIRD LITTLE GIRL, *to the* FIRST LITTLE GIRL. Really? You're growing a bosom?

FIRST LITTLE GIRL. Are we going to recite or not?

STRANGER. Let them recite, gardener.

FIRST LITTLE GIRL. Let's recite Clytemnestra, Electra's mother— You agree? Clytemnestra?

SECOND LITTLE GIRL. We agree.

FIRST LITTLE GIRL. Queen Clytemnestra has a bad color. She uses rouge.

SECOND LITTLE GIRL. Her color is bad because she sleeps badly.

THIRD LITTLE GIRL. She sleeps badly because she's afraid.

FIRST LITTLE GIRL. What is Queen Clytemnestra afraid of?

SECOND LITTLE GIRL. Of everything.

FIRST LITTLE GIRL. What's everything?

SECOND LITTLE GIRL. Silence. Silences.

THIRD LITTLE GIRL. Noise. Noises.

FIRST LITTLE GIRL. The idea that midnight is near. That the spider on its thread is about to pass from the time of day when it brings good luck to the time when it brings bad luck.

SECOND LITTLE GIRL. Of everything red, because blood is red.

FIRST LITTLE GIRL. Queen Clytemnestra has a bad color. She puts on blood.

GARDENER. What a silly story!

SECOND LITTLE GIRL. Good, isn't it?

FIRST LITTLE GIRL. See how the end goes back to the beginning—couldn't be more poetic!

STRANGER. Very interesting.

FIRST LITTLE GIRL. As you're interested in Electra we can recite about her. You agree, sisters? We can recite what she was like at our age.

SECOND LITTLE GIRL. We certainly do agree!

THIRD LITTLE GIRL. Even before we were born, before yesterday, we agreed.

FIRST LITTLE GIRL. Electra amuses herself by making Orestes fall out of his mother's arms.

SECOND LITTLE GIRL. Electra waxes the steps of the throne so her uncle Aegisthus, will measure his length on the marble.

THIRD LITTLE GIRL. Electra is preparing to spit in the face of her little brother, Orestes, if he ever returns.

FIRST LITTLE GIRL. Of course, *that* isn't true, but it'd be a good story.

SECOND LITTLE GIRL. For nineteen years she's prepared poisonous spittle in her mouth.

THIRD LITTLE GIRL. She's thinking of your slugs, gardener, to make her mouth water more.

GARDENER. Now stop, you dirty little vipers!

SECOND LITTLE GIRL. Oh, ha, ha, the bridegroom gets mad!

STRANGER. He's right. Get out!

GARDENER. And don't come back!

FIRST LITTLE GIRL. We'll come back tomorrow.

GARDENER. Just try to! The palace is forbidden to girls of your age.

FIRST LITTLE GIRL. Tomorrow we'll be grown up.

SECOND LITTLE GIRL. Tomorrow will be the day after Electra's marriage to the gardener. We'll be grown up.

STRANGER. What are they saying?

FIRST LITTLE GIRL. You've not defended us, stranger. You'll be sorry for that.

GARDENER. Horrible little beasts! You'd think they were three little Fates. Dreadful to be a child Fate!

SECOND LITTLE GIRL. Fate shows you her tail, gardener. Watch out if it grows.

FIRST LITTLE GIRL. Come, sisters. Let's leave them both in front of their tainted wall.

The little EUMENIDES *go out, the* GUESTS *shrinking away from them in terror.*

SCENE 2 *The* STRANGER. *The* GARDENER. *The* PRESIDENT OF THE COUNCIL *and his young wife,* AGATHA THEOCATHOCLES. *Villagers*

STRANGER. What did these girls say? That you are marrying Electra, gardener?

GARDENER. She'll be my wife an hour from now.

AGATHA. He'll *not* marry her. We've come to prevent that.

PRESIDENT. I'm your distant cousin, gardener, and the Vice President of the Council; so I've a double right to advise you. Run away to your radishes and squashes. Don't marry Electra.

GARDENER. Aegisthus orders me to.

STRANGER. Am I crazy? If Agamemnon were alive, Electra's wedding would be a festival for all Greece—and Aegisthus gives her to a gardener, whose family, even, objects! Don't tell me Electra is ugly or hunch-backed!

GARDENER. Electra is the most beautiful girl in Argos.

AGATHA. Oh, she's not too bad looking.

PRESIDENT. And she's perfectly straight. Like all flowers that grow in the shade.

STRANGER. Is she backward? Feeble-minded?

PRESIDENT. She's intelligence personified.

AGATHA. An especially good memory. Not always for the same thing, though. I don't have a good memory. Except for your birthday, darling, *that* I never forget.

STRANGER. What can she have done, or said, to be treated this way?

PRESIDENT. She does nothing, says nothing. But she's always *here*.

AGATHA. She's here now.

STRANGER. She has a right to be. It's her father's palace. It's not her fault he's dead.

GARDENER. I'd never have dreamed of marrying Electra, but as Aegisthus orders me to, I don't see why I'd be afraid.

PRESIDENT. You have every reason to be afraid. She's the kind of woman that makes trouble.

AGATHA. And you're not the only one! Our family has everything to fear.

GARDENER. I don't understand you.

PRESIDENT. You will understand. Life can be pleasant, can't it!

AGATHA. Very pleasant! Immensely so!

PRESIDENT. Don't interrupt me, darling, especially just to repeat what I say. It *can* be very pleasant. Everything has a way of settling itself in life—spiritual suffering can be cured more quickly than cancer, and mourning than a sty. Take any group of human beings at random, each will have the same per centage of crime, lies, vice and adultery.

AGATHA. That's a horrid word, adultery, darling.

PRESIDENT. Don't interrupt me, especially to contradict! How does it happen that in one group life slips by softly, conventionally, the dead are forgotten, the living get on well together, while in another there's hell to pay? It's simply that in the latter there's a woman who makes trouble.

STRANGER. That means there's a conscience in the second group.

AGATHA. I can't help thinking of your word, adultery—such a horrid word!

PRESIDENT. Be quiet, Agatha. A conscience, you say! If criminals don't forget their sins, if the conquered don't forget their defeats, if there are curses, quarrels, hatreds, the fault is not with humanity's conscience, which always tends toward compromise and forgetfulness, it lies with ten or fifteen women who make trouble.

STRANGER. I agree with you. Those ten or fifteen women save the world from egoism.

PRESIDENT. They save it from happiness! I know Electra. Let's agree that she is what you say—justice, generosity, duty. But it's by justice, generosity, duty, and not by egoism and easy going ways, that the state, individuals, and the best families are ruined.

AGATHA. Absolutely! But why, darling? You've told me, but I forget.

PRESIDENT. Because those three virtues have in common the one element fatal to humanity—implacability. Happiness is never the lot of implacable people. A happy family makes a surrender. A happy epoch demands unanimous capitulation.

STRANGER. You surrendered at the first call?

PRESIDENT. Alas, no! Some one else got in first. So I'm only the vice-president.

GARDENER. Against what is Electra implacable? She goes every night to her father's tomb, is that all?

PRESIDENT. I know. I've followed her. Along the same road which my duty made me take one night, pursuing our most dangerous murderer, along the same river I followed and saw the greatest innocent in Greece. A horrible walk, behind the two of them. They stopped at the same places, at the yew, at the corner of the bridge, at the thousand year old milestone, all made the same signs to innocence and to crime. But because the murderer was there, the night was bright, peaceful, clear. He was the kernel taken out of the fruit, which, in a tart, might have broken your tooth. Electra's presence, on the contrary, confused light and darkness, even spoiled the full moon. Have you seen a fisherman, who before going out to fish, arranges his bait? All the way along the river, that was she. Every evening she spreads her net for everything that without her would have abandoned this pleasant, agreeable earth—remorse, confessions, old blood stains, rust, bones of murdered men, a mass of accusations. In a short time everything will be ready for the fisherman to pass by.

STRANGER. He always comes, sooner or later.

PRESIDENT. That's not so.

AGATHA, *much taken by the* STRANGER. A mistake!

PRESIDENT. This child herself sees the leak in your argument. A triple layer of earth daily piles up over our sins, our failures, our crimes, and stifles their worst effects! Forgetfulness, death, human justice. It is madness to remember those things. A horrible country, one where because of an avenger of wrongs, ghosts walk, dead men, half asleep,— where no allowance is ever made for human weakness, or perjury, where a ghost and an avenger constantly threaten.

When guilty men's sleep continues to be more troubled after legal prosecution than the sleep of an innocent, society is terribly disturbed. When I look at Electra, I'm troubled by the sins I committed in my cradle.

AGATHA. And I by my future sins. I'll never commit them, darling. You know that. Especially that adultery, which you will talk about. But those other sins already bother me.

GARDENER. I'm rather of Electra's opinion. I don't much care for wicked people. I love truth.

PRESIDENT. Do you know what truth is for our family that you proclaim it so openly? A quiet, well-thought-of family, rising fast. You'll not deny my assertion that you are the least important member of it. But I know by experience that it's not safe to venture on thin ice. It won't be ten days, if you marry Electra, before the discovery—I'm just inventing this—that our old aunt, when a young girl, strangled her baby so her husband wouldn't find out about it, and in order to quiet suspicion, stopped hushing up the various aspersions on her grandfather's virtue. My little Agatha, in spite of being gaiety itself, can't sleep because of all this. You are the only one who doesn't see Aegisthus' trick. He wants to pass on to the Theocathocles family everything that might some day throw a sinister light on the Atrides.

STRANGER. And what have the Atrides to fear?

PRESIDENT. Nothing. Nothing that I know of, it's like every happy family or couple, every satisfied person. Yet it does have to fear the most dangerous enemy in the world, who would eat it through to the bone, Electra's ally, uncompromising justice.

GARDENER. Electra loves my garden. If she's a little nervous, the flowers will do her good.

AGATHA. But she'll not do the flowers good.

PRESIDENT. Certainly. You'll get to know your fuchias and geraniums. You'll see that they're not just pretty symbols. They'll show their knavery and their ingratitude. Electra in the garden is justice and memory among the flowers—that means hatred.

GARDENER. Electra is devout. All the dead are for her.

PRESIDENT. The dead! The murdered, half melted into the murderers, the shades of the robbed mingled with those of the thieves, rival families scattered among each other, and saying, "Oh, Heavens! here's Electra! And we were so peaceful."

AGATHA. Here comes Electra!

GARDENER. No, not yet. It's Aegisthus. Leave us, stranger, Aegisthus doesn't like strange faces.

PRESIDENT. You, too. Agatha. He's rather too fond of well-known women's faces.

AGATHA, *with marked interest in the stranger's good looks.* Shall I show you the way, handsome stranger?

AEGISTHUS *enters, to the hurrahs of the* GUESTS, *as* SERVANTS *set up his throne, and place a stool beside a pillar.*

SCENE 3   AEGISTHUS. *The* PRESIDENT. *The* GARDENER. SERVANT.

AEGISTHUS. Why the stool? What's the stool for?

SERVANT. For the beggar, my lord.

AEGISTHUS. What beggar?

SERVANT. The god, if you prefer. This beggar has been wandering through the city for several days. We've never seen a beggar who's so much a beggar, so it's thought he must be a god. We let him go wherever he likes. He's prowling around the palace now.

AEGISTHUS. Changing wheat to gold? Seducing the maids?

SERVANT. He does no harm.

AEGISTHUS. A queer god! The priests haven't found out yet whether he's a rascal or Jupiter?

SERVANT. The priests don't want to be asked.

AEGISTHUS. Friends, shall we leave the stool here?

PRESIDENT. I think it will be better to honor a beggar than to insult a god.

AEGISTHUS. Leave the stool there. But if he comes, warn us. We'd like to be just a group of human beings for a few minutes. And don't be rude to him. Perhaps he is delegated by the gods to attend Electra's marriage. The gods invite themselves to this marriage, which the President considers an insult to his family.

PRESIDENT. My lord . . .

AEGISTHUS. Don't protest. I heard everything. The acoustics in this palace are extraordinary. The architect apparently wanted to listen to the council's discussions of his salary and bonus, he built it full of echoing passages.

PRESIDENT. My lord . . .

AEGISTHUS. Be quiet. I know everything you're about to say on the subject of your fine honest family, your worthy sister-in-law, the baby-killer, your uncle, the satirist and our nephew, the slanderer.

PRESIDENT. My lord . . .

AEGISTHUS. An officer, in a battle, to whom the King's standard is given to turn the enemy's fire on him, carries it with more enthusiasm. You're losing your time. The gardener will marry Electra.

SERVANT. Here is the beggar, my lord.

AEGISTHUS. Detain him a moment. Offer him a drink. Wine is appropriate for a beggar or a god.

SERVANT. God or beggar, he's drunk already.

AEGISTHUS. Then let him come in. He'll not understand us,

though we must speak of the gods. It might even be amusing to talk about them before him. Your notion of Electra, President, is true enough, but it's peculiar, definitely middleclass. As I'm the Regent, allow me to give you more elevated philosophical ideas. You believe in the gods, President?

PRESIDENT. Do you, my lord?

AEGISTHUS. My dear President, I've often asked myself if I believe in the gods. Asked myself because it's the only problem a statesman must decide for himself. I do believe in the gods. Or rather, I believe I believe in the gods. But I believe in them, not as great caretakers and great watchmen, but as great abstractions. Between space and time, always oscillating between gravitation and emptiness, there are the great indifferences. Those are the gods. I imagine them, not constantly concerned with that moving mould on the earth which is humanity, but as having reached the stage of serenity and universality. That is blessedness, the same thing as unconsciousness. They are unconscious at the top of the ladder of being, as the atom is at the bottom. The difference is that theirs is the unconsciousness of lightning, omniscient, thousand-faceted, so that in their normal state, like diamonds, powerless and deaf, they only *react* to light, to omens, without understanding them.

BEGGAR, *at last seated, feels he must applaud.* Well said! Bravo!

AEGISTHUS. Thanks. On the other hand, President, it's undeniable that sometimes there seem to be interruptions in human life so opportune and extensive that it's possible to believe in an extraordinary superhuman interest or justice. Such events have something superhuman or divine about them, in that they are like coarse work, not at all well designed. The plague breaks out in a town which has sinned by impiety or folly, but it also ravages the neighboring city, a particularly holy one. War breaks out when a nation becomes degenerate and vile, but it destroys all the just, the brave, and preserves the cowards. Or, whose ever the fault, or by whom committed, it's the same family that pays, innocent or guilty. I know a mother of seven children, who al-

ways spanked the same child—she was a divine mother. This
fits our idea of the gods, that they are blind boxers, always
satisfied by finding the same cheeks to slap, the same bot-
toms to spank. We might even be surprised if we understood the confusion that comes from a sudden waking to
beatitude, that their blows weren't given more at random;
that the wife of a good man, and not a perjurer's, is brained
by a shutter in a wind storm; that accidents strike down pil-
grims and not troops. Always humanity suffers . . . I'm speaking generally. We see crows or deer struck down by an inexplicable epidemic—perhaps the blow intended for mankind went astray, either up or down. However it be, it's certain that the chief duty of a statesman is to watch fiercely
that the gods are not shaken out of their lethargy, and to
limit the harm they do to such reactions as sleepers snoring,
or to thunder.

BEGGAR. Bravo! That's very clear! I understand it very well!

AEGISTHUS. Charmed, I'm sure!

BEGGAR. Its truth itself. For example, look at the people walking along the roads. Sometimes every hundred feet you'll
see a dead hedgehog. They go over the roads at night by
tens, male and female, and get crushed. You'll say they're
fools, that they could find their mates on their side of the
road. I can't explain it, but love, for hedgehogs, begins by
crossing a road. What the devil was I trying to say? I've lost
the thread . . . Go on, it'll come back to me.

AEGISTHUS. Indeed! What is he trying to say!

PRESIDENT. Shall we talk about Electra, my lord?

AEGISTHUS. What do you think we've been talking about? Our
charming little Agatha? We were talking only about Electra, President, and about the need I feel to get her out of the
royal family. Why, since I've been Regent, while other cities
are devoured by dissension, other citizens by moral crises,
are we alone satisfied with other people and with ourselves?
Why are we so rich? Why in Argos alone are raw materials
so dear and retail prices so low? Why, when we're exporting

more cows, does butter go down in price? Why do storms
pass by our vineyards, heresies our temples, animal diseases
our barns? Because, in this city, I wage merciless war against
all who signal to the gods.

PRESIDENT. What do you mean, signal to the gods?

BEGGAR. There! I've found it!

AEGISTHUS. Found what?

BEGGAR. My story, the thread of my story. I was speaking of the
death of hedgehogs.

AEGISTHUS. One moment, please. We're speaking of the gods.

BEGGAR. To be sure! Gods come first, hedgehogs second. But I
wonder if I'll remember.

AEGISTHUS. There are no two ways of signaling, President: it's
done by separating one's self from the crowd, climbing a hill
and waving a lantern or a flag. The earth is betrayed, as is a
besieged city, by signals. The philosopher signals from his
roof, the poet or a desperate man signals from his balcony
or his swimming pool. If for ten years the gods have not
meddled with our lives, it's because I've kept the heights
empty and the fairgrounds full. I've ordered dreamers,
painters, and chemists to marry; and because, in order to
avoid racial trouble between our citizens—something that
can't help marking human beings as different in the eyes of
the gods—I've always given great importance to misde-
meanors and paid slight attention to crimes. Nothing keeps
the gods so quiet as an equal value set on murder and on
stealing bread. I must say the courts have supported me
splendidly. Whenever I've been forced to be severe, they've
overlooked it. None of my decisions has been so obvious as
to allow the gods to avenge it. No exile. I kill. An exile tends
to climb up a steep road, just like a ladybird. I never execute
in public. Our poor neighboring cities betray themselves by
erecting their gallows on the top of a hill; I crucify at the
bottom of a valley. Now I've said everything about Electra.

GARDENER. What have you said?

AEGISTHUS. That there's just one person in Argos now to give a signal to the gods, and that's Electra. What's the matter?

BEGGAR *moves about among the* GUESTS.

BEGGAR. Nothing's the matter. But I'd better tell you my story now. In five minutes, at the rate you're talking, it won't make sense. It's just to support what you say. Among those crushed hedgehogs you'll see dozens who seem to have died a hedgehog's death. Their muzzles flattened by horse's hoofs, their spines broken under wheels, they're just smashed hedgehogs, nothing more. Smashed because of the original sin of hedgehogs—which is crossing the main or side road on the pretext that the snail or partridge egg on the far side tastes better but actually to make hedgehog love. That's their affair. No one stops them. Suddenly you see a little young one, not flattened like the others, not so dirty, his little paw stretched out, his lips closed, very dignified, and you feel that he's not died a hedgehog's death, but was struck down for someone else, for you. His cold little eye is your eye. His spikes, your beard. His blood, your blood. I always pick up those little ones, they're the youngest, the tenderest to eat. A year goes by, a hedgehog no longer sacrifices himself for mankind. You see I understand. The gods were mistaken, they wanted to strike a perjurer, a thief, and they kill a hedgehog. A young one.

AEGISTHUS. Very well understood.

BEGGAR. And what's true of hedgehogs holds for other species.

PRESIDENT. Of course! Of course!

BEGGAR. Why, of course? That all wrong. Take the martin. Even though you're a President of the Council, you'll never pretend to have seen birds dying for you?

AEGISTHUS. Will you let us go on talking about Electra?

BEGGAR. Talk! Talk! But I must add, when you see dead men, many seem to have died for bulls or pigs or turtles, not many for mankinds. A man who seems to have died for man, he's hard to find, or even for himself. Are we going to see her?

AEGISTHUS. See whom?

BEGGAR. Electra. I'd like to see her before she's killed.

AEGISTHUS. Electra killed? Who says Electra's to be killed?

BEGGAR. You.

PRESIDENT. There's been no thought of killing Electra.

BEGGAR. I have one gift. I don't understand words—I've had no education—but I do understand people. You want to kill Electra.

PRESIDENT. You don't understand at all, stranger. This man is Aegisthus, Agamemnon's cousin, and Electra's his darling niece.

BEGGAR. Are there two Electras? The one he was talking about who ruins everything, and the other one, his darling niece?

PRESIDENT. No! There's only one.

BEGGAR. Then he wants to kill her. No doubt of it. He wants to kill his darling niece.

PRESIDENT. I repeat, you don't understand in the least.

BEGGAR. Oh, I move about a lot. I knew a family, name of Narses. She was better than he. She was sick, her breathing bad. But a great deal better than he. No comparison.

GARDENER. He's drunk, a beggar, you know.

PRESIDENT. He's raving. He's a god.

BEGGAR. No. I started to tell you they had a wolf cub. It was their darling little pet. But one day around noon, wolf cubs, you know, grow up. They couldn't fortell the day. Two minutes before noon they were petting her, one minute after twelve she jumped at their throats. I didn't mind about him!

AEGISTHUS. Well?

BEGGAR. Well, I was just passing by. And I killed the wolf. She was beginning to eat Narses' cheeks, she liked them.

Narses' wife got away, not too badly hurt. Thanks! You'll
see her. She's coming for me pretty soon.

AEGISTHUS. What's the connection . . . ?

BEGGAR. Oh, don't expect to see an Amazon queen. Varicose
veins age a person.

PRESIDENT. He asked, what's the connection?

BEGGAR. The connection? It's because I think this man, as he's
head of the state, must be more intelligent than Narses. No
one could imagine such stupidity as Narses'. I never could
teach him to smoke a cigar except by the lighted end. And
what about knots? It's terribly important to know how to
make knots. If you make a curlycue where you ought to
have a knot, and vice versa, you're lost. You lose your
money, you catch cold, you choke, your boat veers away or
collides, you can't pull off your shoes. I mean if you want to
pull them off. And the laces? You know Narses was a
poacher.

PRESIDENT. We've asked you, what is the connection?

BEGGAR. Here's the connection. If this man distrusts his niece,
if he knows that one of these days she'll give a signal, as he
said, she'll begin to bite, to turn the city upside down, push
up the price of butter, start a war, et cetera, he can't hesitate.
He ought to kill her dead before she reveals herself. When
will she reveal herself?

PRESIDENT. What do you mean?

BEGGAR. What day, at what time will she reveal herself? When
will she turn into a wolf? When will she become Electra?

PRESIDENT. But nothing tells us she'll turn into a wolf.

BEGGAR, *pointing to* AEGISTHUS. Yes. He thinks so. He says so.

GARDENER. Electra is the gentlest of women.

BEGGAR. Narses' wolf cub was the gentlest of wolves.

PRESIDENT. Your expression "reveals herself" doesn't make sense.

BEGGAR. My expression doesn't make sense? You know nothing about life. The 29th of May, when you see the hills astir with thousands of little red, yellow, and green balls flying, squawling, quarreling over every little bit of thistle fluff, never making a mistake nor going after dandelion down, aren't the butterflies revealing themselves? And June 14th when you see on the river bank two reeds move without wind or wave till June 15th, and, too, without bubbles made by carp, isn't the pike revealing himself? And judges like you, the first time they condemn to death, when the condemned man appears, distraught, don't they reveal themselves by the taste of blood on their lips? Everything in nature reveals itself. Even the king. And the question today, if you'll believe me, is whether the king will reveal himself as Aegisthus before Electra reveals herself as Electra. So he has to know the day when it will happen to the girl, so he can kill her on the eve, down in a valley, as he said, down in a little valley, the handiest and least visible, in her bath.

PRESIDENT. Isn't he awful?

AEGISTHUS. You're forgetting the wedding, beggar.

BEGGAR. True. I am forgetting the wedding. But a wedding, if you want to kill someone, isn't as sure as death. Especially as a girl like her, sensitive, rather retarded et cetera, will reveal herself the moment a man takes her in his arms for the first time. You're marrying her?

AEGISTHUS. At once. Right here.

BEGGAR. Not to the king of a neighboring city, I hope?

AEGISTHUS. Not on your life! To this gardener.

PRESIDENT. To this gardener.

BEGGAR. She'll take him? I'd not reveal myself in the arms of a gardener. But everyone to his taste. I revealed myself in Corfu, at the fountain near the bakery, under the plane trees. You should have seen me that day! In each tray of the scales I weighed a hand of the baker's wife. They never weighed the same. I evened them up in the right tray with flour, in the left with oatmeal ... Where does the gardener live?

GARDENER. Outside the walls.

BEGGAR. In a village?

GARDENER. No. My house stands alone.

BEGGAR, *to* AEGISTHUS. Bravo! I catch your idea. Not bad! It's quite easy to kill a gardener's wife. Much easier than a princess in a palace.

GARDENER. Whoever you are, I beg you ...

BEGGAR. You'll not deny that it's easier to bury someone in compost than in marble?

GARDENER. What are you imagining? For one thing she'll not be a minute out of my sight.

BEGGAR. You'll bend down to plant a pear tree. Transplant it again because you hit a hard clod. Death has passed by.

PRESIDENT. Stranger, I fear you don't know where you are. You're in Agamemnon's palace, in his family.

BEGGAR. I see what I see, I see this man is afraid, he lives with fear, fear of Electra.

AEGISTHUS. My dear guest, let's not misunderstand each other. I'll not deny I'm anxious about Electra. I know misfortunes and troubles will come to the family of the Atrides the day she reveals herself, as you say. And to us all, for every citizen is affected by what happens to the royal family. That's why I'm handing her over to a lowly family, unseen by the gods, where her eyes and gestures will not inflame, where the harm will be only local and in the middle class, the Theocathocles family.

BEGGAR. A good idea, a good idea! But the family ought to be especially lowly.

AEGISTHUS. It is, and I'll see that it stays so. I'll see that no The-ocathocles distinguishes himself by talent or courage. As for boldness and genius, I'm not afraid they'll make their mark.

BEGGAR. Take care! This little Agatha is not exactly ugly. Beauty too can give a signal.

PRESIDENT. I beg you to leave Agatha out of our argument.

BEGGAR. Of course it's possible to rub her face with vitriol.

PRESIDENT. My lord!

AEGISTHUS. The case has been argued.

PRESIDENT. But I'm thinking of fate, Aegisthus! It's not a dis-ease. You think it's infectious?

BEGGAR. Yes. Like hunger among the poor.

PRESIDENT. I can hardly believe that fate will be content with one obscure little clan instead of the royal family, or that it will become the fate of the Theocathocles instead of the Atrides.

BEGGAR. Don't worry. A royal cancer spreads to the middle classes.

AEGISTHUS. President, if you don't want Electra's entrance into your family to mark the disgrace of its members, don't add a word. In a third-class zone the most implacable fate will do only third-class harm. I personally am distressed, because of my great esteem for the Theocathocles family, but the dynasty, the state, and the city can no longer take risks.

BEGGAR. And perhaps she can be killed a little anway, if an occasion arises.

AEGISTHUS. I have spoken. You may fetch Clytemnestra and Electra. They're waiting.

BEGGAR. It's not too soon. Without blaming you, I must say our talk lacks women.

AEGISTHUS. You'll have two, and talkers!

BEGGAR. And they'll argue with you a little, I hope?

AEGISTHUS. You like arguing women?

BEGGAR. Adore them. This afternoon I was in a house where a dispute was going on. Not a very high-toned discussion. Not compared to here. Not a plot of royal assassins as here. They were arguing whether they ought to serve guests chickens with or without livers. And the neck, of course. The women were furious. Had to be separated. Now I think of it, it was a fierce dispute. Blood flowed.

SCENE 4 *The Same.* CLYTEMNESTRA, ELECTRA, MAIDS.

PRESIDENT. Here they both are.

CLYTEMNESTRA. Both! That's a manner of speaking. Electra is never more absent than when she's present.

ELECTRA. No. Today I'm here.

AEGISTHUS. Then let's make the most of it. You know why your mother has brought you here?

ELECTRA. It's her habit. She's already led a daughter to sacrifice.

CLYTEMNESTRA. There's Electra to the life! Never a word that's not treason or insinuation.

ELECTRA. Excuse me, mother. The allusion is quite apropos in the family of the Atrides.

BEGGAR. What does she mean? Is she angry with her mother?

GARDENER. It would be the first time anyone has seen Electra angry.

BEGGAR. All the more interesting!

AEGISTHUS. Electra, your mother has told you of our decision. We've been anxious about you for a long time. I hardly think you realize that you're like a sleepwalker in broad daylight. In the palace and the city people speak of you only in whispers, they're so afraid you'd wake and fall if they raised their voices.

BEGGAR, *shouting*. Electra!

AEGISTHUS. What's the matter with him?

BEGGAR. Oh, I'm sorry, it's just a joke. Excuse it. But you were scared, not she. Electra's no sleepwalker.

AEGISTHUS. Please——

BEGGAR. At least the experiment has been made. You were the one who flinched. What would you have done if I'd shouted, "Aegisthus?"

PRESIDENT. Let our Regent speak.

BEGGAR. I'll shout "Aegisthus" pretty soon, when nobody expects it.

AEGISTHUS. You must get well, Electra, no matter what it costs.

ELECTRA. To cure me, that's easy. Give life to a dead man.

AEGISTHUS. You're not the only one who grieves for your father. But he'd not ask you to make your mourning an offense to the living. We wrong the dead to attach them to our lives, for that deprives them of the freedom of death, if they know it.

ELECTRA. He's free. That's why he comes.

AEGISTHUS. Do you really think he's pleased to see you weep for him, not like a daughter but like a wife?

ELECTRA. I am my father's widow, for lack of another.

CLYTEMNESTRA. Electra!

AEGISTHUS. Widow or not, today we'll celebrate your marriage.

ELECTRA. Yes, I know your plot.

CLYTEMNESTRA. What plot? Is it a plot to marry a twenty-one year old daughter? At your age I had the two of you in my arms, you and Orestes.

ELECTRA. You carried us badly. You let Orestes fall on the marble floor.

CLYTEMENSTRA. What could I do? You pushed him.

ELECTRA. That's a lie. I never pushed him.

CLYTEMNESTRA. What do you know about it? You were only fifteen months old.

ELECTRA. I did *not* push Orestes! I remember it, far back in my memory. Oh, Orestes, wherever you are, hear me! I did not push you.

AEGISTHUS. That's enough, Electra.

BEGGAR. This time they're really at it! It'd be funny if the little girl revealed herself right in front of us.

ELECTRA. She lies. Orestes, she lies!

AEGISTHUS. Please, Electra!

CLYTEMNESTRA. She did push him. Obviously at her age she didn't know what she was doing. But she did push him.

ELECTRA. With all my strength I tried to hold him: by his little blue tunic, by his arm, by the end of his fingers, by his shadow. I sobbed when I saw him on the floor, with the red mark on his forehead.

CLYTEMNESTRA. You shouted with laughter. The tunic, by the way, was mauve.

ELECTRA. It was blue. I know Orestes' tunic. When it was drying you couldn't see it against the sky.

AEGISTHUS. Can *I* get a word in? Haven't you had time these twenty years to settle this debate?

ELECTRA. For twenty years I've waited for this chance. Now I have it.

CLYTEMNESTRA. Why can't she understand that she might be wrong, even honestly?

BEGGAR. That're both honest. That's the truth.

PRESIDENT. Princess, I beg of you! Of what interest is this question today?

CLYTEMNESTRA. Of none, I grant you.

ELECTRA. What interest? If I had pushed Orestes I'd rather die, I'd kill myself. My life would have no meaning.

AEGISTHUS. Must I force you to keep quiet? Are you as mad as she, queen?

CLYTEMNESTRA. Electra, listen. Let's not quarrel. This is exactly what happened: he was on my right arm.

ELECTRA. On your left!

AEGISTHUS. Have you finished, Clytemnestra, or haven't you?

CLYTEMNESTRA. We've finished. But a right arm is a right arm, a mauve tunic is mauve, not blue.

ELECTRA. It was blue. As blue as Orestes' forehead was red.

CLYTEMNESTRA. That is true. Very red. You touched the wound with your finger and danced around the little prone body. You laughed as you tasted the blood.

ELECTRA. I? I wanted to bruise my head on the step that hurt him. I trembled for a week.

AEGISTHUS. Silence!

ELECTRA. I'm still trembling.

BEGGAR. Narses' wife tied hers with an elastic rope that had some play. Often it was askew, but he didn't fall.

AEGISTHUS. Enough. We'll soon see how Electra will carry hers. For you agree, don't you? You accept this marriage?

ELECTRA. I agree.

AEGISTHUS. I must admit not many suitors throng around you.

BEGGAR. They say ...

AEGISTHUS. What do they say?

BEGGAR. They say you've threatened to kill the princes who might marry Electra. That's what they say in the city.

ELECTRA. Good! I don't want any prince.

CLYTEMNESTRA. You'd rather have a gardener?

ELECTRA. I know you two have decided to marry me to my father's gardener. I accept.

CLYTEMNESTRA. You shall not marry a gardener.

AEGISTHUS. Queen, we settled that. Our word is given.

CLYTEMNESTRA. I take mine back. It was a wicked word. If Electra is ill we'll care for her. I'll not give my daughter to a gardener.

ELECTRA. Too late, mother. You have given me.

CLYTEMNESTRA. Gardener, you dare to aspire to Electra?

GARDENER. I'm unworthy, queen, but Aegisthus commands me.

AEGISTHUS. I do command you. Here are the rings. Take your wife.

CLYTEMNESTRA. If you persist, gardener, it's at the risk of your life.

BEGGAR. Then don't persist. I'd rather see soldiers die than gardeners.

CLYTEMNESTRA. What's that man saying? Marry Electra, gardener, and you die.

BEGGAR. It's your business. But go into the garden a year after the death of the gardener. You'll see something. You'll see what's happened to the endive, widowed by its gardener. Its not like kings' widows.

CLYTEMNESTRA. That garden won't suffer. Come, Electra.

GARDENER. Queen, you can deny me Electra, but it's not nice to say bad things about a garden you don't know.

CLYTEMNESTRA. I know it—empty land, with scattered plantings.

GARDENER. Empty? The best tended garden in Argos.

PRESIDENT. If he begins to talk about his garden we'll never finish.

AEGISTHUS. Spare us your descriptions!

GARDENER. The queen provoked me, and I answer. My garden is my dowry and my honor.

AEGISTHUS. Never mind! Enough of quarrels.

GARDENER. Empty, indeed! It covers ten acres of hilly land, and six of valley. No, no, you'll not silence me! Not a sterile inch, is there, Electra? On the terraces I have garlic and tomatoes, on the slopes grape vines and peach trees. On the level land vegetables, strawberries, and raspberries. A fig tree at the bottom of each slope against the wall, which warms the figs.

AEGISTHUS. Fine! Let your figs get warm and take your wife.

CLYTEMNESTRA. You dare talk of your garden! I've seen it from the road. It's all dry, a bald skull. You shall not have Electra.

GARDENER. All dry! A brook flows between the box and the plane trees, never dry in hottest weather; I've dug two little trenches from it—one turned on the meadow, the other cut in the rock. Try to find skulls like that! And scattered plantings! In spring it's full of narcissus and jonquils. I've never seen Electra really smile, but in my garden, I saw something on her face almost like a smile.

CLYTEMNESTRA. See if she's smiling now!

GARDENER. I call that Electra's smile.

CLYTEMNESTRA. Smiling at your dirty hands, your black nails ...

ELECTRA. Dear gardener ...

GARDENER. My black nails? Look, see if my nails are black! Don't believe it, Electra. You're unlucky today, queen, I spent this morning whitewashing my house, so there's not a sign of mice there, and my nails came out, not black, as you say, but mooned with white.

AEGISTHUS. That's enough, gardener.

GARDENER. I know, I know it's enough. And my dirty hands! Look! Look at these dirty hands! Hands that I washed after taking down the dried mushrooms and onions, so nothing would trouble Electra's nights. I'll sleep in the outhouse, Electra; there I'll keep guard so that nothing disturbs your sleep, whether an owl, or the open floodgate, or a fox, hunting the hedge, with a chicken in his mouth. I've said my say.

ELECTRA. Thanks, gardener.

CLYTEMNESTRA. And that's how Electra will live, Clytemnestra's daughter, watching her husband going around his border, two pails in his hands. . . .

AEGISTHUS. There she can weep for her dead to her heart's content. Get ready your wreaths of everlasting tomorrow.

GARDENER. And there she'll escape from anxiety, torture, and perhaps tragedy. I don't understand people, queen, but I do know the seasons. It's time, full time, to transplant misfortune from our city. The Atrides wont be grafted on our poor family, but on the seasons, the fields, the winds. I think they'll lose nothing by that.

BEGGAR. Be persuaded, queen. Don't you see that Aegisthus hates Electra so much he'll be driven to kill her, giving her to the earth by a kind of play on words: he gives her to a garden. She gains by that, she gains life.

AEGISTHUS *rises*.

What? Was I wrong to say that?

AEGISTHUS, *to* ELECTRA *and the* GARDENER. Come here, both of you.

CLYTEMNESTRA. Electra, I beg you!

ELECTRA. You're the one who wanted it, mother.

CLYTEMNESTRA. I no longer want it. You see I don't want it now.

ELECTRA. Why don't you want it? Are you afraid? Too late!

CLYTEMNESTRA. How can I make you remember who I am and who you are?

ELECTRA. You'll have to tell me I didn't push Orestes.

CLYTEMNESTRA. Stupid girl!

AEGISTHUS. Are they beginning again?

BEGGAR. Yes, yes, let them begin again.

CLYTEMNESTRA. And unjust! And stubborn! I let Orestes fall! I who never break anything! Never let fall a glass or a ring! I'm so steady that birds light on my arms. It's possible to fly away from me but not to fall. That's just what I said when he lost his balance, "Why, why did an ill fate bring his sister so near him?"

AEGISTHUS. They're crazy!

ELECTRA. And I said to myself, as soon as I saw him slipping, "IF she's a true mother she'll stoop to soften his fall, or she'll bend to make a slope and catch him on her thigh or her knees. We'll see if they'll catch him, the noble knees and thighs of my mother. I'm not sure. I'll see."

CLYTEMNESTRA. Be quiet!

ELECTRA. "Or she'll bend backward, so little Orestes will slip off her like a child from a tree where he's picked off a nest, or she'll fall so *he* won't, or so he'll fall on her. She knows all the ways a mother uses to catch her son, she still knows them. She can still be a curve, a shell, a motherly slope, a cradle." But she stood fixed, straight, and he fell right down from the full height of his mother.

AEGISTHUS. The case is heard. Clytemnestra, we'll leave.

CLYTEMNESTRA. Just let her remember what she saw when she was fifteen months old and what she didn't see. That's the point.

AEGISTHUS. Who but you believes her or listens to her?

ELECTRA. There are a thousand ways of preventing a fall, and she did nothing.

CLYTEMNESTRA. The slightest movement, and *you* would have fallen.

ELECTRA. Just as I said. You calculated. You figured it all out. You were a nurse, not a mother.

CLYTEMNESTRA. My little Electra . . .

ELECTRA. I'm not your little Electra. your motherly feeling is tickled awake by your rubbing your two children against you. But it's too late.

CLYTEMNESTRA. Please——!

ELECTRA. There you are! Open your arms, see what you've done. Look, everybody. That's just what you did.

CLYTEMNESTRA. Let's go, Aegisthus.
She leaves.

BEGGAR. I believe the mother is frightened.

AEGISTHUS, *to the* BEGGAR. What's that you say?

BEGGAR. I? I say nothing. I never say anything. When I'm hungry I talk, everyone hears me. Today I've drunk a little something.

SCENE 5   ELECTRA.   BEGGAR,   GARDENER,
STRANGER, AGATHA.

AGATHA. This is the right time, Aegisthus isn't here. Get out, gardener.

GARDENER. What do you mean?

AGATHA. Get out, fast. This man will take your place.

GARDENER. My place with Electra?

STRANGER. Yes, I'll marry her.

ELECTRA. Let go my hand.

STRANGER. Never.

AGATHA. Just look at him, Electra. Before you turn your back
on a man, at least look at him. I'm sure you'll lose nothing
by that.

ELECTRA. Gardener, help!

STRANGER. I owe you nothing, gardener. But look me in the
eye. You understand species and kinds. Look at me and see
the kind I am. So! Look, with your poor peasant eyes, with
the gaze of humble folk, a blear-eyed mixture of devotion
and fear, the sterile look of the poor, unchanged by sunshine
or misfortune, see if I can give way to you. Fine! Now give
me your ring. Thanks!

ELECTRA. Agatha, cousin! Help me! I swear I'll not tell about
your rendezvous, your quarrels, I'll tell nothing.

AGATHA, *leading off the* GARDENER. Come, the Theocathocles
are saved. Let the Atrides work it out.

BEGGAR. She runs away—like a wood-louse, hiding under a
stone to escape from the sun.

SCENE 6   ELECTRA, STRANGER, BEGGAR.

STRANGER. Struggle no more.

ELECTRA. I'll struggle till I die.

STRANGER. You think so? In a minute you'll take me in your
arms.

ELECTRA. No insults!

STRANGER. In a minute you'll embrace me.

ELECTRA. Shame on you for profiting from two infamies!

STRANGER. See how I trust you. I let you go.

ELECTRA. Farewell forever!

STRANGER. No! I'll say one word to you and you'll come back to me, tenderly.

ELECTRA. What lie is this?

STRANGER. One word, and you'll be sobbing in my arms. One word, my name.

ELECTRA. There's only one name in the world that could draw me to anyone.

STRANGER. That's the one.

ELECTRA. Are you Orestes?

ORESTES. Ungrateful sister, only recognizing me by my name!
    CLYTEMNESTRA *appears*.

SCENE 7   CLYTEMNESTRA. ELECTRA.
                ORESTES. BEGGAR.

CLYTEMNESTRA. Electra!

ELECTRA. Mother?

CLYTEMNESTRA. Come back to your place in the palace. Leave the gardener. Come!

ELECTRA. The gardener has left, mother.

CLYTEMNESTRA. Where is he?

ELECTRA. He's given me to this man.

CLYTEMNESTRA. What man?

ELECTRA. This man. He's my husband now.

CLYTEMNESTRA. This is no time for jokes. Come!

ELECTRA. How can I come? He's holding my hand.

CLYTEMNESTRA. Hurry!

ELECTRA. You know, mother, those clogs they put on the legs of foals to prevent their running away? This man has put them on my ankles.

CLYTEMNESTRA. This time I command you. You must be in your room by tonight. Come!

ELECTRA. What? Leave my husband the night of my wedding?

CLYTEMNESTRA. What are you doing? Who are you?

ELECTRA. He'll not answer you. This evening my husband's mouth belongs to me, and all the words he speaks.

CLYTEMNESTRA. Where do you come from? Who is your father?

ELECTRA. A misalliance maybe. But not such a bad one.

CLYTEMNESTRA. Why do you look at me like that? Why the challenge in your eyes? Who was your mother?

ELECTRA. He never saw her.

CLYTEMNESTRA. She's dead?

ELECTRA. Perhaps what you see in his eyes is that he never saw his mother. Handsome, isn't he?

CLYTEMNESTRA. Yes. He looks like you.

ELECTRA. If our first married hours make us look alike, that's a good omen, isn't it, mother?

CLYTEMNESTRA. Who are you?

ELECTRA. What does it matter to you? Never was a man less yours.

CLYTEMNESTRA. Whatever or whoever you are, stranger, don't give in to her caprice. We'll see tomorrow if you're worthy of Electra. I'll win over Aegisthus. But I've never known a less propitious night. Leave this man, Electra.

ELECTRA. Too late! His arms hold me.

CLYTEMNESTRA. You can break iron if you want to.

ELECTRA. Iron, yes *this* iron, no!

CLYTEMNESTRA. What has he said against your mother that you accept him this way?

ELECTRA. We've had no time yet to speak of my mother or his. Go, we'll begin!

ORESTES. Electra!

ELECTRA. That's all he can say. If I take my hand from his mouth, he just says my name without stopping. You can't get anything else out of him. Oh, husband, now that your mouth is free, kiss me!

CLYTEMNESTRA. Shame! So this madness is Electra's secret!

ELECTRA. Kiss me, before my mother.

CLYTEMNESTRA. Farewell! But I didn't think you were a girl to give yourself to the first passer-by.

ELECTRA. Nor I. But I didn't know what the first kiss was like.

SCENE 8   ELECTRA. ORESTES. BEGGAR.

ORESTES. Why do you hate our mother so, Electra?

ELECTRA. Don't speak of her, above all not of her! Let's imagine for a minute that we were born without a mother. Don't talk.

ORESTES. I have everything to tell you.

ELECTRA. You tell me everything just by being here. Be quiet. Close your eyes. Your words and your look touch me too poignantly, they wound me. I often wished that I'd find you in your sleep, if I ever found you. Now I can't bear to have all at once the look, the voice, the life of Orestes. I ought to have stumbled on your image, dead at first, then coming alive little by little. But my brother was born like the sun, a golden animal at his rising. Either I'm blind or I find my brother by groping—oh, the joy of being blind for a sister who finds her brother! For twenty years my hands have fumbled over mean or indifferent things, and now they touch—a brother—a brother in whom everything is true. Some dubious or some false bits might have been in this

head, this body, but by a wonderful chance, everything in
Orestes is brotherly, everything is Orestes.

ORESTES. You smother me.

ELECTRA. I don't smother you. I don't kill you. I caress you. I'm
calling you to life. From this brotherly shape which my
dazzled eyes have scarcely seen I'm making my brother in
all his features. See, how I've made my brother's hand, with
its straight thumb. See how I've made my brother's chest,
which I'm animating so it swells and breathes, giving life
to my brother. See how I make this ear, little, curled, trans-
parent like a bats wing. One last touch and the ear is finished. I make the two alike. Quite a success, these ears!
And now I'll make my brother's mouth, gentle and dry, and
fasten it on his face. Take your life from me, Orestes, not
from our mother.

ORESTES. Why do you hate her? Listen . . .

ELECTRA. What's the matter with you? Are you pushing me
away? That's the ingratitude of sons. They're hardly finished before they get away and escape.

ORESTES. Someone is watching us from the staircase.

ELECTRA. Its she, certainly she. From jealousy or fear. It's our
mother.

BEGGAR. Yes, yes, it's she.

ELECTRA. She suspects we're here, creating ourselves, freeing
ourselves from her. She thinks that my caresses will cover
you, wash you clear of her, make you an orphan. Oh,
brother, who else could do me such a service!

ORESTES. How can you speak so of her who bore you? Though
she was harsh to me, I'm less hard on her.

ELECTRA. That's just what I can't stand about her, that she bore
me. That's my shame. I feel that I came into life in a dubious way, that her motherhood is only a plot to bind us together. I love everything that comes from my father. I love
the way he put off his fine wedding garment and lay down

to beget me, from his thought and from his body. I love his eyes, and his surprise the day I was born; I came from him far more than from my mothers pains. I was born from his nights of deep sleep, his nine month's emancipation, the comfort he found with other women while my mother was carrying me, his fatherly smile when I was born. I hate everything about my birth that comes from my mother.

ORESTES. Why do you detest women so?

ELECTRA. I don't detest women, I detest my mother. And I don't detest men, I detest Aegisthus.

ORESTES. Why do you hate him?

ELECTRA. I don't know yet. I only know it's the same hatred. That's why it's so hard to bear, that's why I'm suffocating. Many times I've tried to find out why I hate both of them with a special hatred. Two little hatreds could be borne—like sorrows—one balances the other. I tried to think I hated my mother because she let you fall when you were a baby, and Aegisthus because he stole your throne. But it's not true. I really pitied this great queen, who ruled the world, yet suddenly, frightened and humble, let her child fall, like a feeble grandmother. I pitied Aegisthus, that cruel tyrant, whose fate is to die miserably from your blows. All the reasons I had for hating them made me think them human, pitiable, but no sooner had my hatred washed them clean and re-clothed them and I found myself gentle, obedient before them, than a yet heavier wave, charged with a yet more virulent hatred, flowed over them. I hate them with a hatred that is not really me.

ORESTES. I'm here. It will vanish.

ELECTRA. You believe that? I used to think your return would free me of this hatred. I thought my illness was because you were far away. I prepared for your return by becoming all tenderness, tenderness for everyone, for them too. I was wrong. My pain tonight is caused by your being here and all the hatred in me laughs and welcomes you, it is my love for you. It caresses you as a dog does the hand that frees him. I know that you have given me the sight, the smell of hatred. The first scent, and now I follow the trail. Who's there? Is it she?

BEGGAR. No, me. You're forgetting the time. She's gone up. She's undressing.

ELECTRA. She's undressing. Before her mirror, looking long at herself, our mother, Clytemnestra, undresses. Our mother, whom I love for her beauty and pity because she's aging, whose voice and looks I admire, our mother, whom I hate.

ORESTES. Electra, sister darling, please calm yourself.

ELECTRA. Then I'm to follow the trail?

ORESTES. Calm yourself.

ELECTRA. I? I'm perfectly calm. I'm all sweetness. Sweet to my mother, very sweet. It's this hatred for her that swells up and kills me.

ORESTES. Now it's your turn not to talk. We'll think about that hatred tomorrow. This evening let me taste for an hour at least, the sweetness of the life I've never known and now return to.

ELECTRA. An hour. All right, one hour.

ORESTES. The palace is so beautiful beneath the moon. My palace. All the power of our family is emanating from it. My power. In your arms let me imagine all the happiness these walls might have held for calmer, more reasonable people. Oh, Electra, how many of our family's names were originally sweet and tender, and should have been happy names!

ELECTRA. Yes, I know. Medea, Phaedra.

ORESTES. Even those, why not?

ELECTRA. Electra. Orestes.

ORESTES. Isn't there still time? I've come to save them.

ELECTRA. Silence! She's there.

ORESTES. Who?

ELECTRA. She with the happy name: Clytemnestra.

SCENE 9   ELECTRA. ORESTES. CLYTEM-
NESTRA, *then* AEGISTHUS.

CLYTEMNESTRA. Electra?

ELECTRA. Mother?

CLYTEMNESTRA. Who is this man?

ELECTRA. Guess.

CLYTEMNESTRA. Let me see his face.

ELECTRA. If you can't see it at a distance you'd see him less
well near to.

CLYTEMNESTRA. Electra, let's stop fighting. If you really want
to marry this man, I'll agree. Why do you smile? Wasn't
it I who wanted you to marry?

ELECTRA. Not at all. You wanted me to be a woman.

CLYTEMNESTRA. What's the difference?

ELECTRA. You wanted me in your camp. You didn't want the
face of your worst enemy constantly before you.

CLYTEMNESTRA. You mean my daughter's?

ELECTRA. Chastity, rather!

ORESTES. Electra. . !

ELECTRA. Let me alone, let me alone. I've found the trail.

CLYTEMNESTRA. Chastity! This girl who's devoured by desire
talks about chastity! This girl at two years old couldn't see
a boy without blushing. It was because you wanted to embrace Orestes, if you want to know, that you pulled him out
of my arms.

ELECTRA. Then I was right. I'm proud of it. It was worth while.

Trumpets. Shouts. Faces in the windows. AEGISTHUS *leans down from a balcony.*

AEGISTHUS. Are you there, queen?

BEGGAR. Yes, she's here.

AEGISTHUS. Great news, queen. Orestes is not dead. He's escaped. He's coming toward Argos.

CLYTEMNESTRA. Orestes!

AEGISTHUS. I'm sending my bodyguard to meet him. I've posted my most faithful men around the walls. You say nothing?

CLYTEMNESTRA. Orestes is coming back?

AEGISTHUS. Coming back to seize his father's throne, to prevent my being regent, and you being queen. His emissaries are preparing a revolt. But don't worry. I'll keep order. Who's down there with you?

CLYTEMNESTRA. Electra.

AEGISTHUS. And her gardener?

BEGGAR. And her gardener.

AEGISTHUS. I hope you're not still trying to separate them? You see how well founded my fears were! You agree now?

CLYTEMNESTRA. No. I'm not trying any more.

AEGISTHUS. Don't let them leave the palace. Them especially. I've ordered the gates closed till the soldiers return. You hear me, gardener?

ELECTRA. We'll not leave.

AEGISTHUS. Queen, come upstairs. Go back to your room. It's late and the Council is to meet at dawn. I wish you a good-night.

ELECTRA. Thanks, Aegisthus.

AEGISTHUS. I was speaking to the queen, Electra. This is no time for irony. Come, queen.

CLYTEMNESTRA. Good-bye, Electra.

ELECTRA. Good-bye, mother.

CLYTEMNESTRA *goes, then turns back.*

CLYTEMNESTRA. Good-bye, my daughter's husband.

BEGGAR. What you see in families! You see everything!

ELECTRA. Who spoke?

BEGGAR. No one! No one spoke. You think someone would speak at a time like this?

SCENE 10 ELECTRA. ORESTES. BEGGAR.

ORESTES. Tell me, Electra! Tell me!

ELECTRA. Tell you what?

ORESTES. Your hatred. The reason for your hatred. You know it now, when you were talking to Clytemnestra a moment ago you almost fainted in my arms. It might have been from joy—or horror.

ELECTRA. It was both joy *and* horror. Are you strong or weak, Orestes?

ORESTES. Tell me your secret and I'll find out.

ELECTRA. I don't know my secret yet. I hold only one end of the thread. Don't worry. Everything will follow. Take care! Here she is.

CLYTEMNESTRA *appears at the back of the stage.*

SCENE 11 ELECTRA. CLYTEMNESTRA.
ORESTES. BEGGAR.

CLYTEMNESTRA. So it's you, Orestes?

ORESTES. Yes, mother, it's I.

CLYTEMNESTRA. Is it sweet to see a mother when you're twenty?

ORESTES. A mother who sent you away? Sad and sweet.

CLYTEMNESTRA. You look at her from far away.

ORESTES. She's just as I imagined her.

CLYTEMNESTRA. My son. Handsome. Regal. And yet I draw near.

ORESTES. Not I. At a distance she's a magnificent mother.

CLYTEMNESTRA. Who tells you that near to her magnificence remains?

ORESTES. Or her motherliness? That's why I don't move.

CLYTEMNESTRA. The mirage of a mother is enough for you?

ORESTES. I've had so much less until today. At least I can tell the mirage what I'd never tell my real mother.

CLYTEMNESTRA. If the mirage deserves it, that's all right. What will you tell her.

ORESTES. Everything I never tell you. Everything that would be a lie if said to you.

CLYTEMNESTRA. That you love her?

ORESTES. Yes.

CLYTEMNESTRA. That you respect her?

ORESTES. Yes.

CLYTEMNESTRA. That you admire her?

ORESTES. That the mother and the mirage can share.

CLYTEMNESTRA. It's the opposite for me. I don't love the mirage of my son. But when my son is actually before me, speaking, breathing, I lose my strength.

ORESTES. Think of hurting him, you'll recover it.

CLYTEMNESTRA. Why are you so hard? You don't look cruel. Your voice is gentle.

ORESTES. Yes, I'm exactly like the son I might have been. You too, of course. You look so like a wonderful mother. If I weren't your son, I'd be deceived.

ELECTRA. Why are you both talking? Where does this horrible maternal coquetry get you, mother? At midnight the little window which allows a mother and son to see each other as they are not opens for a minute. Shut it, the minute has passed.

CLYTEMNESTRA. Why so quickly? How do you know one minute of maternal love is enough for Orestes?

ELECTRA. Everything tells me you have no right to more than a minute of your son's love in your whole life. You've had it. And that's the end. What a comedy you're playing! Go!

CLYTEMNESTRA. Very well. Good-bye.

FIRST LITTLE GIRL, *appearing from behind the columns.* Good-by, truth of my son!

ORESTES. Good-by.

SECOND LITTLE GIRL. Good-by, mirage of my mother!

ELECTRA. You might say au revoir. You'll meet again.

SCENE 12 ELECTRA *and* ORESTES *asleep. The little* EUMENIDES. BEGGAR. *The* EUMENIDES *now seem to be about twelve or thirteen years old.*

FIRST GIRL. They're asleep. It' our turn to play Clytemnestra and Orestes. But not the way they played. Let's play it truly.

BEGGAR, *to himself, though out loud.* The story of push or not push—I'd like to know . . .

SECOND GIRL. You there, let us play. We're playing.

The three little EUMENIDES *take the positions of the actors in the preceding scene and play it as a parody. Masks could be used.*

FIRST GIRL. So it's you, Orestes?

SECOND GIRL. Yes, it's me, mother.

FIRST GIRL. You've come to kill me and Aegisthus?

SECOND GIRL. News to me!

FIRST GIRL. Not to your sister. You've done some killing, little Orestes?

SECOND GIRL. The things one kills when one is good! A doe. And to be a little kind, I killed her fawn too, so it wouldn't be an orphan. But to kill my mother, never! That would be—parricide.

FIRST GIRL. Was that the sword you did your killing with?

SECOND GIRL. Yes. It will cut iron. See, it went through the fawn so fast he felt nothing.

FIRST GIRL. I'm not suggesting anything. I don't want to influence you. But if a sword like that were to kill your sister, we'd all be at peace!

SECOND GIRL. You want me to kill my sister?

FIRST GIRL. Never! That would be—fratricide. If the sword were to kill her by itself, that would be ideal. Let it come out of its scabbard, like this, and kill her by itself. I'd just quietly marry Aegisthus. We'd call you home, Aegisthus is getting old. You'd succeed him very soon. You'd be King Orestes.

SECOND GIRL. A sword doesn't kill by itself. It needs an assassin.

FIRST GIRL. Certainly! I should know! But I'm talking about the times when swords will kill by themselves. People who avenge wrongs are the curse of the world. And they get no better as they get older, I beg you to believe that. As criminals improve with age, good people always become criminals. Surely this is a fine moment for a sword to think for itself, move of itself, and kill by itself. They'd marry you to Alcmena's second daughter, the laughing one, with the fine teeth—you'd be Orestes, the married man.

SECOND GIRL. I don't want to kill my sister, I love her, nor my mother, I detest her.

FIRST GIRL. I know, I know. In a word you're weak and you have principles.

THIRD GIRL. Why are you two talking? Because the moon is rising, the nightingale singing here in the middle of this night of hatred and threats; take your hand off the hilt of your sword, Orestes, and see if it will have the intelligence to act by itself.

FIRST GIRL. That's right. Take it off . . . it's moving, friends, it's moving!

SECOND GIRL. It really is! It's a thinking sword. It thinks so hard it's half out!

ORESTES, *asleep*. Electra!

BEGGAR. Off with you, screech owls! You're waking them.

ELECTRA, *asleep*. Orestes!

SCENE 13 ELECTRA, ORESTES, BEGGAR.

BEGGAR. I'd love to get straight that story of pushed or not pushed. For whether it's true or false, it would show whether Electra is truthful or lying and whether she lies knowingly or whether her memory plays her false. I don't believe she pushed him. Look at her: two inches above ground she's holding her sleeping brother as tight as if they were over an abyss. He's dreaming that he's falling, evidently, but that's not her fault. Now the queen looks like those bakers' wives who never stoop, even to pick up their money, or like those bitches who smother their prettiest pup while they sleep. Afterward they lick it as the queen licked Orestes, but no one ever made a child with saliva. I can see the story as if I'd been there. It's understandable, if you imagine the queen had put on a diamond pin and a white cat had passed by. She's holding Electra on her right arm, for the girl was getting heavy, and the baby on the left, a bit away from her so he'll not scratch himself on the brooch or drive it into him. It's a queen's pin, not a nurse's. And the child sees the white cat, a magnificent creature—a white life, white hair—his eyes follow it, he rocks himself, and she's an egotistical woman. Anyway, seeing the child capsizing, in order to hold him she need only free her arm of little Electra, throw little Electra off on the marble floor, get rid of little Electra. Let little Electra break her neck, so the son of the king of kings be unhurt! But she's an egotist. For her a woman is as good as a man, she's a woman; the womb as good as the phallus, and she's a womb; she wouldn't dream for a second of destroying her daughter to save her son, so she keeps Electra. Now look at Electra. She's revealed herself in her brother's arms, and she's right. She couln't wish for a better moment. Fraternity is the mark of human beings. Beasts know only love . . . cats, parrots, et cetera, they only recognize fraternity by the hair. To find brothers they have to love men, to turn to men. . . . What does the duckling do when he gets away from the other ducks and, with his tender little eye shining on his slanting duck's cheek, he looks at us humans, eating and playing games, because he knows men and women are his brothers? I've taken little ducks in my hands, and could have wrung their necks, because they came to me so fraternally, trying to understand what I was doing, I, their brother, cutting my bread and cheese and adding an onion. Brother of ducks, that's our real title, for when they raise the little heads they've plunged into the water and look at a man, they're all neatness, intelligence and tenderness—not eatable except for their brains. I could teach those little duck heads to weep! . . . So Electra didn't push Orestes! That makes everything she says legitimate, everything she undertakes irrefutable. She's unadulterated truth, a lamp without a wick. So if she kills, as looks likely, all happiness and peace around her, it's because she's right. It's as if the soul of a girl, in bright sunlight, felt a moment of anguish, as if she sniffed escaping gas in the midst of splendid festivals, and had to go after it, for the young girl is the guardian of truth; she has to go after it whether or not the world bursts and cracks down to its foundations, whether innocents die the death of innocents to let the guilty live their guilty lives. Look at those two innocents! What will be the fruit of their marriage? To bring to life, for the world and for ages to come, a crime already forgotten, the punishment of which will be a worse crime? How right they are to sleep away this hour that is still theirs! Leave them. I'm going for a walk. If I stayed, I'd wake them. I always sneeze three times when the moon is full, and, right now, to sneeze would be taking a frightful risk. But all you who remain here, be quiet, now. This is Electra's first rest, and the last rest of Orestes.

CURTAIN.

INTERLUDE: THE GARDENER'S LAMENT

I'm not in the play any more. That's why I'm free to come and tell you what the play can't tell you. In stories like this the people won't stop killing and biting each other in order to tell you that the one aim of life is to love. It would be awkward to see the parricide stop, with upraised, dagger, and make a speech praising love. That would seem artificial. A lot of people wouldn't believe him. But I really don't see what else I can do here in this loneliness and desolation. And I speak impartially. I'll never marry anyone but Electra, and I'll never have her. I was made to live with a woman day and night, but I'll always live alone. I was meant to give myself fully, and yet I have to keep myself to myself. This is my wedding night that I'm living through, all alone—but thank you for being here—and the orangeade I'd prepared for Electra I had to drink up myself; there's not a drop left, and this was a long wedding night. Now who will doubt my word? The trouble is that I always say the opposite of what I mean, and that would be miserable today when my heart is so heavy and my mouth so bitter—oranges are really bitter—and if I forgot for an instant that I must speak to you of joy. Yes, love and joy. I come to tell you they're preferable to bitterness and hate. That's a motto to carve on a porch, or to put on a handkerchief, or better, in dwarf begonias in a clump. Of course, life is a failure, yet it's very, very good. Of course nothing ever goes right, never is well planned, yet you must confess, sometimes everything comes out splendidly, is splendidly planned. . . . Not for me . . .

or perhaps just for me. . . . If I can judge from my wish to love
everything and everyone, which is the result of the greatest misfortune in my life! What will happen to people who've had less
bad luck? How much love must men feel who marry wives they
don't love, what joy must those feel who leave a wife they
adore, after having had her in their home one hour? And people
whose children are ugly? Of course, tonight in my garden, I
wasn't very happy. As a little festival it didn't come off. I pre-
tended sometimes that Electra was near me, I talked to her and
said: "Come in, Electra! Are you cold, Electra?" But no one was
deceived, not even the dog, not to say myself. The dog thought:
"He promised us a bride, and he only gives us a word. My
master has married a word; he put on his white garment, the
one my paws soil, which keeps me from caressing him, just to
marry a word! He gives his orangeade to a word. He scolds me
for barking at shadows, real shadows which aren't alive, yet he
tries to embrace a word."

And I didn't lie down: to sleep with a word was impossible. I
can speak with a word, that's all! But if you were sitting like me
in this garden, where everything is confused at night, where the
moon is shining on the sundial, and the blind owl tries to drink
the cement walk instead of the brook, you'd understand what
I've understood: the truth! You'd understand that the day your
parents died, that day your parents were born; the day you
were ruined, that day you were rich; when your child was ungrateful, he was gratitude itself; when you were abandoned, the
whole world was coming to you in rapture and tenderness. That
was what happened to me in this empty, silent suburb. All these
stony trees, these immovable hills, rushed toward me. This all
applies to our play. To be sure, we can't say Electra is all love
for Clytemnestra. But note the difference: she tries to find a
mother and would see one in the first comer. She was marrying
me because I was the only man who could be a kind of mother
to her, though I'm not *really* the only one. There are men who'd
be glad to carry a child nine months, if they had to, just to have
daughters. All men, actually. Nine months are rather long,
but . . . a week, or a day . . . any man would be proud. Perhaps
to find a mother in *her* mother she'd have to cut her breast open,
though with royalty that's rather theoretical. Among kings there

are experiences never found among humble folk, pure hatred, for instance, and pure wrath. Always purity. That's tragedy, with its incests and parricides: purity, meaning—innocence. I don't know if you're like me, but to me, in tragedy, Pharoah's daughter killing herself means hope, the treasonous Marshall means faith, the Duke-Assassin speaks of tenderness. Cruelty is a deed of love—excuse me, I mean: tragedy is a deed of love. That's why I'm sure this morning, that if I asked, Heaven would approve me, would give a sign that a miracle is near, which would show you that joy and love are written in heaven, and that they echo my motto, though I'm abandoned and alone. If you wish, I'll ask. I'm as sure as I'm here that a voice from on high would answer me, that loud speakers and amplifiers and God's thunder are all prepared by God himself to shout, if I ask: "love and joy." But I'd rather you didn't ask. First it would be indecent. It's not the gardener's role to demand of God a storm, even a storm of tenderness. Moreover it would be useless. We know so well that at this moment, and yesterday and tomorrow and always, they're all up there, as many as there are, or perhaps only one, or even if that one is absent, they're all ready to shout: love and joy. It's much better for a man to take the gods at their word—this is euphemism—without forcing them to underline it, or to be held by it, or to create among themselves obligations of creditor and debtor. I'm always convinced by silences. Yes, I've begged them, haven't I? not to shout love and joy. But let them shout it if they really want to. Yet I'd rather conjure them, I conjure you, God, as a proof of your affections, of your voice and all your shouting, to keep silent, silent for one second. . . . That's much more convincing. . . . Listen! . . . Thanks!

ACT TWO

SCENE 1 *The same setting,*
shortly before dawn.

ELECTRA, *seated, holding* ORESTES, *asleep.* BEGGAR. *A cock.*
Sound of a trumpet in the distance.

BEGGAR. It won't be long now, eh, Electra?

ELECTRA. No. It's not far away.

BEGGAR. I said "it," I meant the day.

ELECTRA. I meant the light.

BEGGAR. It's not enough for you that liars' faces are shining in
the sun? That adulterers and murderers move about freely?
That's what the day brings—not too bad.

ELECTRA. No. But I want their faces to look blank at noon, and
their hands red. That's what light brings out. I want their
eyes to be rotten, their mouths diseased.

BEGGAR. As you say, one can't ask too much!

ELECTRA. There's the cock . . . shall I wake him?

BEGGAR. Wake him if you wish, but if I were you, I'd give him
another five minutes.

ELECTRA. Five minutes of nothingness! A poor gift!

BEGGAR. You never know. I believe there's an insect that lives
only five minutes. In five minutes he's young, adult, noisy; he
runs through childhood and adolescence, to the time of lame
knees and cataract, and legitimate and morganatic unions.
While I'm speaking he must be having measles and growing
to puberty.

ELECTRA. Let's wait till he dies. That's all I'll agree to.

BEGGAR. Our brother sleeps well.

ELECTRA. He went to sleep right away. He escaped from me. He slipped into sleep as though that were his real life.

BEGGAR. He's smiling. It *is* his real life.

ELECTRA. Tell me anything you like, beggar, except that Orestes' real life is a smile.

BEGGAR. Loud laughter, love, fine clothes, happiness. I guessed that as soon as I saw him. Orestes would be gay as a lark, if life were good to him.

ELECTRA. He has bad luck.

BEGGAR. Yes, he's not very lucky. All the more reason for not hurrying him.

ELECTRA. Good! As he was made to laugh, to dress well, as he's a lark, I'll give Orestes five minutes, for he'll wake to a lifetime of horror.

BEGGAR. In your place, since you can choose, I'd see to it that this morning light and truth depart at the same time. That doesn't mean much, but it would be a young girl's role and would please me. Man's truth is part of his habits, it leaves him somehow, whether at nine o'clock in the morning when workers strike, or at six in the evening, when women confess, et cetera; these are always bad things, always unclear. Now I'm used to animals. They know when to leave. A rabbit's first jump in the heather, the very second the sun rises, the plover's first flight, the young bear's first run from his rock, these, I can tell you, go toward the truth. If they don't get there, that's because they don't have to. A mere nothing distracts them, a gudgeon, a bee. Do as they do, Electra, go toward the dawn.

ELECTRA. A fine kingdom where gudgeons and bees are liars! But your animals are moving already!

BEGGAR. No. Those are the night creatures turning in. Owls. Rats. The night's truth turning in. Hush! Listen to the last two, the nightingales, of course the nightingales' truth.

SCENE 2 *The same.* AGATHA. A YOUNG MAN.

AGATHA. Darling, you do understand, don't you?

YOUNG MAN. Yes, I have an answer for everything.

AGATHA. If he sees you on the stairs?

YOUNG MAN. I have come to see the doctor on the top floor.

AGATHA. You forget already! He's a veterinary. Buy a dog. . . .
If he finds me in your arms?

YOUNG MAN. I've picked you up in the street, you've sprained
your ankle.

AGATHA. If it's in our kitchen?

YOUNG MAN. I'll pretend to be drunk—I don't know where I am.
I'll break the glasses.

AGATHA. One will be enough, darling, a small one, the large
ones are crystal. If it's in our room and we're dressed?

YOUNG MAN. I'm looking for him, to talk politics. I had to go
there to find him.

AGATHA. If it's in our room and we're undressed?

YOUNG MAN. I entered unexpectedly, your're resisting me, you
are perfidy itself, you treat as a thief a man who's pursued
you six months. . . . You're a tart!

AGATHA. Darling!

YOUNG MAN. A real tart!

AGATHA. I understand. It's almost day, my love, and I've hardly
had you for an hour, and how many more times do you
think he'll believe I walk in my sleep, and that it's less dangerous to let me stroll in the grove than on the roof? Oh, my
love, can you think of any pretext for letting me have you in
our bed at night, me between you two, so it would seem
quite natural to him?

YOUNG MAN. Think! You'll invent something.

AGATHA. A pretext for letting you two talk about your elections and the races over the body of your Agatha, so he'd not suspect anything. That's what we need—that's all.

YOUNG MAN. All!

AGATHA. Oh dear! Why is he so vain? Why is his sleep so light? Why does he adore me?

YOUNG MAN. The eternal litany! Why did you marry him? Why did you love him?

AGATHA. I? Liar! I never loved anyone but you!

YOUNG MAN. I? Remember in whose arms I found you day before yesterday!

AGATHA. That was only because I'd sprained my ankle. The man you mention was picking me up.

YOUNG MAN. First I've *heard* of any sprain.

AGATHA. You! You understand nothing. You don't realize that accident gave me an idea for us to use.

YOUNG MAN. When I meet him on the stairs he has no dogs, I can tell you, and no cats.

AGATHA. He rides horseback. You can't take a horse to the doctor upstairs.

YOUNG MAN. And he's always leaving your room.

AGATHA. Why do you force me to betray a state secret? He comes to consult my husband. They're afraid of a plot in the city. Please don't tell anyone, that would mean his dismissal. You'd bring me to the stake.

YOUNG MAN. One evening he was hurrying, his scarf not fastened, his tunic half unbuttoned. . . .

AGATHA. Of course, that was the day he tried to kiss me. I fixed him!

YOUNG MAN. You didn't let him kiss you, and he so powerful? I was waiting downstairs. He stayed two hours. . . .

AGATHA. He did stay two hours, but I didn't let him kiss me.

YOUNG MAN. Then he kissed you without your leave. Confess, Agatha, or I'll go away.

AGATHA. Force me to confess! That's a fine reward for my frankness. Yes, he did kiss me . . . once . . . on my forehead.

YOUNG MAN. And that seems dreadful to you?

AGATHA. Dreadful? Frightful!

YOUNG MAN. And you don't suffer for it?

AGATHA. Not at all! . . . Ah, do I suffer? It's killing me, killing me! Kiss me, darling. Now you know everything, and I'm glad of it. Aren't you happy everything is cleared up between us?

YOUNG MAN. Yes. Anything is better than a lie.

AGATHA. What a nice way you have of saying you prefer me to everything else, darling!

SCENE 3 ELECTRA, ORESTES. BEGGAR. *Then the* EUMENIDES. *They are taller than before, and seem fifteen years old.*

BEGGAR. A dawn song, at the dawn of such a day! It's always like this.

ELECTRA. The insect is dead, beggar?

BEGGAR. Dispersed in the universe. His great-grandchildren are now fighting gout.

ELECTRA. Orestes!

BEGGAR. You see he's no longer asleep. His eyes are open.

ELECTRA. Where are you, Orestes? What are you thinking about?

FIRST FURY. Orestes, there's just time. Don't listen to your sister.

SECOND FURY. Don't listen to her. We have learned what life holds for you, it's wonderful!

THIRD FURY. Just by chance. As we grew up during the night.

SECOND FURY. We're not saying anything about love to you, does that seem strange?

FIRST FURY. She's going to spoil everything with her poison.

THIRD FURY. Her poison of *truth*, the only one that has no antidote.

FIRST FURY. You're right. We know what you're thinking. Royalty is magnificent, Orestes: young girls in the royal parks, feeding bread to the swans, King Orestes' miniature hanging on their blouses—they kiss it secretly; soldiers going to war, the women on the roofs, the sky like a veil over them, a white horse prancing to music; the return from war, the king's face looking like the face of a god, just because he's chilly or hungry or a little frightened, or pitying his people. If the truth is going to spoil all that, let it perish!

SECOND FURY. You're right. And love is magnificent. Orestes! Lovers, it seems, will never part. They're never separated but they rush back to each other, to clasp hands. Or if they go away, they find each other face to face again immediately. The earth is round for the sake of lovers. Everywhere I run into him I love, though he's not yet alive. All this Electra wants to take from you, and from us too, with her Truth. We want to love. Flee Electra!

ELECTRA. Orestes!

ORESTES. I'm awake, sister.

ELECTRA. Wake from your awakening. Don' listen to these girls.

ORESTES. Are you sure they aren't right? Are you sure that it's not the worst kind of arrogance for a human being to try to retrace his steps? Why not take the first road and go forward, at random? Trust yourself to me. At this moment I can see so clearly the track of the game called happiness.

ELECTRA. Alas! That's not what we're hunting today.

ORESTES. The only thing that's important is not to leave each other. Let's go to Thessaly. You'll see my house, covered with roses and jasmin.

ELECTRA. Darling Orestes, you've saved me from the gardener not just to give me to flowers!

ORESTES. Be persuaded! Let's slip out of the trap which will soon catch us! Let's rejoice that we woke up before it did! Come!

FIRST FURY. It's awake! Look at its eyes!

THIRD FURY. You're right. The spring is wonderful, Orestes. When you can see over the hedges only the moving backs of the beasts grazing in the new grass, and the donkey's head looking at you over them. That donkey's head would look funny if you murdered your uncle. Pretty funny, a donkey looking at you when your hands are red with your uncle's blood—

ORESTES. What's she saying?

THIRD FURY. Talk on about the spring! The buttery mould that floats on the watercress in the brooks—you'll see what a comfort that will be for a man who kills his mother. Spread your butter that day with a knife, even if it's not the knife that killed your mother, and you'll see!

ORESTES. Help. Electra!

ELECTRA. So! You're like all men, Orestes! The least little flattery relaxes them, the slightest breath captivates them. Help you? I know what you'd like me to say.

ORESTES. Then tell me.

ELECTRA. That on the whole human beings are good, that life, too, after all, is good.

ORESTES. Isn't that true?

ELECTRA. That it's not a bad fate to be young, handsome, and a prince, to have a young sister who's a princess. That it's enough to leave men alone in their mean, vain business—not lancing human ulcers, but living for the beauty of the earth.

ORESTES. Isn't that what you're telling me?

ELECTRA. No! I'm telling you our mother has a lover.

ORESTES. You lie! That's impossible.

FIRST FURY. She's a widow. She has the right.

ELECTRA. I'm telling you our father was murdered.

ORESTES. Agamemnon! Murdered!

ELECTRA. Stabbed, by assassins.

SECOND FURY. Seven years ago. It's ancient history.

ORESTES. You knew that and let me sleep all night!

ELECTRA. I didn't know it. It's the night's gift to me. These truths were tossed to me by the night. Now I know how prophetesses work. They hold their brother close to their heart through one night.

ORESTES. Our father killed! Who told you?

ELECTRA. He himself.

ORESTES. He spoke to you before he died?

ELECTRA. Dead, he spoke to me. The very day of his death, but it's taken seven years for his word to reach me.

ORESTES. He appeared to you?

ELECTRA. No. His corpse appeared to me last night, looking like him the day he was murdered, but illuminated; I just had to read. There was a fold of his garment which said, I'm not a fold of death but of murder. And on his shoe there was a buckle which repeated, I'm not an accidental buckle but a criminal buckle. And on his eyelid there was a wrinkle which said, I didn't see death, I saw regicides.

ORESTES. And about our mother, who told you that?

ELECTRA. She herself, herself again.

ORESTES. She confessed?

ELECTRA. No. I saw her dead. Her body betrayed her. There's no possible doubt. Her eyebrow was the eyebrow of a dead woman who'd had a lover.

ORESTES. Who is this lover? Who is this murderer?

ELECTRA. I've waked you so you can find out. Let's hope they're both the same, then you'll have to strike just one blow.

ORESTES. Girls, I think you'll have to clear out. My sister presents me as I wake with a harlot queen and a murdered king . . . my parents.

FIRST FURY. That's not too bad. Add nothing more.

ELECTRA. Forgive me, Orestes.

SECOND FURY. Now she's excusing herself.

THIRD FURY. I'm killing you, but excuse it, please.

BEGGAR. She's wrong to excuse herself. This is the kind of awakening we generally reserve for our wives and sisters. They seem to be made for that.

ELECTRA. They are made just for that. Wives, sisters-in-law, mothers-in-law, they're the ones to shake up the men who, barely awake, see nothing but purple and gold, till the women give them, with their coffee and hot water, a hatred of injustice and a scorn for small joys.

ORESTES. Forgive me, Electra!

SECOND FURY. It's his turn to beg pardon. Aren't they polite in this family!

FIRST FURY. They take off their heads and bow to each other.

ELECTRA. And they watch for their waking. For men put on the armor of happiness if they sleep no more than five minutes: and with it satisfaction, indifference, generosity,

appetite. And a spot of sunlight reconciles them to all blood
spots. And a bird song to all lies. But the women are there,
all of them, worn by insomnia, with jealousy, envy, love,
memory and truth. Are you awake, Orestes?

FIRST FURY. And we'll be as old as he in an hour! Let's hope
heaven makes us different!

ORESTES. I believe I'm waking up.

BEGGAR. Here comes our mother, children.

ORESTES. Where's my sword?

ELECTRA. Bravo! That's what I call a good awakening. Take up
your sword. Take up your hatred. Take up your strength.

SCENE 4   *The same.* CLYTEMNESTRA.

CLYTEMNESTRA. Their mother appears. And they turn into
statues.

ELECTRA. Orphans, rather.

CLYTEMNESTRA. I'm not going to listen to an insolent daughter
any longer.

ELECTRA. Listen to your son.

ORESTES. Who is it, mother? Confess.

CLYTEMNESTRA. What kind of children are you, turning our
meeting into a melodrama? Leave me, or I'll call.

ELECTRA. Whom will you call? Him?

ORESTES. You struggle too much, mother.

BEGGAR. Be careful, Orestes. An innocent creature struggles as
much as a guilty.

CLYTEMNESTRA. Creature? What kind of creature am I for my
children? Speak, Orestes, speak!

ORESTES. I don't dare.

CLYTEMNESTRA. Electra, then, She'll dare.

ELECTRA. Who is it, mother?

CLYTEMNESTRA. Of whom, of what are you speaking?

ORESTES. Mother, it is true you have . . . ?

ELECTRA. Don't specify, Orestes. Just ask who it is. There's a name somewhere in her. However you ask your question, the name will come out.

ORESTES. Mother, is it true you have a lover?

CLYTEMNESTRA. That's your question too, Electra?

ELECTRA. It might be put that way.

CLYTEMNESTRA. My son and daughter ask if I have a lover?

ELECTRA. Your husband can't ask it now.

CLYTEMNESTRA. The gods would blush to hear you.

ELECTRA. That would surprise me. They've not been doing much blushing lately.

CLYTEMNESTRA. I have no lover. But watch your step. All the evil in the world is caused by the so-called pure people trying to dig up secrets and bring them to light.

ELECTRA. Rottenness is born of sunshine, I grant that.

CLYTEMNESTRA. I have no lover, I couldn't have a lover if I wanted one. But take care. Curious people have had no luck in our family: they tracked down a theft and found a sacrilege; they carried on a love affair and ran into an incest. You'll not find out I have a lover, because I haven't, but you'll stumble on a stone which will be fatal to your sisters and yourselves.

ELECTRA. Who is your lover?

ORESTES. Electra, at least listen to her.

CLYTEMNESTRA. I have no lover. But who would call it a crime if I had?

ORESTES. Oh, mother, you're a queen.

CLYTEMNESTRA. The world is not old and day is just dawning. But it would take us at least till twilight to recite the list of queens who've had lovers.

ORESTES. Mother, please! Fight on this way. Convince us. If this struggle restores a queen to us, it's blessed, everything is restored.

ELECTRA. Don't you see you're giving her weapons, Orestes?

CLYTEMNESTRA. That's enough. Orestes, leave me alone with Electra, will you?

ORESTES. Must I, sister?

ELECTRA. Yes, Yes. Wait there, under the arch. And run back to me as soon as I call, Orestes. Run as fast as you can. It will mean I know all.

SCENE 5   CLYTEMNESTRA. ELECTRA.
The BEGGAR.

CLYTEMNESTRA. Help me, Electra!

ELECTRA. Help you to what? To tell the truth or to lie?

CLYTEMNESTRA. Protect me.

ELECTRA. It's the first time you stoop to your daughter, mother. You must be afraid.

CLYTEMNESTRA. I'm afraid of Orestes.

ELECTRA. You lie. You're not the least afraid of Orestes. You see what he is: passionate, changeable, weak—still dreaming of an idyl in the Atrides' family. It's I you're afraid of, it's for me you're playing this game, the meaning of which still escapes me. You have a lover, haven't you? Who is he?

CLYTEMNESTRA. He knows nothing. And he's not in question.

ELECTRA. He doesn't know he's your lover?

CLYTEMNESTRA. Stop acting like a judge, Electra. Stop this pursuit. After all, you're my daughter.

ELECTRA. After all! Exactly after all! That's why I'm questioning you.

CLYTEMNESTRA. Then stop being my daughter. Stop hating me. Just be what I look for in you—a woman. Take up my cause, it's yours. Defend yourself by defending me.

ELECTRA. I'm not a member of the Women's Association, and someone other than you would have to recruit me.

CLYTEMNESTRA. You're wrong. If you betray your equal in body, in misfortune, you're the first one Orestes will loathe. Scandal always strikes back at the people who start it. What good does it do you to bespatter all women by bespattering me? In Orestes' eyes you'll sully all the qualities you get from me.

ELECTRA. I'm not like you in anything. I never look in my mirror except to be certain of that piece of luck. All the shiny marble, all the fountains of the palace have cried out to me, your own face cries it: Electra's nose is not the least like Clytemnestra's nose. My forehead is my own. My mouth's my own. And I have no lover.

CLYTEMNESTRA. Listen! I have no lover. I'm in love.

ELECTRA. Don't try that trick. You throw love at me the way drivers pursued by wolves throw them a dog. Dog meat is not my food.

CLYTEMNESTRA. We're women, Electra. We have a right to love.

ELECTRA. There are many rights in the sisterhood of women. I know. If you pay the entrance fee, which is steep, which means admission only for weak, lying, base women, you have a right to be weak, lying, and base. Unfortunately women are strong, loyal, and noble, so you're wrong. You had the right to love my father only. Did you? On your wedding night, did you love him?

CLYTEMNESTRA. What are you driving at? Do you want me to say that your birth owes nothing to love, that you were conceived in indifference? Be satisfied. Not everyone can be like your Aunt Leda, and lay eggs. You never spoke in me. We were indifferent to each other from the first. You didn't even cause me pain at your birth. You were small and withdrawn, your lips tight. When you were a year old, your lips were sealed, so "mother" wouldn't be your first word. Neither of us cried that day. We've never wept together.

ELECTRA. Weeping parties don't interest me.

CLYTEMNESTRA. You'll weep soon, perhaps over me.

ELECTRA. Eyes can weep by themselves. That's what they're there for.

CLYTEMNESTRA. Yes, even yours, which look like two stones. Some day tears will drown them.

ELECTRA. I hope that day comes! But why are you trying to hold me by cold words instead of by love?

CLYTEMNESTRA. So you'll understand I have a right to love. So you'll know that my whole life has been as hard as my daughter from her very first day. Since my marriage I've never been alone, never at peace. I never went to the forest except for festivals. No rest, even for my body which was covered every day by golden robes and at night by a king. Always mistrust, even of things, animals, plants. I often said to myself, as I looked at cross, silent lindens, smelling like a wet nurse: "They're like Electra's head, the day she was born." No queen has ever suffered so deeply the fate of queens, a husband's absence, a son's suspicions, a daughter's hatred. What had I left?

ELECTRA. What the others had left: waiting.

CLYTEMNESTRA. Waiting, for what? Waiting is horrible.

ELECTRA. For her who has caught you today, perhaps.

CLYTEMNESTRA. Can you tell me what you're waiting for?

ELECTRA. I no longer wait. For ten years I've waited—for my father. Waiting is the only happiness in the world.

CLYTEMNESTRA. A virgin's happiness, a solitary happiness.

ELECTRA. You think so? Except for you and the men, everything in the palace awaited my father with me, everything was party to my waiting. It began in the morning with my early walk under the lindens which hate you, which waited for my father with an eagerness they tried in vain to repress; they were sorry to live by the year and not by the decade, ashamed every spring that they couldn't hold back their flowers and perfume, that they grew weak with me over his absence. It went on till noon when I went to the brook that was the luckiest of us all, for it awaited my father as it ran to the river that ran to the sea. And in the evening, when I wasn't strong enough to wait near his dogs and his horses, poor short-lived beasts, that couldn't wait for centuries, I took refuge with the columns and the statues. I modeled myself on them. I waited in the moonlight for hours, motionless like them, without thought, lifeless. I awaited him with a stony heart—marble, alabaster, onyx—though it was beating, shattering my breast. Where would I be if there weren't still hours to wait, to wait for the past, wait for him still!

CLYTEMNESTRA. I'm no waiting. I love.

ELECTRA. Everything goes well with you now?

CLYTEMNESTRA. Very well.

ELECTRA. Flowers obey you? Birds talk to you?

CLYTEMNESTRA. Yes, your lindens signal to me.

ELECTRA. Quite likely. You've robbed me of everything in life.

CLYTEMNESTRA. Fall in love. We'll share.

ELECTRA. Share love with you?! Are you offering to share your lover with me? Who is he?

CLYTEMNESTRA. Electra, have pity! I'll tell you his name, though it will make you blush. But wait a few days. What good will a scandal do you? Think of your brother. Can you imagine the Argives letting Orestes succeed an unworthy mother?

ELECTRA. An unworthy mother? What are you getting at with this confession? What time do you want to gain? What trap are you setting for me? What brood are you hoping to save, limping off like a partridge, toward love and unworthiness?

CLYTEMNESTRA. Spare me public disgrace! Why do you force me to confess I love someone below me in rank?

ELECTRA. Some little nameless lieutenant?

CLYTEMNESTRA. Yes.

ELECTRA. You're lying. If your lover were some little nameless inglorious officer, or a bathhouse attendant, or a groom, you'd love him. But you're not in love, you've never loved. Who is it? Why do you refuse to name him, as you'd refuse a key? What piece of furniture are you afraid of opening with that name?

CLYTEMNESTRA. Something of my own, my love.

ELECTRA. Tell me the name of your lover, and I'll tell you if you love. And we'll keep it to ourselves forever.

CLYTEMNESTRA. Never!

ELECTRA. You see! It's not your lover but your secret that you're hiding from me. You're afraid his name would give me the one proof I'm lacking in my pursuit.

CLYTEMNESTRA. What proof? You're mad.

ELECTRA. The proof of the crime. Everything tells me, mother, that you committed it. But what I don't yet see, what you must tell me, is why you committed it. I've tried all the keys, as you say. Not one opens it—yet. Not love. You love nothing. Not ambition. You scoff at queenship. Not anger. You're deliberate, calculating. But our lover's name would clear up everything, tell us everything, wouldn't it? Who do you love? Who is he?

SCENE 6 *The same.* AGATHA, *pursued
by the* PRESIDENT.

PRESIDENT. Who is he? Who do you love?

AGATHA. I hate you.

PRESIDENT. Who is it?

AGATHA. I tell you that's enough. Enough lies. Electra's right.
I'm on her side. Thanks, Electra, you give me life.

PRESIDENT. What is this song?

AGATHA. Wives' song. You'll soon know it.

PRESIDENT. So, she's going to sing!

AGATHA. Yes, we're all here, with our unsatisfactory husbands
or our widowhood. And we all kill ourselves, trying to make
life and death pleasant. And if they eat cooked lettuce they
have to have salt and a smile with it. And if they smoke
we have to light their horrid cigars with the flame of our
hearts.

PRESIDENT. Who are you talking about? I never ate cooked lettuce.

AGATHA. Sorrel, if you prefer.

PRESIDENT. Your lover doesn't eat sorrel or smoke cigars?

AGATHA. The sorrel my lover eats turns into ambrosia, and I
lick up what's left. And everything soiled by my husband's
touch is purified by his hands or lips. I myself! God knows!

ELECTRA. I've found out, mother, I've found out!

PRESIDENT. Collect yourself, Agatha.

AGATHA. Precisely. I've done just that. Twenty-four hours a day
we kill ourselves to please someone whose displeasure is our
only joy, for a husband whose absence is our only delight, for
the vanity of the only man who humiliates us daily by show-

ing us his toes and his shirt tails. And he has the gall to reproach us for stealing from him one hour a week of this hell! But, sure enough, he's right. When this wonderful hour comes, we don't greet it with a dead hand!

PRESIDENT. Electra, this is your work. This very morning she kissed me!

AGATHA. I'm pretty and he's ugly. I'm young and he's old. I'm bright and he's stupid. I have a soul and he hasn't. Yet he has everything. At least he has me. And I have nothing, though I have him! Until this morning, I gave everything and had to seem grateful. Why? I black his shoes. Why? I brush off his dandruff. Why? I make his coffee. Why? The truth might be that I'm poisoning him, rubbing his collar with pitch and ashes. Of course you can understand about the shoes. I spit on them. I spit on you. But it's all over, finished. Welcome, truth! Electra has given me her courage. I'm through. I'd as soon die.

BEGGAR. Don't these wives sing well!

PRESIDENT. Who is it?

ELECTRA. Listen, mother! Listen to yourself. It's you talking.

AGATHA. Who is it? All husbands think it's just one person.

PRESIDENT. Lovers? You have lovers?

AGATHA. They think we deceive them only with lovers. Of course we have lovers, too. But we deceive you with everything. When I wake and my hand slips along the wooden bedstead, that's my first adultery. Let's use your word for once, adultery. How often, when I'm wakeful, I've caressed that wood—olive wood, so soft! What a pretty name! I start when I hear an olive tree mentioned in the street—I hear my lover's name! And my second adultery is when I open my eyes and see daylight through the blinds. And my third, when my foot touches the bathwater and when I jump in. I betray you with my fingers, with my eyes, with the soles of my feet. When I look at you, I deceive you. When I listen to you and pretend to admire you in court, I'm deceiving

you. Kill the olive trees, the pigeons, the five year old children, boys and girls, and water and earth and fire! Kill this
beggar. You're betrayed by all of them.

BEGGAR. Thanks!

PRESIDENT. And yesterday this woman was still pouring my tea!
And finding it too cool, having the water boiled again! You're
all pleased, aren't you? This little scandal within a great one
can't displease you!

BEGGAR. No. It's like the squirrel in a big wheel. It gives the
right rhythm.

PRESIDENT. And this scene before the queen herself. You'll pardon it?

ELECTRA. The queen envies Agatha. The queen would give her
live to have the chance Agatha has today. Who is it, mother?

BEGGAR. Sure! Don't let anything distract you, president. It's
almost a minute since you asked her who it is.

PRESIDENT. Who is it?

AGATHA. I've told you, Everybody. Everything.

PRESIDENT. It's enough to drive me to suicide, to make me bash
my head against the wall.

AGATHA. Don't stop on my account. The Mycenean wall is solid.

PRESIDENT. Is he young? Or old?

AGATHA. A lover's age—between 16 and 80.

PRESIDENT. And she thinks she's disgracing me by insulting me!
Your insults only hurt yourself, abandoned woman!

AGATHA. I know, I know. Outrage is called majesty. In the
streets the most respectable people slip on dung.

PRESIDENT. At last you'll find out who I am! Whoever your
lovers are, I'll kill the first one I find here.

AGATHA. The first one you find here? You choose the place
badly.

PRESIDENT. I'll make him kneel down and kiss the marble.

AGATHA. You'll see how he'll kiss the marble when he comes into this court in a minute and sits on the throne.

PRESIDENT. Wretch, what are you saying?

AGATHA. I'm saying that at present I have two lovers, and one is Aegisthus.

CLYTEMNESTRA. Liar!

AGATHA. What! She too!

ELECTRA. You too, mother?

BEGGAR. That's funny. I'd have thought, if Aegisthus had a liking, it was for Electra.

PAGE, *announcing.* Aegisthus!

ELECTRA. At last!

THE FURIES. Aegisthus!

AEGISTHUS *comes in. Much more majestic and calm than in the first act. Far above him, a bird hovers in the air.*

SCENE 7 *The same.* AEGISTHUS.
A CAPTAIN. SOLDIERS.

AEGISTHUS. Electra is here. . . . Thanks, Electra! I'll stop here, Captain. Headquarters are here.

CLYTEMNESTRA. I, too, am here.

AEGISTHUS. I'm glad. Welcome, queen!

PRESIDENT. I too, Aegisthus!

AEGISTHUS. Good, president. I need your help.

PRESIDENT. And now he insults us!

AEGISTHUS. What's the matter with you all, that you stare at me so?

BEGGAR. What's the matter is that the queen is waiting for a perjurer, Electra for an infidel, Agatha for a faithless lover. He's
more humble, he's waiting for the man who seduced his
wife. They're all waiting for you, but it's not you that's come!

AEGISTHUS. They have no luck, have they, beggar?

BEGGAR. No, they have no luck. Waiting for a rascal, they see
a king enter! I don't care about the others, but for our little
Electra, the situation is complicated.

AEGISTHUS. You think so? I think not.

BEGGAR. I knew it would happen. I told you so yesterday. I
knew the king would reveal himself in you. He has your
strength and your years. He finds the right moment. Electra
is near. That might have involved a bloody act. But you've
revealed yourself. Fine for Greece! But not so gay for the
family.

CLYTEMNESTRA. What do these riddles mean? What are you
talking about?

BEGGAR. Lucky for us, too! Since there has to be *some* kind of
meeting, better let Electra meet nobility than wickedness.
How did you get this way, Aegisthus?

AEGISTHUS, *looking at* ELECTRA. Electra is here! I knew I'd find
her looking toward me, her statuesque head, her eyes which
see only when the lids are closed, deaf to human speech.

CLYTEMNESTRA. Listen to me, Aegisthus!

PRESIDENT. How well you choose your lovers, Agatha! What
impudence!

CAPTAIN. Aegisthus, there's no time!

AEGISTHUS. Your ears are ornaments, aren't they, Electra? Mere
ornaments. . . . The gods said, we gave her hands so she'd
not touch, eyes so she'd be seen, we can't let her head be
without ears! People would soon discover that she hears only
us. . . . Tell me, what would we hear if we placed our ears
near hers? What roaring! And where from?

CLYTEMNESTRA. Are you mad? Take care! Electra's ears do hear you.

PRESIDENT. They blush for it.

AEGISTHUS. They hear me. I'm sure of that. Since what happened to me just now in the outskirts of Argos, my words come from beyond myself. And I know she sees me too, she's the only one who does see me. The only one to guess what I've become since that moment.

CLYTEMNESTRA. You're talking to your worst enemy, Aegisthus!

AEGISTHUS. She knows why I galloped toward the city from the mountains. Electra, you'd have thought my horse understood. He was beautiful, that light chestnut, charging toward Electra, followed by the thunder of the squadron, in which the knowledge of rushing toward Electra grew less, from the white stallions of the trumpeters to the piebald mares of the rear guard. Don't be surprised if my horse sticks his head between the pillars, neighing to you. He knew that I was strangling, with your name in my mouth like a golden stopper. I had to shout your name, and to you—shall I shout it, Electra?

CLYTEMNESTRA. Stop this outrageous behavior, Aegisthus.

CAPTAIN. Aegisthus! The city is in danger!

AEGISTHUS. True! Pardon me! Where are they now, Captain?

CAPTAIN. You can see their lances coming over the hills. I've never seen a harvest grow so fast. Nor so thick. There are thousands of them.

AEGISTHUS. The cavalry's no use against them?

CAPTAIN. Repulsed, prisoners taken.

CLYTEMNESTRA. What's happening, Aegisthus?

CAPTAIN. The Corinthians are surrounding us, no declaration of war, no reason for it. Their regiments entered our territory last night. The suburbs are on fire already.

AEGISTHUS. What do the prisoners say?

CAPTAIN. Their orders are to leave no stone standing in Argos.

CLYTEMNESTRA. Show yourself, Aegisthus, and they'll flee!

AEGISTHUS. I fear, queen, that wouldn't be enough.

CAPTAIN. They have friends in the city. The reserves of pitch have been stolen, so the middle-class quarters can be burned. Gangs of beggars are gathering around the markets ready to start pillaging.

CLYTEMNESTRA. If the guard is loyal, what is there to fear?

CAPTAIN. The guard is ready to fight. But they're muttering. You know, they've never willingly obeyed a woman. The city's the same way. They both demand a king, a man.

AEGISTHUS. They're right. They shall have one.

PRESIDENT. Whoever wants to be king of Argos, Aegisthus, must first kill Clytemnestra.

BEGGAR. Or simply marry her.

PRESIDENT. Never!

AEGISTHUS. Why, never? The queen can't deny that's the only way to save Argos. I don't doubt she'll consent. Captain, tell the guard the wedding has this moment taken place. Keep me informed of events. I'll wait here for your bulletins. And do you, president, go meet the rioters and tell them this news most enthusiastically.

PREIDENT. Never! I must first speak to you, man to man, no matter what happens.

AEGISTHUS. No matter if Argos falls, if war comes? You're outrageous.

PRESIDENT. My honor, the honor of all Greek judges, is at stake.

BEGGAR. If Greek justice lies in Agatha's lap, that's just what it deserves. Don't hinder us at such a time. Look at Agatha, see if she cares for the honor of Greek judges, with her nose in the air.

PRESIDENT. Her nose in the air! Agatha is your nose in the air?

AGATHA. My nose *is* in the air. I'm looking at that bird hovering over Aegisthus.

PRESIDENT. Lower it!

AEGISTHUS. Queen, I'm waiting for your reply.

CLYTEMNESTRA. A bird? What is that bird? Get from under that bird, Aegisthus.

AEGISTHUS. Why? He's not left me since sunrise. He must have his reasons. My horse noticed him first. He kicked without any provocation. I looked all around and then up there. He was kicking at that bird, and plunging and rearing. It's exactly above me, isn't it, beggar?

BEGGAR. Exactly above. If you were a thousand feet tall, your head would be there.

AEGISTHUS. Like a mark on a page, isn't it? A black mark.

BEGGAR. Yes, at the moment you're the most marked man in Greece. We'll have to find out whether the mark is over the word "human" or the word "mortal."

CLYTEMNESTRA. I don't like this hovering bird. What is it? A kite or an eagle?

BEGGAR. He's too high up. I might recognize him by his shadow, but so high up we can't see it, it's lost.

CAPTAIN, *returning*. The guards are delighted, Aegisthus. They're joyfully getting ready to fight. They're waiting for you to appear on the balcony with the queen, so they can cheer you.

AEGISTHUS. My oath, and I'll go.

PRESIDENT. Electra, help me! Why should this rake teach us courage?

BEGGAR. Why? Listen! . . .

AEGISTHUS. Oh, Heavenly Powers, since I must pray to you on the eve of battle, I thank you for the gift of this hill which

overlooks Argos the moment the fog evaporates. I dis-
mounted, weary from the night patrol, I leant against the
battlement, and suddenly I saw Argos as I had never before
seen it—new, rebuilt by me; you have given it to me. You've
given it all to me, its towers, its bridges, the smoke from its
farm machines, the flying pigeons, its first movements, the
grinding of its locks, its first cry. Everything in your gift has
equal value, Electra, the sunrise over Argos, the last lantern
in the city, the temple, the ruins, the lake, the tanneries. And
the gift is forever! This morning I was given my city for
eternity, as a mother her child, and in agony I asked myself
if the gift were not even greater, if you hadn't given me far
more than Argos. In the morning God never counts his gifts:
he might even have given me the whole world. That would
have been dreadful. I should have felt a despair like that of
a man who expects a diamond on his birthday and is given
the sun. Electra, you see my anxiety! I anxiously stretched
my foot and my thoughts beyond Argos. What joy! I had not
been given the Orient, its plagues, earthquakes, famines: I
realized that with a smile. My thirst was not like that of men
who quench it in the great, warm rivers flowing through the
desert, but, I discovered, I could quench it at an icy spring.
And nothing in Africa is mine! Negresses can pound millet
at the doors of their huts, the jaguar drive his claws into the
crocodile's flank, not a drop of their soup or their blood is
mine. I'm as happy over the gifts not given me as over the
gift of Argos. In a fit of generosity the Gods have not given
me Athens or Olympia or Mycenae. What joy! They have
given me the Argive cattle markets, not the treasures of
Corinth, the short noses of the Argive girls, not the nose of
Athena; the wrinkled prune of Argos, not the golden fig of
Thebes! That's what they gave me this morning; me, the
wastrel, the parasite, the knave, a country where I feel myself pure, strong, perfect; a fatherland; a country where, instead of being a slave, I am king, where I swear to live and
die—you hear me, judge—a country I swear to save.

PRESIDENT. I rely on you only, Electra!

ELECTRA. Rely on me. No one should save his fatherland with
impure hands.

BEGGAR. A coronation purifies everything.

ELECTRA. Who crowned you? Who witnessed your coronation?

BEGGAR. Can't you guess? Just what he begged of you. For the first time he sees you in your truth and power. The thought has suddenly dawned on him that Electra is included in this gift of Argos.

AEGISTHUS. Everything on my way consecrated me, Electra. As I galloped I heard the trees, the children, the streams shout to me: I was king. But the holy oil was lacking. I was a coward yesterday. A rabbit, whose trembling ears showed over a furrow, gave me courage. I was a hypocrite. A fox crossed the road, his eyes crafty, and I became frank. And a couple of magpies gave me independence, an ant hill, generosity. And if I hurried back to you, Electra, it was because you are the only creature who can give me her very being.

ELECTRA. And that is——?

AEGISTHUS. I think it is rather like duty.

ELECTRA. My duty is certainly the mortal enemy of yours. You shall not marry Clytemnestra.

PRESIDENT. You shall not marry her.

CLYTEMNESTRA. And why shan't we marry? Why should we sacrifice our lives to ungrateful children? Yes, I love Aegisthus. For ten years I've loved Aegisthus. For ten years I've postponed this marriage for your sake, Electra, and in memory of your father. Now you force us to it. Thanks! But not under that bird. That bird annoys me. As soon as the bird flies away. I consent.

AEGISTHUS. Don't worry, Queen. I'm not marrying you in order to create new lies. I don't know if I still love you, and the whole city doubts that you ever loved me. For ten years our liaison has dragged along between indifference and neglect. But marriage is the only way to cast a little truth over our past lies, and it will safeguard Argos. It must take place, this very hour.

ELECTRA. I don't believe it will take place.

PRESIDENT. Bravo!

AEGISTHUS. Will you be quiet? Who are you in Argos? A deceived husband or the chief justice?

PRESIDENT. Both, of course.

AEGISTHUS. Then choose. I have no choice. Choose between duty and prison. Time is short.

PRESIDENT. You took Agatha from me.

AEGISTHUS. I'm not the one who took Agatha.

PRESIDENT. Weren't you given all the deceived husbands in Argos this morning?

BEGGAR. Yes. But he's not the man who deceived them.

PRESIDENT. I understand. The new king forgets the outrages he committed as regent.

BEGGAR. Agatha looks like a rose. Outrages make her rosy?

AEGISTHUS. A king begs you to pardon today the insult a rake inflicted on you yesterday. That must satisfy you. Listen to my orders. Go quickly to your courtroom, try the rebels, and be severe with them.

AGATHA. Be severe. I have a little lover among them.

PRESIDENT. Will you stop looking at that bird? You irritate me.

AGATHA. I'm sorry. It's the only thing in the world that interests me.

PRESIDENT. Idiot! What will you do when it goes away?

AGATHA. That's what I'm wondering.

AEGISTHUS. Are you disobeying me, president? Don't you hear those shouts?

PRESIDENT. I'll not go. I'll help Electra prevent your marriage.

ELECTRA. I don't need your help, president. Your role ended

when Agatha gave me the key to everything. Thanks, Agatha!

CLYTEMNESTRA. What key?

AEGISTHUS. Come, queen.

CLYTEMNESTRA. What key did she give you? What new quarrel are you trying to start?

ELECTRA. You hated my father! Oh, everything is clear in the light of Agatha's lamp.

CLYTEMNESTRA. There she goes again! Protect me, Aegisthus!

ELECTRA. How you envied Agatha just now! What joy to shout out your hatred to the husband you hate! That joy was not allowed you, mother. Never in your life will you have it. Till the day of his death he believed you admired and adored him. At banquets and festivals I've often seen your face harden, your lips move soundlessly, because you wanted to cry out you hated him. You wanted passers-by, guests, the servant pouring wine, the detective guarding the silver, to hear you, didn't you? Poor mother, you could never go to the country alone to cry out to the bushes! All the bushes say you adored him!

CLYTEMNESTRA. Listen, Electra!

ELECTRA. That's right, mother, cry it out to me! Though he's not here, I'm his substitute. Cry to me! That will do you as much good as to say it to him. You're not going to die without letting him know you hated him.

CLYTEMNESTRA. Come, Aegisthus! Never mind the bird!

ELECTRA. If you take one step, mother, I'll call.

AEGISTHUS. Whom will you call, Electra? Is there anyone in the world who can take from us the right to save our city?

ELECTRA. Save our city from hypocrisy, from corruption? There are thousands. The purest, the handsomest, the youngest is here, in this courtyard. If Clytemnestra takes a step, I'll call.

CLYTEMNESTRA. Come, Aegisthus!

ELECTRA. Orestes! Orestes!

The EUMENIDES *appear and bar the way.*

FIRST FURY. Poor girl! You're too naive! Do you think we'll let Orestes run around sword in hand? Accidents happen too quickly in this palace. We've gagged him and chained him up.

ELECTRA. That's not true! Orestes! Orestes!

SECOND FURY. You, too, it will happen to you.

AEGISTHUS. Electra, dear Electra, listen to me. I want to persuade you.

CLYTEMNESTRA. You're losing precious time, Aegisthus.

AEGISTHUS. I'm coming! Electra, I know you're the only one who understands what I am today. Help me! Let me tell you why you must help me!

CLYTEMNESTRA. What is this craze to explain, to argue? Are we roosters in this courtyard or human beings. Do we have to go on explaining till our eyes are gouged out? Must the three of us be carried off by force, to separate us?

PRESIDENT. I think that's the only way, queen.

CAPTAIN. I beseech you, Aegisthus! Hurry!

BEGGAR. Don't you understand? Aegisthus must settle once and for all the business about Agamemnon—Clytemnestra—Electra. Then he'll come.

CAPTAIN. In five minutes it will be too late.

BEGGAR. We'll all do our bit. It will be settled in five minutes.

AEGISTHUS. Take this man away.

Guards take out the PRESIDENT. *All the spectators leave. Silence.*

AEGISTHUS. Now, Electra, what do you want?

SCENE 8 ELECTRA. CLYTEMNESTRA.
AEGISTHUS. BEGGAR.

ELECTRA. She's not late, Aegisthus. She just won't come.

AEGISTHUS. Of whom are you speaking?

ELECTRA. Of her you're waiting for. The messenger of the gods. If divine justice absolves Aegisthus because he loves his city, and is marrying Clytemnestra because he despises lies and wants to save the middle class and the rich, this is the moment for her to appear before the two of you, bearing her diplomas and her laurels. But she'll not come.

AEGISTHUS. You know she has come. This morning's sunbeam on my head was she.

ELECTRA. That was a morning beam. Every scurvy child thinks he's a king when a morning sunbeam touches him.

AEGISTHUS. Do you doubt my sincerity?

ELECTRA. I don't doubt it. I recognize in it the hypocrisy and malice of the gods. They change a parasite into a just man, an adulterer into a husband, a usurper into a king. They thought my task not painful enough, so they made a figure of honor out of you, whom I despise! But there's one change they can't carry through! They can't transform a criminal into an innocent man. They bow to me there.

ELECTRA. You have an inkling. Listen to the small voice beneath your heroic soul. You'll understand.

AEGISTHUS. Who can explain what you're talking about?

CLYTEMNESTRA. Of whom *can* she talk? What has she always talked about her whole life long? Of a father she never knew.

ELECTRA. I? I never knew my father?

CLYTEMNESTRA. You touched a corpse, ice that had been your father. But not your father.

AEGISTHUS. Please, Clytemnestra! How can you quarrel at such a moment!

CLYTEMNESTRA. Everyone must have a turn in this debate. It's my turn now.

ELECTRA. For once you're right. We've come to the heart of the matter. If I'd not touched my living father, from whom would I have drawn my strength, my truth?

CLYTEMNESTRA. Precisely. But now you're talking wildly. I wonder if you ever kissed him. I took care he didn't lick my children.

ELECTRA. I never kissed my father?

CLYTEMNESTRA. Your father's dead body, perhaps, not your father.

AEGISTHUS. I beg you . . . !

ELECTRA. Ah, now I see why you're so firm as you face me. You thought me unarmed, you thought I'd never touched my father. What a mistake!

CLYTEMNESTRA. You're lying.

ELECTRA. The day my father came home you two waited for him a minute too long on the palace stairs, didn't you?

CLYTEMNESTRA. How do you know? You weren't there!

ELECTRA. I was holding him back. I was in his arms.

AEGISTHUS. Now listen, Electra . . .

ELECTRA. I'd waited in the crowd, mother. I rushed toward him. His escorts were frightened, they feared an attempt on his life. But he recognized me, smiled at me. He understood Electra's attempt, and, brave father, went to meet it. And I touched him.

CLYTEMNESTRA. You may have touched his leg armor, his horse, leather and hair!

ELECTRA. He got down, mother. I touched his hands with these fingers, his lips with these lips. I touched a skin you'd never touched, purified from you by ten years of absence.

AEGISTHUS. That's enough. She believes you!

ELECTRA. My cheek on his, I felt my father's warmth. Sometimes in summer the whole world is just as warm as my father. I faint from it. And I did hug him in these arms. I thought I was taking the measure of my love—it was also that of my vengeance. He freed himself, mounted his horse, more agile, more resplendent than before. Electra's attempt on his life was over. He was more alive, more golden, because of it. And I ran to the palace to see him again, but I was really running not toward him, but toward you, his murderers.

AEGISTHUS. Pull yourself together, Electra!

ELECTRA. Perhaps I am out of breath. I've reached my goal.

CLYTEMNESTRA. Rid us of this girl, Aegisthus. Give her back to the gardener. Or turn her over to her brother.

AEGISTHUS. Stop, Electra! Why, at the very moment that I see you, that I love you, when I'm at the point of understanding you—your scorn for abuses, your courage, your disinterestedness—why do you persist in fighting?

ELECTRA. I have only this moment.

AEGISTHUS. Don't you know Argos is in danger?

ELECTRA. We don't see the same dangers.

AEGISTHUS. Don't you know that if I marry Clytemnestra, the city will quiet down, the Atrides will be saved? If not, riots, conflagrations?

ELECTRA. Perhaps.

AEGISTHUS. Don't you know that I alone can defend the city against the Corinthians who are already at the gates? If not, pillage, massacre?

ELECTRA. Yes. You'd be victor.

AEGISTHUS. Yet you are obstinate! You ruin my work. And you sacrifice your family and your country to a dream!

ELECTRA. You're mocking me, Aegisthus! You pretend to know me yet you think I'm the kind to whom you can say, "If you lie and let other people lie, you'll have a prosperous country. If you hide your crimes, your country will be victorious." What is this poor country that you're all of a sudden placing between us and truth?

AEGISTHUS. Your country—Argos.

ELECTRA. You're wrong, Aegisthus. This morning, at the very hour you were given Argos, I also received a gift. I expected it, it had been promised me, but I still didn't know just what it would be. I had already been given a thousand gifts, which seemed incomplete, I couldn't see their appropriateness, but last night, near Orestes as he slept, I saw they were all one and the same gift. I'd been given the back of a truck driver, the smile of a laundress suddenly stopped in her work, watching the river. I'd been given a fat, naked little child, running across the street as his mother and the neighbors shouted to him, I'd been given the cry of a caged bird set free, and that of a mason I one day saw fall from a scaffold, his legs sprawling. I was given the water plant, resisting the current, fighting and dying; the sick young man, coughing, smiling and coughing; and my maid's red cheeks, puffed up each winter morning as she blows on the ashes of the fire. I too thouht I was given Argos, everything in Argos that is modest, tender, beautiful and wretched, but just now I found out that it's not so. I knew I'd been given all the servants' cheeks as they blow on wood or coal, all the laundresses' eyes, whether round or almond-shaped, all the falling masons, all the water plants which seem lost and grow again in streams or the sea. But Argos is only a speck in this universe, my country only a village in that country. All the light and the cries in sad faces, all the wrinkles and shadows on joyful faces, all the desires and despair on indifferent faces—these are my new country. And this morning, at dawn, when you were given Argos and its narrow borders, I also saw it as tremendous, and I heard its name, which is not to be spoken, but which is both tenderness and justice.

CLYTEMNESTRA. So that's Electra's motto! Tenderness! That's enough. Let's go.

AEGISTHUS. And you dare call this justice, that makes you burn your city, damn your family, you dare call this the justice of the gods?

ELECTRA. Far from it! In this country of mine, concern for justice is not the gods' business. The gods are only artists. A beautiful light from a conflagration, beautiful grass on a battle field, such is their justice. A magnificent repentance for a crime is the gods' verdict on your case. I don't accept it.

AEGISTHUS. Electra's justice consists in re-examining every sin, making every act irreparable?

ELECTRA. Oh, no! Some years, frost is justice for the trees, other times it's injustice. There are criminals we love, murderers we embrace. But when the crime is an assault on human dignity, infects a nation, corrupts its loyalty, then—no pardon is possible.

AEGISTHUS. Have you any idea what a nation is, Electra?

ELECTRA. When you see a huge face fill the horizon and you look straight at it with pure, brave eyes, that's a nation.

AEGISTHUS. You talk like a young girl, not like a king. There's also a huge body to rule and to nourish.

ELECTRA. I speak like a woman. There's a bright look to sift, to gild. And the only gold is truth. Those great eyes of truth, they're so beautiful, when you think of the real nations of the world.

AEGISTHUS. There are truths that can kill nations, Electra.

ELECTRA. Sometimes, the eyes of a dead nation shine forever. Pray Heaven that will be the fate of Argos! But since my father's death, since our people's happiness came to be founded on injustice and crime, since everyone has become a cowardly accomplice in murder and lies, the city can prosper, sing, dance, conquer, heaven may shine on it, but it will be only a cellar where eyes are useless. Infants suck the beast without seeing it.

AEGISTHUS. A scandal can only destroy it.

ELECTRA. Possibly. But I can no longer endure the dim, lustreless look in its eyes.

AEGISTHUS. That will cost thousands of glazed, dead eyes.

ELECTRA. That's the price. It's not too high.

AEGISTHUS. I must have this day. Give it to me. Your truth, if there is such a thing, will find a way to be revealed at a time more suitable for it.

ELECTRA. The revolt shows this day is made for it.

AEGISTHUS. I beseech you! Wait till tomorrow.

ELECTRA. No. This is the day for it. I've seen too many truths fade away because they were a day too late. I know young girls who waited one second before saying no to an ugly, vile thing, and could then say nothing but yes, yes. The beautiful and cruel thing about truth is that she is eternal, but is also like a flash of lightning.

AEGISTHUS. I must save the city and Greece.

ELECTRA. That's a small duty. I'm saving their soul.—You did kill him, didn't you?

CLYTEMNESTRA. How dare you say that, daughter? Everyone knows your father slipped on the tiles.

ELECTRA. Everyone knows it because you said so.

CLYTEMNESTRA. Crazy girl, he slipped and fell.

ELECTRA. He did not slip. For one obvious reason. Because my father never slipped.

CLYTEMNESTRA. How do you know?

ELECTRA. For eight years I've been asking the grooms, the maids, his escort in rain and hail. He *never* slipped.

CLYTEMNESTRA. The war came after.

ELECTRA. I've asked his fellow soldiers. He crossed Scamander without slipping. He took the battlements by assult without slipping. He never slipped, in water or in blood.

CLYTEMNESTRA. He was in haste that day. You had made him late.

ELECTRA. I'm the guilty one, am I? That's Clytemnestra's kind of truth. Your opinion, too, Aegisthus? Electra murdered Agamemnon?

CLYTEMNESTRA. The maids had soaped the tiles too well. I know. I almost slipped myself.

ELECTRA. Ah, you were in the bathroom, too, mother? Who held you up?

CLYTEMNESTRA. What's wrong in my being there?

ELECTRA. With Aegisthus, of course?

CLYTEMNESTRA. With Aegisthus. And we weren't alone. Leo, my counsellor, was there, wasn't he, Aegisthus?

ELECTRA. Leo, who died the next day?

CLYTEMNESTRA. Did he die the next day?

ELECTRA. Yes. Leo slipped, too. He lay down on his bed and in the morning was found dead. He found a way to slip into death—sleeping, not slipping! You had him killed, didn't you?

CLYTEMNESTRA. Aegisthus, defend me. I call on you for help.

ELECTRA. He can do nothing for you. You've come to the place where you must defend yourself.

CLYTEMNESTRA. Oh, God! Have I come to this? A mother! A queen!

ELECTRA. Where is "this"? Tell us where you've come.

CLYTEMNESTRA. Brought there by this heartless, joyless daughter! Happily, my little Chrysothemis loves flowers.

ELECTRA. Don't I love flowers?

CLYTEMNESTRA. To come to this! Through this idiotic journey called life, to come to this! I, who as a girl loved quiet, tending my pets, laughing at meal time, sewing! . . . I was so gentle, Aegisthus, I swear I was the gentlest. . . . There are still old men in my birthplace who call gentleness Clytemnestra.

ELECTRA. If they die today, they needn't change their symbol. If they die this morning!

CLYTEMNESTRA. To come to this! What injustice! Aegisthus, I spent my days in the meadows behind the palace. There were so many flowers I didn't have to stoop to pick them, I sat down. My dogs lay at my feet, the one who barked when Agamemnon came to take me away. I teased him with flowers and he ate them to please me. If I only had him! Anywhere else, if my husband had been a Persian, or an Egyptian, by now I'd be good, careless, gay! When I was young I had a voice, I trained birds! I might have been an Egyptian queen, singing gaily; I'd have had an Egyptian aviary! And we've come to this! What has this family, what have these walls done to us?

ELECTRA. Murderers! . . . These are wicked walls.

MESSENGER. My lord, they've forced an entrance. The postern gate gave way.

ELECTRA. All right. Let the walls crumble.

AEGISTHUS. Electra, heed my final word. I forgive everything,— your foolish fancies, your insults. But can't you see your country is dying?

ELECTRA. And I don't love flowers! Do you imagine flowers for a father's grave are picked sitting down?

CLYTEMNESTRA. Well, let this father return! Let him stop being dead! What nonsense, this absence, this silence! Let him come back, in his pomp, his vanity, his beard! That beard must have grown in the grave—a good thing, too!

ELECTRA. What are you saying?

AEGISTHUS. Electra, I promise that tomorrow, as soon as Argos is saved, the guilty, if there are any, shall disappear, for good and all. But don't be stubborn. You're gentle, Electra, in your heart you're gentle. Listen! The city will perish.

ELECTRA. Let it! I can already feel my love for a burnt and conquered Argos! No! My mother has begun to insult my father, let her finish!

CLYTEMNESTRA. Why are you talking about the guilty! What do you mean, Aegisthus?

ELECTRA. He's just told me in a word all that you deny!

CLYTEMNESTRA. And what do I deny?

ELECTRA. He's told me that you let Orestes fall, that I love flowers, and that my father didn't slip.

CLYTEMNESTRA. He did slip. I swear he slipped. If there's a truth in the world, let lightning from heaven show it to us. You'll see it revealed in all its brilliance.

AEGISTHUS. Electra, you're in my power. Your brother too. I can kill you. Yesterday I should have killed you. Instead of that I promise, as soon as the enemy is repulsed, to step down from the throne and place Orestes on it.

ELECTRA. That's no longer the question, Aegisthus. If the gods for once change their methods, if they make you wise and just in order to ruin you, that's their affair. The question now is, will she dare tell us why she hated my father!

CLYTEMNESTRA. Oh, you want to know that?

ELECTRA. But you'll not dare tell.

AEGISTHUS. Electra, tomorrow, before the altar where we celebrate our victory the guilty man shall stand, for there is only one guilty man, in a parricide's coat. He'll confess his crime publicly and determine his punishment himself. First let me save the city.

ELECTRA. You've "saved" yourselves today, Aegisthus, and in my presence. That's enough. Now I want her to finish!

CLYTEMNESTRA. So, you want me to finish!

ELECTRA. I dare you to!

MESSENGER. They're entering the court yards, Aegisthus!

AEGISTHUS. Come, queen!

CLYTEMNESTRA. Yes, I hated him. Yes, you shall know what this fine father was like. Yes, after twenty years I'll have the joy that Agatha had today. A woman might belong to anyone, but there was just one man in the world to whom I couldn't belong. That man as the king of kings, father of fathers! I hated him from the first day he came to wrench me from my home, with his curly beard and the hand with the little finger always sticking up. He raised it when he drank, when he drove, when he held his sceptre . . . and when he held me close I felt on my back only four fingers. It drove me wild, and the morning he sacrificed your sister, Iphigenia,—horrible—I saw the little fingers of both his hands sticking out, dark against the sun—king of kings! What nonsense! He was pompous, indecisive, stupid. He was the fop of fops, the most credulous creature. The king of kings was never anything more than that little finger and the beard that nothing could soften. The bathwater I soaked his head in didn't soften it, nor did the nights of false love when I pulled and tangled it, nor the storm at Delphi which turned the dancers' hair into manes; it came out in gold ringlets from water, bed, and rain. He would beckon me with his little finger and I would go smiling. . . . Why? He would tell me to kiss his mouth in that fleece and I would run to kiss it. . . . Why? And when I woke and was unfaithful to him, like Agatha, with the wooden bedstead—a royal bed—and he bade me talk to him, though I knew he was vain, empty, tiresome, I told him he was modest, strange, even splendid.

. . . Why? And if he persisted, stammering, pathetic, I swore to him he was a god. King of kings! The only excuse for that title is that it justifies a hatred of hatreds. Do you know what I did, Electra, the day of his departure, when his ship was still in sight? I sacrificed the curliest ram I could find and toward midnight I stole into the throne room quite alone, and took the sceptre in my hands! Now you know everything. You wanted a hymn to truth, and here's a beautiful one.

ELECTRA. Oh, father, forgive!

AEGISTHUS. Come, queen.

CLYTEMNESTRA. Take this girl first and chain her up.

ELECTRA. Father, will you ever forgive me for listening to her? Aegisthus, should she not die?

AEGISTHUS. Farewell, Electra.

ELECTRA. Kill her, Aegisthus. And I'll forgive you.

CLYTEMNESTRA. Don't let her go free, Aegisthus. They'll stab you in the back.

AEGISTHUS. We'll see about that. Leave Electra alone. . . . Unbind Orestes.

AEGISTHUS *and* CLYTEMNESTRA *go out.*

ELECTRA. The bird is coming down, beggar, the bird is coming down.

BEGGAR. Look, it's a vulture!

SCENE 9   ELECTRA. NARSES' WIFE.
BEGGAR. *Then* ORESTES.

BEGGAR. You here, Narses' wife?

NARSES' WIFE. All of us beggars, the lame, the halt and the blind, have come to save Electra and her brother.

BEGGAR. Justice, eh?

NARSES' WIFE. There they are, untying Orestes.

A crowd of BEGGARS *enter, a few at a time.*

BEGGAR. This is how they did the killing, listen, woman. This
is the way it all happened, I never invent anything. It was
the queen who had the steps soaped that go down to the
bath; the two of them did it. While all the housewives in
Argos scrubbed their thresholds, the queen and her lover
soaped the door-sill to his death. Think how clean their
hands were when they greeted Agamemnon at his entrance!
And your father slipped, Electra, as he reached out his arms
to her. You were right except on this one point. He slipped
on the steps, and the noise of his fall, because of his golden
cuirass and helment, was that of a king falling. And she
threw herself on him, he thought, to raise him up, but she
held him down. He didn't understand why his darling wife
was holding him down, he wondered if it was a love trans-
port, but then why did Aegisthus stay? Young Aegisthus
was awkward and indiscreet. (We'll consider his promotion.)
The ruler of the world, the conqueror of Troy, who had just
reviewed the army and navy parade, must have been humiliated, to fall like that, on his back and in his noisy armor, even
if his beard was untouched, in the presence of his loving
wife and the young ensign. All the more annoyed because
this might be a bad omen. The fall might mean he'd die in a
year, or in five years. And he was surprised that his beloved
wife caught his wrists and threw herself on him to hold him
down, as fisherwomen do with big stranded turtles on the
shore. She was wrong, and not so beautiful, her face flushed,
her neck wrinkled. Not like young Aegisthus, who was trying to extricate his sword for fear he'd hurt himself, apparently, he looked handsomer every minute. What was
strange, though, was that the two of them were silent. He
said "Dear wife, how strong you are!" "Young man," he said,
"Pull out the sword—by its handle!" But they said nothing,
the queen and the squire had become mutes in the last ten
years, and no one had told him. They were as mute as
travellers hurrying to pack a trunk when time is short. They
had to do something quickly, before anyone else came in.

What was it? Suddenly Aegisthus kicked his helmet as a dying man kicks his dog, and the truth was plain. And he cried, "Wife, let me go. Wife, what are you doing?" She took care not to answer, she couldn't say aloud, "I'm killing you, murdering you!" But she said to herself, "I'm killing you because there's not one gray hair on your beard, because it's the only way to murder that little finger."

She undid the laces of his cuirass with her teeth, and the gold turned scarlet, and Aegisthus—beautiful with the beauty of Achilles killing Hector, of Ulysses killing Dolon— approached, with drawn sword. Then the king of kings kicked Clytemnestra's back, and she shook all over, her silent hand shook, and he shouted so loud Aegisthus had to roar with laughter to cover the noise. Then he drove in the sword. And the king of kings was no longer the mass of bronze and iron he'd thought himself, he was just soft flesh, as easy to pierce as a lamb, and the sword cut so deep it split the marble. The murderers were wrong to hurt the marble, for it revenged itself. I found out about the crime from that split tile.

So he stopped struggling, let himself go, between the woman, who became uglier every moment, and the man, who was handsomer and handsomer. One good thing about death is that you can trust yourself to her, death is your only friend in an ambush, she has a familiar look, he saw that and called on his children, first the boy, Orestes, then the girl, Electra, to thank them for avenging him in future, lending their hands of death. Clytemnestra, foam on her lips, did not let go of him, and Agamemnon as willing to die but not to have this woman spit in his face, on his beard. She didn't spit because she was walking around the corpse, trying not to get blood on her sandals; her red dress looked to the dying man like the sun. Then the shadow fell, because each of them took an arm and turned him over on the floor. On his right hand four fingers were already stiff. Then, as Aegisthus had pulled out the sword without thinking, they turned him over again and put it gently, deliberately, back in the wound. Aegisthus was grateful to the dead man for having let himself be killed so very easily. Dozens of kings of kings could be killed like that, if murder was so easy.

But Clytemnestra's hatred of the man who'd struggled so fiercely, so stupidly, grew as she foresaw how every night she would dream of this murder. That's just what happened. It's seven years since she killed, she's killed him three thousand times.

ORESTES *has come in during this speech.*

NARSES' WIFE. Here's the young man! Isn't he handsome?

BEGGAR. As beautiful as Aegisthus when young.

ORESTES. Where are they, Electra?

ELECTRA. Dear Orestes!

NARSES' WIFE. In the southern courtyard.

ORESTES. I'll see you soon, Electra, and we'll never part.

ELECTRA. Go, my lover.

ORESTES. Don't stop, beggar. Go on, tell him about the death of Clytemnestra and Aegisthus.
He goes out, sword in hand.

NARSES' WIFE. Tell us, beggar.

BEGGAR. In two minutes. Give him time to get there.

ELECTRA. He has his sword?

NARSES' WIFE. Yes, daughter.

BEGGAR. Are you crazy? Calling the princess your daughter!

NARSES' WIFE. I call her daughter, I don't say she's my daughter. I've often seen her father, though. Heavens, what a fine man!

ELECTRA. He had a beard, hadn't he?

NARSES' WIFE. Not a beard, a sun. A wavy, curly sun, a sun just rising from the sea. He stroked it with his hand. The most beautiful hand in the world.

ELECTRA. Call me your daughter, Narses' wife! I am your daughter. . . . I heard a cry!

NARSES' WIFE. No, my daughter.

ELECTRA. You're sure he had his sword? He didn't go to them without a sword?

NARSES' WIFE. You saw him going. He had a thousand swords. Be calm, be calm!

ELECTRA. What a long minute, mother, you waited at the edge of the bath!

NARSES' WIFE. Why don't you tell us? Everything will be over before we know it.

BEGGAR. One minute! He's looking for them. Now! He's found them.

NARSES' WIFE. Oh, I can wait. Little Electra is soft to touch. I had only boys, gangsters. Mothers who only have girls are happy.

ELECTRA. Yes . . . happy. . . . This time I do hear a cry!

NARSES' WIFE. Yes, my daughter.

BEGGAR. So, here's the end. Narses' wife and the beggars untied Orestes. He rushed across the courtyard. He didn't touch or embrace Electra. He was wrong, for he'll never touch her again. He found the murderers on the marble balcony, calming the rioters. As Aegisthus leaned down to tell the leaders that everything was going well, he heard behind him the cry of a wounded beast. But it wasn't a beast crying, it was Clytemnestra. She was bleeding. Her son had stabbed her. He struck at the couple blindly, his eyes closed. A mother, though, even when unworthy, is sensitive and human. She didn't call on Electra or Orestes but on her youngest daughter, Chrysothemis, so Orestes thought he had killed another, and an innocent, mother. She clung to Aegisthus' arm; she was right, that gave her a last chance to stand up. But she prevented Aegisthus from drawing his sword. He shook her, to free his arm. She was too heavy to serve as a shield. And that bird was beating his head with its wings and attacking him with its beak, so he struggled. Just with his unarmed left arm, the dead queen, loaded with necklace

and pendants, on his right arm. He was in despair over dying
like a criminal, when he had become pure and holy; to be
fighting because of a crime which was no longer his; to find
himself, though loyal and innocent, infamous before this parricide. He struggled with one hand, which the sword was
cutting little by little, but the lacing of his cuirass caught
on a brooch of Clytemnestra's, and it opened. Then he resisted no longer; he only shook his right arm to rid himself of
the queen, not only to fight but to die alone, to lie far from
Clytemnestra in death. He didn't succeed. Forever Clytemnestra and Aegisthus will be coupled. He died, calling a
name I'll not repeat.

AEGISTHUS' *voice off stage.* Electra!

BEGGAR. I talked too fast. He caught up with me.

SCENE 10   ELECTRA. BEGGAR. NARSES' WIFE
the EUMENIDES, *who are of exactly the same height
and figure as* ELECTRA.

SERVANT. Flee, everybody, the palace is on fire!

FIRST FURY. That's what Electra wanted. Three things: daylight, truth—and this fire!

SECOND FURY. Satisfied, Electra? The city's dying.

ELECTRA. I'm satisfied. I know now that it will be born again.

THIRD FURY. And the people killing each other in the streets,
will they be born again? The Corinthians have started the
attack, and it's a massacre.

FIRST FURY. Your pride has brought you to this, Electra. You
have nothing left, nothing.

ELECTRA. I have my conscience, I have Orestes, I have justice,
I have everything.

SECOND FURY. Your conscience! Will you listen to your conscience in the early mornings to come? For seven years

you've not slept because of a crime that others committed. Now you're the guilty one.

ELECTRA. I have Orestes, I have justice I have everything.

THIRD FURY. Orestes! You'll never see Orestes again. We're leaving *you*—to pursue *him*. We've taken on your age and your shape—to pursue him. Good-bye! We'll not leave him until he's been driven to madness or suicide, cursing his sister.

ELECTRA. I have justice. I have everything.

NARSES' WIFE. What are they saying? They're back. What have we come to, my poor Electra, what have we come to?

ELECTRA. What have we come to?

NARSES' WIFE. Yes, tell me. I'm not very quick to understand. I know something's happened but I don't know just what. How can you explain it, when a day begins like today, and everything's ruined and pillaged—though we're still breathing, we've lost everything, the city's burning, innocent people are killing each other, the guilty are dying, too—and the sun still rises?

ELECTRA. Ask the beggar. He knows.

BEGGAR. It all has a beautiful name, Narses' wife, it is called the dawn.

Curtain

NOTES

WOYZECK was unfinished and unpublished at Büchner's death in 1837. In fact nearly a hundred years passed before the MS was properly edited first by G. Witkowski, Leipzig, 1920, then by Fritz Bergemann, Leipzig, 1922. The first English translation was that of Geoffrey Dunlop in Büchner's *Plays* (New York, 1928), the second that of Henry Schnitzler and Seth Ulman in *New Directions in Prose and Poetry XII* (New York, 1950). The libretto of Alban Berg's opera *Wozzeck*, translated by Eric Blackall and Vida Harford, has been published by Alfred A. Kalmus (London, 1952). The Hoffman version of Büchner's play was commissioned for the present volume. Mr Hoffman writes: "Büchner based *Woyzeck* quite literally on the case of Johann Christian Woyzeck, a barber and soldier who was executed in Leipzig in 1824 for murdering his mistress in a fit of jealousy. The case was well publicized, since it was the first public execution in Leipzig for thirty years, and precipitated a legal and medical controversy as to whether or not Woyzeck was insane. . . . It is impossible to present a definitive text. Büchner did not number his scenes, was vague about stage directions and locale, and left several drafts of some scenes, fragments of others. I have tried to follow the text agreed on by his most recent editors, and, aside from an occasional idiomatic liberty, have tampered only with fragments and transitional material that would not otherwise fall into place. Producers usually see fit to adapt, cut, and interpolate; I have assigned the speeches of two characters, a Concessionaire and a Charlatan, to one, the Barker, but elsewhere have resisted temptation. Marie's Child was introduced into Scene 25 by Büchner's first editor, Franzos, who was inspired by one of the fragments that won't fit in at all . . . The songs present a difficulty since the original music is not easily traced. I have translated them literally—and, for the most part, have kept the same meter."

The only book-length presentation of Büchner in English is *Georg Büchner* by A. H. J. Knight, Blackwell, Oxford (England), 1951.

CAVALLERIA RUSTICANA first appeared in a collection of short stories by Giovanni Verga in 1880 (*Vita dei campi*). The story was published in English, translated by D. H. Lawrence, in 1928 (*Cavalleria Rusticana and Other Stories*). In Lawrence's fine preface to his fine translations, there is a small error of fact. He wrote: "Everybody knows, of course, that Verga made a dramatized version of *Cavalleria Rusticana*, and that this dramatized version is the libretto of the ever popular little opera of the same name. So that Mascagni's rather feeble music has gone to immortalize a man like Verga, whose only popular claim to fame is that he wrote the aforesaid libretto. —But that is fame's fault, not Verga's." The libretto is not by Verga but by a couple of nonentities. What Verga did make out of his story was the one-act play here for the first time printed in English. Eleanora Duse created the role of Santuzza in 1884, and one of the most famous portraits of the actress—drawn in America, incidentally—shows her in the role. The short play has a most important place in Italian theater, and in at least one history of the Italian drama is described as the most original play in the language.

WOMAN OF PARIS, was first performed in 1885 and played at the Comédie Francaise in 1890. The first English version, by C. A. Byrne, was published in New York in 1904, a second, by Freeman Tilden, in New York in 1913. A third, entitled *Parisienne*, is by Ashley Dukes and was performed and published in England in the early nineteen-forties; Faye Emerson played in it in America in 1950. The Barzun version first appeared in *From the Modern Repertoire*, Series One, edited by Eric Bentley (Denver, 1949).

THE THREEPENNY OPERA, 1928, was first produced in New York in 1933, English version by Gifford Cochran and Jerrold Krimsky; in 1954 it was again produced in New York, English version by Marc Blitzstein. Neither of these versions has been published. The Bentley-Vesey version, as published in the present volume, is new; but it has the following history. It began as an unpublished version by Mr. Vesey alone, entitled *A Penny For the Poor*. Somewhat revised by Eric Bentley, it appeared as *The Threepenny Opera* in *From the Modern Repertoire*, Series One, edited by Eric Bentley, (Denver, 1949), and was subsequently performed in various parts of the U.S. All changes from the 1949 to the present text have been made by Eric Bentley alone (with the exceptions noted in the acknowledgments above).

Kurt Weill's music for the play is published by Universal Edition, Vienna. Bertolt Brecht's Notes are appended to the 1949 text.

ELECTRA was first produced by Louis Jouvet in Paris in 1937. Electra was played by Renée Devillers, Aegisthus by Pierre Renoir, the Beggar by Jouvet. The first appearance of the play in English was in *From the Modern Repertoire*, Series Two, edited by Eric Bentley (Denver, 1952). It was revised for the present book.

ADAPTATION
VS
TRANSLATION

In the theatrical business, the term Translation is applied to a first, rough English draft prepared by a linguist with no gift for writing; the term Adaptation being reserved for the final stage version which is made by a "playwright."

Both conceptions are fraught with fallacy. The fallacy of the Translation is that you might still claim to be accurate when you have translated a beautiful phrase with an ugly one. The Adaptor tends to make the opposite mistake, and assume that the more changes he makes the better. Sometimes the changes do show the Adaptor to be a very smart fellow, but is his smartness apropos? If you paid your money to see Girandoux, you may not be willing to settle for Mr. Behrman.

Obviously, there is no fixed rule. If an adaptor is a much better writer than his author, we should be glad to have him show the latter a due disrespect: some of Shakespeare's plays are adaptations. Or there may be a relationship of parity, as when an Anouilh comes to us through the mediation of a Fry.

But these cases are the exception, not the rule. Normally one wishes to believe one is reading a version *of an original:* God (not Lancelot Andrewes), Plato (not Jowett), Proust (not Scott Moncrieff). Is not the job of an Andrewes, a Jowett, or a Scott Moncrieff noble enough? Coleridge was modest in his rendering of Schiller, Shelley in his rendering of Goethe; they did not adapt.

In short, commercial usage has made of both terms—translation and adaptation—a downright derogation. That is why I have freed my writers from either imputation by calling each text, noncommittally and incontrovertibly, an "English version." This is not to say that they all approach their material in the same way. Temperaments—as well as circumstances—alter cases. When the editor had a choice of version he did not on principle "go for" the more literal or the more free. To repeat: there is no fixed rule. Mr. Barzun's version of *La Parisienne* is more literal than Mr. Ashley Dukes's; it is also better English dialogue. Mr. Ackland's version of *Enough Stupidity in Every Wise Man* is less literal than either of the earlier versions; yet it is the only one of the three that impresses the reader as a drama at all. Not one or two but a dozen or so factors are involved: and, at that, not only such things as the talent of the translator but such things as the distance at which another culture stands from ours. Moscow is further off than Paris; he who would bring us a Russian play may have more work to do. Then there is the *relation* between the author's temperament and his translator's. There is the question of differing theatrical conventions. There is the question of.... Perhaps a dozen is too low an estimate. It must be left to the scholarly and polygot to refer each "version" here reprinted to the original and judge how much has successfully been imported and also if anything has successfully been added to make up for what has inevitably been lost.

ANCHOR BOOKS